D1600976

The Volcano Registry

ALSO BY HARRIS M. LENTZ III

*Encyclopedia of Heads of States and
Governments, 1900 through 1945* (1999)

Obituaries in the Performing Arts
(volumes from 1994 on)

Biographical Dictionary of Professional Wrestling (1997)

*Television Westerns Episode Guide:
All United States Series, 1949–1996* (1997)

*Western and Frontier Film and Television
Credits: 1903–1995* (two volumes, 1996)

*Heads of States and Governments:
A Worldwide Encyclopedia of Over 2,300
Leaders, 1945 through 1992* (1994)

Science Fiction, Horror & Fantasy Film and Television Credits
(four volumes, 1983–1994)

*Assassinations and Executions:
An Encyclopedia of Political Violence, 1865–1986* (1988)

The Volcano Registry

Names, Locations, Descriptions and History for Over 1500 Sites

by
Harris M. Lentz III

McFarland & Company, Inc., Publishers
Jefferson, North Carolina, and London

British Library Cataloguing-in-Publication data are available

Library of Congress Cataloguing-in-Publication Data

Lentz, Harris M., III.
    The volcano registry : names, locations, descriptions and history for
over 1500 sites / by Harris M. Lentz III.
      p.   cm.
    Includes bibliographical references and index.
    ISBN 0-7864-0732-8 (library binding : 50# alkaline paper) ∞
    1. Volcanoes.   I. Title.
    QE522.L46   1999
    551.21—dc21   99-19961
                                                                  CIP

Manufactured in the United States of America

McFarland & Company, Inc., Publishers
  Box 611, Jefferson, North Carolina 28640

To Adrian Room,
without whom this book would not exist.

Acknowledgments

I would like to thank Adrian Room for supplying much of the information found in this volume. I would also like to thank Carla Clark for her invaluable help in assisting me with this work. Thanks to my mother, Helene Lentz, my sister, Nikki Walker, and my friends Paul Geary, Kent Nelson, Glinda and Mark Gressel, Nina and Mark Heffington, Anne Taylor, Dia Barbee and Andy Branham for their support and assistance. I would also like to thank the kind folks at J. Alexander's, especially Laura Hunt, Denise Tansil and Gary Holder.

Contents

Introduction

And all the people saw the thunderings, and the lightnings, and
the noise of the trumpet, and the mountain smoking: and when
the people saw it, they removed, and stood afar off.
(Exodus 20:18)

This handbook gives particulars of more than 1,500 of the world's major volcanoes. All entries contain the following core information: (1) volcano name, (2) region of location, (3) geographical coordinates and (4) physical description and type. Many entries then continue with (5), a summary of the dates of particular eruptions or activity, and a note of the damage, destruction, or deaths they caused.

This is the place to say a little more about each of these four items.

(1) The *volcano name* is generally as given in Simkin and Siebert (see Select Bibliography, p. 185). It should be noted that the names on the whole are those of the volcanoes or volcanic fields themselves, not their individual features such as cones, craters, domes, and fissure vents, unless these warrant a separate entry, usually for their historical activity. Thus **Methana** volcano, in Greece, is entered, but not its dome *Kameno Vouno*. Similarly, **Ambrym** volcano has its place, but not its crater, *Benbow*, which has done much of the erupting over the past 100 years. However, where a particular feature is well known, and its activity reported and recorded under its own name, it is cross-referred to the volcano of which it is a part. Thus *Sherman* Crater is referred to its parent, Mt. **Baker**, Washington, USA, and *Karua*, as a submarine cone of **Kuwae**, Vanuatu, is similarly directed. Synonymous names are also largely omitted, but alternate names widely encountered in literature are cross-referred, especially when one is linguistically European and the other not. An example is *Quizapu* in Chile, which is commonly known as Cerro **Azul**. This last name, incidentally, is an example of the method of cross-referral when the main name begins with a generic, which is here set in ordinary type. (*Cerro* is Spanish for "peak.") It is also an example of the way such names are entered, with the

1

generic second: **Azul, Cerro**. Alternate names follow the entered name in square brackets, as **Colo** [**Una Una**].

In some cases, the meaning of the name is given in parentheses, together with its language of origin. Where a meaning is not given, it is usually because it is not known. But famous volcanoes such as **Etna**, **Stromboli**, and the "terrible twins" **Mauna Kea** and **Mauna Loa**, are furnished with an etymology. In fact many volcano names do not relate to the volcano itself but to a nearby feature with which they have become identified. Examples are **Villarrica** volcano, Chile, named for the nearby town so called (as is the lake here), and **Curaçoa** submarine volcano, named for the Tongan reef off which it lies. Many volcanoes are on islands, and are simply known by the island name. **Raoul Island** volcano, in the Kermadec Islands, is obviously so designated. Any etymology here would thus be that of the island, not of the volcano, even if the generic *Island* were omitted from its name.

(2) The *region of location* is usually a country name, since the following geographical coordinates will locate the volcano in question precisely. However, in some cases a subregion is additionally given. In island states, such as Japan and Indonesia, the island name is usually supplied as well, and in the USA the state is given (mostly Alaska or California). In the case of submarine volcanoes, an indication of the land feature off which they lie is often supplied. Thus **Kadovar** is located as "northeast of New Guinea."

(3) The *geographical coordinates* are given in degrees and minutes with latitude north or south before longitude east or west. It should be noted that the readings are in *decimal parts of a degree*, not in the conventional duodecimal figures. This facilitates estimation of the distances between points, since one degree of latitude is equal to 111 km. (It also, of course, facilitates computer manipulation of data.) Thus Mt. **Etna** in Sicily, Italy, is located as 37.73N, 15.00E, not 37.45N, 15.00E, and Mt. **Shasta**, California, USA, is at 41.42N, 122.20W, not 41.25N, 122.12W. Where three digits were given in the original source for the minutes, these have been rounded up or down accordingly to two. Thus **Ilimuda**, on Flores Island, Indonesia, is actually 8.478S, 122.671E, but here rounded to 8.48S, 122.67E. An extensive volcanic field, such as the **Chaîne des Puys**, France, is given a location that is the centerpoint of the field, in this case 45.50N, 2.75E. It goes without saying that any given coordinates are not necessarily those of a sole eruption site, since eruptive centers can lie many kilometers apart within a single volcanic field.

(4) The *physical description* and *type* gives the volcano's summit elevation, above sea level, in both feet and meters. A small number of volcanoes, usually submarine volcanos, have unknown elevation, or depth. The term *Holocene* indicates that the volcano has been active in postglacial time.

(5) The *summary* is presented as a concise historical record of a volcano's activity. Since some volcanoes remain active, it should be understood that "most recent eruption" relates to the year of compilation of the data, which for the

most part was 1998. The aim has generally been to be as nontechnical as possible, in order to avoid possibly baffling volcanological terminology. But just about everyone knows what *pumice* and *lava* and *craters* are, and can visualize *vents* and *mud flows*, so these are readily resorted to. The term *caldera* appears in some volcanic names, and should be taken as a large crater, especially one that with breadth greater than that of the vent or vents within it. (**Yellowstone**, better known as the geyser "Old Faithful," is technically a *resurgent caldera*, a vast crater whose floor originally subsided but was heaved up again thousands of years after the eruption.) Other volcanological terms, where they occur, are usually explained, such as *fumarole* and (below) *nuées ardentes*.

Since we are here talking of a geyser in terms of its being a volcano, the time has clearly come to ask the question: what *is* a volcano? The popular notion is of a "fiery mountain," a mountain that erupts, sending flames and smoke into the air and streams of lava down its slopes. This definition is broadly correct but is very general and obviously does not apply to all volcanoes. Some, for example, may send "fire and brimstone" explosively and noisily into the air but discharge little or no lava. Others may quietly spew down sinister rivers of lava to cover the surrounding countryside. Broadly speaking, a volcano is a hole in the Earth's crust, either on land or on the sea floor, from which materials are expelled naturally from below. What the materials are can vary. They mostly include hot lava, cold rock fragments, gases, aerosols, steam, and water. The lava is usually in the form of flows, cinders, blocks, ash, or pumice. Some materials cool and mount up around the original hole, and may form a cone-shaped hill. Other fine materials can be blasted into the stratosphere, where they are carried around the world and then remain as aerosols that may veil the sun for several years.

The word *volcano* itself derives from *Vulcanus*, or *Volcanus*, as he was earlier known, the Latin name of Vulcan, the Roman god of fire. He was one of the three children of Jupiter (Zeus) and Juno, and was blacksmith to the gods. He was worshipped from early times at Rome and had a special shrine at Ostia, the port of Rome. His name was given to Etna before it gained its present name, and is preserved in Vulcano, in the Aeolian Islands. The subterranean fires and rumblings of Etna were believed by the Romans to emanate from Vulcan's forge. They therefore named it for him.

The originally English word for a volcano in the sixteenth century was *volcan* or *vulcan*, adopted from the French or Spanish form of the god's name. A century later, the Italian form of the word, with its final *-o*, became the norm. An early occurrence is in Samuel Purchas's *Purchas his Pilgrimage* (1613): "a Vulcano or flaming hill, the fire whereof may be seene ... aboue 100 miles." Today, some form of the god's name is found for a volcano in many countries of the world: French *volcan*, Spanish *volcán*, Italian *volcano*, Portuguese *vulcao*, German *Vulkan*, Russian *vulkan*, Hungarian *vulkán*, Turkish *volkan*. The term is not fully international, however, since some languages have a word translating as "fire mountain," such as Finnish *tulivuori*, Arabic *jabal nar*, Chinese *huoshan*, and Japanese *yakeyama*.

So where are they to be found, these feared and fearsome giants?

Broadly speaking, the volcanoes of the world are located in three distinct regions. The first is along the margins of continents and on the chains of islands that lead off those continents. The second is in the middle of the ocean. And the third is in the middle of a continent. The reason why they specifically occur in the first two regions is explained by the theory of plate tectonics, according to which the Earth's lithosphere (the rigid outer part) is divided into a number of plates that shift around over the surface. Where they collide, and the Earth's crust splits and faults, mountains are born and volcanoes build up. Around 80 percent of the world's earthquakes and volcanoes thus occur at the margins of the plates, both on land and under the sea, in the latter case along the so called Mid-Atlantic Ridge (see below).

Let us make a grand tour of each of these three regions.

The most familiar of the volcanoes running along the margins of continents and their contiguous islands are those found in the so called "Ring of Fire" that curves rather irregularly around the Pacific. Indeed, around two thirds of all volcanoes are found here. Our tour begins in Antarctica, on Deception Island, off the northern tip of the Antarctic Peninsula. From there we travel to Patagonia, at the southern end of South America, where **Monte Burney**, Chile, can serve as our continental kickoff. We now travel more or less due north up the west coast of South America, taking in such volcanoes as **Osorno**, **Ojos del Salado**, and **El Misti**, until we reach the equator, where we make our first stopover, someplace between two of Ecuador's best known volcanoes, the first inactive, the second active: Chimborazo and Cotopaxi.

We now move on north into Central America, still following the western seaboard, where we admire **Irazú**, **Santa Maria**, **El Chichón**, and **Paracutín** before halting once more at **Popocatépetl**, in Mexico. Meanwhile, we are aware of Mt. **Pelée** to the east in Martinique, at the southern end of the West Indies.

We now head up north into North America. Here, still on the west coast, we note **Lassen Peak** in California and Mt. **St. Helens** and Mt. **Rainier** in Washington, among others. Our course now begins a westward curve, and we leap to Alaska and the Aleutian Islands. There are volcanoes aplenty here, and they continue when we cross to the Kamchatka Peninsula in Russia, then swing south through the Kuril Islands to Japan, where we take another break at the touristically attractive Mt. **Fuji**. From there, the Ring of Fire continues its path through Taiwan and the Philippines to the many islands of Indonesia, a distinctive volcanic chain to the west. (Here, in the Sunda Strait between Java and Sumatra, lies **Krakatau**, the volcanic island which in 1883 caused the world's largest natural explosion.) To the east, our journey takes us down through New Guinea and the New Hebrides to Samoa and the Tonga-Kermadec chain that leads south to New Zealand's North Island. The Ring of Fire virtually fizzles out here, at **Taupo**, but we must not overlook two more southerly volcanoes: **Buckle Island** and Mt. **Erebus**, back down in the Antarctic. Which was where we came in.

Our circular tour skirted an isolated but important group of volcanoes in Hawaii, more or less at the hub of the Ring of Fire. Here are such notorious names as **Mauna Kea, Mauna Loa**, and **Kilauea**. Mauna Kea is inactive, but Mauna Loa and Kilauea have both caused death and destruction in historic times.

But what of Iceland's representation, and Europe's in general? For the former, we must start on our second package tour. In our enthusiasm to see and snap the wonders of the world's volcanoes, we may well overlook (literally) those that are largely unseen. These are the volcanoes in the depth of the ocean, and specifically those along or close to the Mid-Atlantic Ridge (see above). Our journey begins almost at the opposite end of the earth, at the island of Jan Mayen, in the Arctic Ocean, halfway between Greenland and Scandinavia. From there we set off south, and soon reach Iceland, the largest volcanic island in the world. Indeed, it is Iceland's prolific volcanic activity that has kept it above sea level, since it actually forms part of the Mid-Atlantic Ridge. The "Land of Ice and Fire," with its many active volcanoes, is thus geologically young. So young and so active, in fact, that one of its volcanoes can be expected to erupt every five years. In 1963 it threw up a whole new island, Surtsey, while in 1973 lava from **Helga** fell on the island of Heimaey, in the Vestmannaeyjar group, almost destroyed one of Iceland's largest towns.

Setting sail south, we come to several smaller islands known for their volcanic activity: the Azores, the Canaries, the Cape Verde islands, **Ascension, St. Helena, Tristan da Cunha, Bouvet Island**. (These are not properly part of the Mid-Atlantic Ridge, but lie to one side of it.) At the same time we pass over invisible volcanoes deep in the waters of the Atlantic. Many of them are still unnamed, but their eruptions have been recorded. Such volcanoes are known as *seamounts*, as distinct from land-based mountains.

Elsewhere in the world, the most noteworthy groups of volcanoes are in Africa and Europe. Africa's are in two distinct regions: the Rift Valley, in the eastern half of the continent, and the middle of the Sahara Desert, further north. The Rift Valley contains some famous (or infamous) volcanic names: **Mt. Kenya, Kilimanjaro, Meru, Nyamuragira**, and **Nyiragongo**. These last two, in the Democratic Republic of Congo (former Zaire), have been among the most active in the world. In the Sahara, less well known volcanoes exist in three mountain groups: the **Jebel Marra**, in Sudan, **Tibesti**, in Chad, and **Hoggar (Ahaggar)**, in Algeria. If we are visiting African volcanoes we must not bypass Mt. **Cameroon**, in the west of the continent, the only volcano in Africa with a recorded B.C. eruption.

Any volcanic voyage cannot fail to include mainland Europe, for it is here that some of the best known and best documented examples are to be found, notably in Italy. The names of **Etna, Stromboli,** and **Vesuvius** are universally known. France, too, has its **Chaîne des Puys,** Germany its **Eifel,** and Spain its **Olot,** at the eastern end of the Pyrenees, as noted areas of former volcanic activity.

The study of volcanoes is *volcanology,* a science that goes back to the first millennium B.C. Heraclitus was writing about volcanoes in the sixth century B.C., and Aristotle in the fourth century. Strabo took up the study in the first century B.C., and Pliny the Younger continued it in the first century A.D. It was Strabo who described the eruption of Santorín, or Thera, in 196 B.C., and Pliny the Younger the catastrophic eruption of Vesuvius in A.D. 79, an event that cost the life of his uncle, Pliny the Elder, when he inhaled volcanic ash at Stabiae. The first scientific organization devoted to the specialty was a volcanological observatory built on the slopes of Vesuvius in 1842. A similar observatory was opened on Kilauea, Hawaii, in 1911. Further observatories followed in Indonesia and a whole host of them in Japan.

An island group, four volcanoes, and a Roman writer have given the names of six distinctive types of volcanic activity, that is, they describe the type of eruption and what is erupted. In order of strength, the mildest first, they are (1) *Hawaiian,* (2) *Strombolian,* (3) *Vulcanian,* (4) *Vesuvian,* (5) *Plinian,* and (6) *Pelean.*

(1) *Hawaiian* activity is typical of the volcanoes of the Hawaiian Islands, such as **Kilauea, Mauna Kea,** and **Mauna Loa.** Fluid lava flows from the summit and is accompanied by "fire fountains," jets of incandescent liquid rock. Long-lasting lakes of lava may also form.

(2) *Strombolian* activity is typical of **Stromboli.** It consists of intermittent explosive bursts of moderate force that eject gases and bombs of lava some distance into the air. Each burst lasts only a few seconds, and there may be intervals between them of 20 minutes or more. The activity is rather noisier than Hawaiian but is not particularly dangerous. Stromboli itself has had from three to six craters erupting continually like this for the past 2,500 years.

(3) *Vulcanian* activity is typical of **Vulcano.** The eruptions are of small magnitude but their columns rise much higher than Strombolian columns, sometimes reaching 10 to 20 km. This means that rocks and ash are deposited over a wider area. The activity is also more violently explosive, and can even destroy parts of the volcano itself.

(4) *Vesuvian* activity is typical of **Vesuvius.** It is the next step up from Vulcanian activity, with even higher columns (up to 30 km) and wider areas of ash and rock deposits.

(5) *Plinian* activity is comparable to the notorious eruption of Vesuvius in A.D. 79 that was described by the Roman writer Pliny the Younger and that killed his uncle, the famous scholar Pliny the Elder. The eruptions are forceful and reach high in the sky (up to 45 km). Ash, rocks, and pumice are spread with

some thickness over huge areas of ground. Plinian activity is (fortunately) relatively rare, but a recent example was the eruption of **Santa Maria**, Guatamela, in 1902, when thousands were killed.

(6) *Pelean* activity is comparable to the devastating eruption of Mt. **Pelée** in 1902, when the town of St. Pierre was destroyed. It cannot be so neatly pigeon-holed as the types already mentioned, and is essentially a form of either Vulcanian or Plinian activity. It has a distinguishing feature, however, which is the flow or avalanche of solid fragments (boulders mixed with dust) in the form known as *nuées ardentes* (literally, "glowing clouds"). The dust in such *nuées* is swept upwards in the clouds of escaping gas while the boulders roll over the ground at great speed. An example of Pelean activity is the eruption of Mt. **Lamington**, Papua New Guinea, in 1952 that took the lives of some 3,000 people.

Not surprisingly, some eruptions combine different types of activity. That of Mt. Etna in 1971, for example, began with Strombolian activity, continued in a second phase with Hawaiian activity (but without any "fire fountains"), and concluded with Vulcanian activity.

The combination of spectacle and latent danger that volcanoes offer has made them a good subject for the movies. Indeed, they are a true "motion picture" in their own right, with their spectacular displays and streams of glowing lava. They can serve as an appropriately explosive setting for the main story or provide the key interest in a horror or disaster movie. In the 1930s, Paramount (appropriately) used them as the climax of most of Dorothy Lamour's jungle pictures. They also appeared in such adventure movies as *Cobra Woman* (1944), *Mysterious Island* (1961), *The Devil at Four O'Clock* (1961) and *Journey to the Center of the Earth* (1967). In the latter the "journey" was down an extinct Icelandic crater and back up on a fountain of lava inside Etna. The famous eruption of Vesuvius was re-created for *The Last Days of Pompeii* (1935), and that of Krakatau for *Krakatoa, East of Java* (1968). Giant monsters had their lair in an extinct volcano in *The Black Scorpion* (1957), and a volcano was also the climax of *One Million B.C.* (1940) and its remake, *One Million Years B.C.* (1966). More recently, *Joe Versus the Volcano* (1990) concerned a man with a (supposedly) terminal illness who agreed to jump into a volcano after six months of rich living, while *Dante's Peak* (1997) and *Volcano* (1997) were both popular disaster movies. The most memorable footage of *real* volcanoes in action was in the French documentary, *Les Rendezvous du Diable* (1958), also titled *Volcano*. But filming in volcanic locations has its risks. A Hollywood crew was trapped in a Hawaiian volcano while trying to film footage for the 1993 movie *Sliver* and barely escaped with their lives.

Not all volcanoes have names. Appendix 1, p. 175, lists over 70 as yet unnamed. Nor do all supposed volcanoes turn out to be such. Appendix 2 identifies them. Nor are volcanoes only on the earth. Appendix 4 is accordingly devoted to extraterrestrial volcanoes.

This volcanological vade-mecum closes with a Select Bibliography of books and articles that offer further background and more specific information. Some of it is on the technical side, but much of it will be readily accessible to the general reader and budding vulcanophile.

The Volcanoes

A

Abeki (Chad: 21.10N, 17.0E).

Abeki (8,036 ft./2,450 m) is part of a volcanic area in Chad's Tibesti region. There are no reports of modern eruptions in historic time.

Abu (Honshu, Japan: 34.50N, 131.60E).

Abu (1,873 ft./571 m.) is composed of several shield volcanoes. There is evidence of some activity in the post-glacial period.

Acamarchi (Chile: 23.30S, 67.62W).

Acamarchi (19,835 ft./6,046 m.) is a Holocene stratovolcano with no record of eruptions in historic time.

Acatenango (Guatemala: 14.50N, 90.88W).

Acatenango (13,044 ft./3,976 m.) is one of the highest stratovolcanoes in Central America. The earliest recorded eruption was in 1924. There was a second eruption in the 1920s and the most recent eruption occurred in 1972. Acatenango is still active; geologists reported a strong smell of sulfur but no visible fumaroles during an investigation in 1981.

Acigöl-Nevsehir (Turkey: 38.57N, 34.52E).

Acigöl-Nevsehir (5,541 ft./1,689 m.) is a Holocene Maars volcano with no recorded eruptions in historic time.

Aconcagua, Cerro (Araucanian *konka*, "straw stack," *hue*, "abundant in") (Argentina: 32.67S, 70.03W).

Cerro Aconcagua (22,834 ft./6,960 m) is entered in some reference books as the world's highest extinct volcano. Although of volcanic origin, the mountain is not itself actually a volcano.

Acotango (Chile/Bolivia: 18.37S, 69.05W).

Acotango (19,855 ft./6,052 m.) consists of Holocene stratovolcanoes with no record of eruptions in historic time.

Adagdak (Adak I., Aleutian Is., Alaska, USA: 51.98N, 176.60W).

Adagdak (2,115 ft./645 m.) is a small Holocene stratovolcano that forms the northern peninsula of Adak Island with Andrew Bay and Moffett. There is no record of an eruption in historic time.

Adams, Mt. (for John Adams [1735–1826], US president) (Washington, USA: 46.21N, 121.49W).

Mount Adams (12,276 ft./3,742 m) is an andesitic stratovolcano, and one of the largest volcanoes in the Cascade Range. There was volcanic activity somewhere between 520,000 and 3,500 years ago. The volcano's main cone was constructed over 220,000 years ago. It is considered possible that Mt. Adams may erupt again.

Adatara (Honshu, Japan: 37.62N, 140.28E).

Adatara (5,635 ft./1,718 m.) is a stratovolcano near Fukushima City, consisting of three cones — Maegatake, Osoyozan and Adatara. The earliest recorded eruption was in 1899. An eruption in July of 1900 killed 72 sulfur miners in the crater. The most recent eruption was recorded in September of 1996. Four hikers were killed in September of 1997 when they fell into the summit crater and likely died of sulfur inhalation.

Adwa (Ethiopia: 10.07N, 40.84E).

Adwa (7,037 ft./2,145 m.) is a Holocene stratovolcano. There is no record of any eruption in historic time.

Afdera (Ethiopia: 13.08N, 40.85E).

Afdera (4,245 ft./1,295 m.) is a stratovolcano located in the Afar region in Ethiopia near the Red Sea. There is no record of an eruption in historic time, though there is a possibility of eruptions in the past 10,000 years

Agmagan-Karadag (Armenia: 40.21N, 44.75E).

Agmagan-Karadag (11,679 ft./3,560 m.) is a volcanic field. It is unknown when eruptions occurred, but no record of any in historic times.

Agrigan (Mariana Is.: 18.77N, 145.67E).

Agrigan (3,165 ft./965 m.) is a stratovolcano forming a four-mile island. The sole recorded eruption occurred in 1917, depositing nearly 10 feet of ash on a coastal village. The island was evacuated in August of 1990 due to an increase in fumarole activity, though no eruption occurred.

Agua (Guatemala: 14.46N, 90.74W).

Agua (12,333 ft./3,760 m.) is a Holocene stratovolcano that has not erupted in historic time. Although no eruption, at least 1,000 people were killed in 1541 when the draining of a crater lake created mud flows that destroyed the former Guatemalan capital, Ciudad Vieja. Among the dead was Gobermadora Donna Beatrix, the first woman head of government on the American continent.

Agua de Pau (San Miguel, Azores: 37.77N, 25.47W).

Agua de Pau (3,106 ft./947 m.), located in central San Miguel Island, is a stratovolcano with a caldera. The earliest recorded eruption occurred in 1563, although radiocarbon dating indicates eruptions from approximately 6750 B.C. There was a month-long eruption in 1563 and an eruption lasting several days the following year.

Aguas Zarcas Group (Costa Rica: 10.42N, 84.31W).

The Aguas Zarcas Group (2,037 ft./621 m.) is composed of Holocene pyroclastic cones with no record of eruptions in historic time.

Aguilera (Chile: 50.17S, 73.83W).
Aguilera is a likely Holocene stratovolcano with no recorded eruptions in historic time.

Agung (Indonesian, "great") (Bali: 8.34S, 115.51E).
Agung (10,308 ft./3,142 m.) is a stratovolcano whose earliest recorded eruption occurred in 1808. The most recent eruption ended in 1964. This began in 1963 and killed at least 1,000 people, most in falls and flows of pumice and lava and in mud flows. Some were also swept out to sea or perished in landslides. The latest official death toll figure is 1,148.

Ahyi (Mariana Is.: 20.43N, 145.03E).
Ahyi (-230 ft./-70 m.) is a submarine volcano with no record of historical activity.

Akademiya Nauk (Russian, "Academy of Sciences", named by Vladimir Vlodavetz in 1939) (Kamchatka, Russia: 53.98N, 159.45E).
Akademiya Nauk (4,875 ft./1,486 m.) is part of the Karymsky Volcanic Center in Eastern Kamchatka. A Holocene stratovolcano, it began its activity approximately 50,000 years ago. There have been no historical eruptions.

Akagi (Honshu, Japan: 36.53N, 139.18E).
Akagi (5,997 ft./1,828 m.) is a stratovolcano whose sole recorded eruption to date occurred in 1251. There was a possible eruption in 1938 which remains unverified.

Akan (Hokkaido, Japan: 43.38N,144.02E).
Akan (4,916 ft./1,499 m.) is a caldera with four stratovolcanoes, with Me-Akan as the active vent. There have been at least 15 eruptions since the earliest recorded around 1800. Most were short lived, though an explosive phreatic eruption occurred in 1955. The most recent eruption occurred in 1988. The volcano is the home of Hakkaido's National Park.

Akhtang (Kamchatka, Russia: 55.43N, 158.65E).
Akhtang (6,417 ft./1,956 m.) is a Holocene shield volcano with no record of historical eruptions.

Akita-Komaga-Take (Honshu, Japan: 39.75N, 140.80E).
Akita-Komaga-Take (5,370 ft./1,637 m.) is a stratovolcano whose earliest recorded eruption occurred in 1890. The most recent eruption was in 1971.

Akita-Yake-yama (Honshu, Japan: 39.97N, 140.77E).
Akita-Yake-yama (4,481 ft./1,366 m.) is a small andesitic stratovolcano in northeast Honshu. The earliest recorded eruption occurred in 1867. There have been numerous small phreatic eruptions since, including ones in 1948, 1949, 1951 and 1957. The most recent eruption occurred in August of 1997.

Akuseki-jima (Ryukyu Is., Japan: 29.45N, 129.60E).
Akuseki-jima (1,922 ft./586 m.) is a Holocene stratovolcano with no record
of historical eruptions.

Akutan (perhaps Aleut *hakuta*, "I made a mistake") (Aleutian Is., Alaska, USA:
54.13N, 165.97W).
Akutan (4,274 ft./1,303 m.) is a stratovolcano with a summit caldera near
the southwest tip of the Alaska Peninsula. It is one of the most active volcanoes
in the Aleutian arc, with the earliest recorded eruption occurring in 1790. There
have been at least 27 eruptions since, most recently in 1992.

Alaid (Kuril Is.: 50.86N, 155.55E).
Alaid (7,672 ft./2,339 m.) is a stratovolcano on Atlasova, in the northern
Kuril Islands. It is the highest and most northern in the Kuril Islands. The first
recorded eruption occurred in 1790. A major eruption in 1981 produced a plume
that reached a height of seven miles. Recent eruptions occurred in 1986 and in
December of 1996.

Alamagan (Mariana Is.: 17.60N, 145.83E).
Alamagan (2,440 ft./744 m.) is a stratovolcano near Pagan Island. It is suspected that historic eruptions occurred in 1864 and 1887.

Alayta (Ethiopia: 12.88N, 40.57E).
Alayta (4,924 ft./1,501 m.) is a Holocene stratovolcano located in the Afar
region of Ethiopia. Alayta's earliest recorded eruption was in 1907. The most
recent eruption occurred in 1915.

Alban Hills *see* **Monte Albano.**

Albano, Monte [Alban Hills] (Pre-Celtic *alb*, "hill") (Italy: 41.73N, 12.70E).
Monte Albano (3,113 ft./949 m.) is a Holocene caldera with no record of
historic eruptions.

Alcedo, Volcán (Isabela I., Galápagos Is.: 0.43S, 91.12W).
Volcán Alcedo (3,707 ft./1,130 m.) is a shield volcano whose sole recorded
eruption to date occurred in 1953.

Ale Bagu (Ethiopia: 13.52N, 40.63E).
Ale Bagu (3,382 ft./1,031 m.) is a Holocene stratovolcano with no record
of historic eruptions.

Alid (Eritrea: 14.88N, 39.92E).
Alid (2,985 ft./910 m.), once thought to be a stratovolcano, is a dome with
a collapsed summit located in the Danakil depression in Eritrea. There is evidence of explosive eruptions with deposits of pyroclastic flows surrounding the
collapsed dome.

Alligator Lake (Yukon, Canada: 60.42N, 135.42W).
Alligator Lake (7,273 ft./2,217 m.) is a Holocene volcanic field with no record of eruptions in historic time.

Almolonga (Guatemala: 14.82N, 91.48W).
Almolonga (10,488 ft./3,197 m.) is a stratovolcano whose earliest recorded eruption occurred in 1765. The most recent eruption took place in 1818.

Alney-Chashakondzha (Kamchatka, Russia: 56.70N, 159.65E).
Alney-Chashakondzha (8,523 ft./2,598 m.) is a Holocene stratovolcano with no record of historical eruptions.

Alngey (Kamchatka, Russia: 57.70N, 160.40E).
Alngey (6,079 ft./1,853 m.) is a Holocene stratovolcano with no recorded eruptions in historical time.

Altar (Ecuador: 1.68S, 78.42W)
Altar (17,730 ft./5,405 m.) is an extinct volcano in central Ecuador. Named by the Spaniards because of its resemblance to a huge cathedral, the northern summit is called Canon, the eastern summit is Tabernacle, and the southern summit, which is the highest, is called Bishop.

Alu (Ethiopia: 13.82N, 40.55E).
Alu (1,407 ft./429 m.) consists of fissure vents. There is no record of an eruption in historic time, though likely eruptions have occurred in the past 10,000 years.

Aluchin Group (Russia: 66.12N, 165.63E).
The Aluchin Group (3,280 ft./1,000 m.) is comprised of Holocene cones with no record of eruptions in historic time.

Alutu (Ethiopia: 7.77N, 38.78E).
Alutu (7,660 ft./2,335 m.) is a Holocene stratovolcano with no record of eruptions in historic time.

Amak (Aleutian Is., Alaska, USA: 55.42N, 163.15W).
Amak (1,683 ft./513 m.) is a stratovolcano whose earliest recorded eruption occurred in 1700. The most recent eruption took place in 1796.

Ambalatungan Group (Luzon, Philippines: 17.32N, 121.10E).
The Ambalatungan Group is a compound volcano with fumarolic activity. There has been no record of eruptions in historic time.

Ambang (Sulawesi, Indonesia: 0.75N, 124.42E).
Ambang (5,889 ft./1,795 m.) is a volcanic complex whose sole recorded eruption to date occurred in 1845.

Ambitle (New Ireland: 4.08S, 153.65E).

Ambitle (1,476 ft./450 m.) is a Holocene stratovolcano with no evidence of eruptions in historic time.

Amboy (California, USA: 34.55N, 115.78W).

Amboy (984 ft./300 m.) is located west of the town of Amboy in California's Mojave desert. The Amboy Crater is a cinder cone, made of at least four nesting cones, which is thought to be approximately 6,000 years old and has gone through six eruptive phases.

Ambre-Bobaomby (Madagascar: 12.48S, 49.10E).

Ambre-Bobaomby (4,839 ft./1,475 m.) is a Holocene volcanic field with no record of eruptions in historic time.

Ambrym (Vanuatu: 16.25S, 168.12E).

Ambrym (4,375 ft./1,334 m.) is a shield volcano with a caldera forming Vanuatu's Ambrym Island in the Southwest Pacific. The earliest recorded eruption was is 1774. An extremely active volcano, it has erupted nearly 50 times since. Ten people lost their lives in an 1894 eruption, and 21 died in an explosive eruption in 1913, when explosions destroyed the mission hospital at Dip Point. Several hundred were evacuated to Éfaté after the 1950 eruption.

Amiata, Mt. (Italy: 42.90N, 11.63E).

Mount Amiata (5,702 ft./1,738 m.) is a Quaternary volcano with lava domes. It is the highest mountain in Italy's Tuscany region. There is no indication of eruptions in historic times, though geothermal activity is still occurring there.

Amoissa (Ethiopia: 10.07N, 40.84E).

Amoissa (5,684 ft./1,733 m.) is a caldera sometimes known as Abida or Dabita. It is considered a twin to the nearby Ayelu volcano. There is steam activity at Amoissa, indicating thermal activity in its depths.

Amorong (Luzon, Philippines: 15.83N, 120.80E).

Amorong (1,234 ft./376 m.) is a volcano with fumarolic activity but no record of historic eruptions.

Amsterdam I. (Indian Ocean: 37.83S, 77.52E).

Amsterdam Island (2,890 ft./881 m.) is a Holocene stratovolcano with no record of eruptions in historic time.

Amukta (Aleut, meaning unknown) (Aleutian Is., Alaska, USA: 52.50N, 171.25W).

Amukta (3,497 ft./1,066 m.) is an island stratovolcano. The earliest recorded eruption occurred in 1786. There have been four subsequent eruptions recorded, most recently in 1987.

Anallajsi, Nevado (Bolivia: 17.92S, 68.92W).
Nevado Anallajsi (18,864 ft./5,750 m.) is a Holocene stratovolcano with no record of eruptions in historic time.

Anatahan (Mariana Is.: 16.35N, 145.67E).
Anatahan (2,585 ft./788 m.) is a stratovolcano which forms a small island composed of calderas. There have been no historic eruptions, though increased fumarole activity caused the evacuation of the island in March of 1990. The island was declared unsafe following earthquake activity in June of 1993.

Anaun (Kamchatka, Russia: 56.32N, 158.83E).
Anaun (5,997 ft./1,828 m.) is a Holocene stratovolcano with no record of eruptions in historic time.

Andahua Valley (Peru: 15.42S, 72.33W).
The Andahua Valley (15,462 ft./4,713 m.) is composed of Holocene cinder cones with no record of eruptions in historic time.

Andrus (Antarctica: 75.80S, 132.33W).
Andrus (9,770 ft./2,978 m.) is composed of Holocene shield volcanoes with no record of eruptions in historic time.

Aneityum (Vanuatu: 20.20S, 169.83E).
Aneityum (2,794 ft./852 m.) is a group of Holocene stratovolcanoes on Vanuatu in the Southwest Pacific.

Aniakchak (Alaska, USA: 56.88N, 158.17W).
Aniakchak (4,398 ft./1,341 m.) is a caldera surrounded by pyroclastic flows. The earliest recorded eruption of 1931 deposited 0.6 cm. of ash 200 km. distant. Possible later eruptions occurred in 1942 and 1951.

Anjuisky *see* **Anzhuysky.**

Ankaizina Field (Madagascar: 14.30S, 48.67E).
The Ankaizina Field (9,442 ft./2,878 m.) is a cinder cone Holocene volcanic field with no record of eruptions in historic time.

Ankaratra Field (Madagascar: 19.40S, 47.20E).
The Ankaratra Field (8,674 ft./2,644 m.) is a cinder cone Holocene volcanic field with no record of eruptions in historic time.

Antillanca Group (40.77S, 72.15W).
The Antillanca Group (6,528 ft./1,990 m.) is a Holocene stratovolcano with no recorded eruptions in historic time.

Antipodes I. (Southern Pacific: 49.68S, 178.77E).
Antipodes Island (1,319 ft./402 m.) is composed of Holocene pyroclastic cones with no recorded eruptions in historic time.

Antisana (Ecuador: 0.48S, 78.14W).
Antisana (18,871 ft./5,752 m.) had its first recorded eruption in 1801. The most recent occurred the following year in 1802.

Antofagasta de la Sierra (Argentina: 26.08S, 67.50W).
Antofagasta de la Sierra (13,123 ft./4,000 m.) is composed of scoria cones. There have been no recorded eruptions in historic time.

Antofalla, Volcán (Argentina: 25.53S, 68.00W).
Volcán Antofalla (20,013 ft./6,100 m.) is a stratovolcano with fumarolic activity. There have been no eruptions recorded in historic time.

Antuco (Chile: 37.41S, 71.35W).
Antuco (9,773 ft./2,979 m.) is a stratovolcano whose earliest recorded eruption occurred in 1752. The most recent eruption took place in 1869.

Anunciación, Cerro (Costa Rica: 10.47N, 85.07W).
Cerro Anunciación (1,318 ft./402 m.) is composed of Holocene pyroclastic cones. There have been no eruptions recorded in historic time.

Anzhuysky (Russia: 67.17N, 165.20E).
Anzhuysky (3,445 ft./1,050 m.) is a Holocene complex volcano with no record of eruptions in historic time.

Aoba (Vanuatu: 15.40S, 167.83E).
Aoba (4,907 ft./1,496 m.) is a shield volcano on Vanuatu in the Southwest Pacific. A large shallow crater, Manaro, contains several lakes and gas vents. Legend tells of an eruption in 1670 in which lava flow caused many deaths. There were reports of volcanic unrest in 1995.

Aoga-shima (Izu Is., Japan: 32.45N, 139.77E).
Aoga-shima (1,387 ft./423 m.) is a stratovolcano whose earliest recorded eruption occurred in 1652. An eruption in 1783 reportedly killed seven (or possibly 14) people, while explosions in the last month of the five-year 1780 eruption caused deaths of around 130. The island was subsequently abandoned for 50 years.

Apastepeque Volcanic Field (El Salvador: 13.72N, 88.77W).
The Apastepeque Volcanic Field (2,300 ft./700 m.) is a Holocene volcanic field with no record of eruptions in historic time.

Api Siau *see* **Karangetang.**

Apo (Mindanao, Philippines: 6.99N, 125.27E).
Apo (9,691 ft./2,954 m.) is a stratovolcano with fumarolic activity. There have been no recorded eruptions in historic time.

Apoyeque (Nicaragua: 12.42N, 86.34W).
Apoyeque (1,535 ft./468 m.) is a caldera with no recorded eruptions in historic time.

Apoyo (Nicaragua: 11.92N, 86.03W).
Apoyo (1,535 ft./468 m.) is a Holocene caldera with no record of historical eruptions.

Ara Shatan *see* **Butajiri.**

Aracar (Argentina: 24.27S, 67.77W).
Aracar (19,954 ft./6,082 m.) is a stratovolcano whose sole recorded eruption to date occurred in 1993.

Aragats (Armenia: 40.55N, 44.12E).
Aragats (13,418 ft./4,090 m.) is a Holocene stratovolcano with no evidence of eruptions in historic time.

Ararat, Mt. (Pre-Indoeuropean *ar,* "mountain") (Turkey: 39.70N, 44.28E).
Ararat (16,940 ft./5,165 m.) is the largest volcano in Turkey. There have been no recorded eruptions in historical time, though there are indications that there has been volcanic activity in the last 10,000 years. The stratovolcano is considered by many to be the resting place of the biblical Noah's Ark.

Arayat (Luzon, Philippines: 15.20N, 120.74E).
Arayat (3,366 ft./1,026 m.) is a Holocene stratovolcano with no recorded eruptions in historic time.

Ardoukoba (Djibouti: 11.38N, 42.47E).
Ardoukoba (978 ft./298 m.) consists of fissure vents. The sole recorded eruption to date occurred in 1978.

Arenal (Costa Rica: 10.46N, 84.70W).
Arenal (5,435 ft./1,657 m.) was a dormant stratovolcano before the sole recorded eruption to date in 1968, although radiocarbon dating indicates eruptions from Cerro Chato (Spanish, "low hill") from approximately 3190 B.C. The eruption of 1968 propelled lava blocks up to 5 km. from the vent, and in the first three days around 80 people were killed by pumice and lava flows and falling rocks. It has been continuously active since then. Two people died in 1975 and

a climber was killed in 1988 when he was struck on his head by rocks from an explosion when he was only 3 meters from the crater rim.

Arhab, Harrat (Yemen: 15.63N, 44.08E).

Harrat Arhab (6,890 ft./2,100 m.) is a volcanic field whose earliest recorded eruption occurred in approximately A.D. 500.

Arintica, Volcán (Chile: 1873S, 69.05W).

Volcán Arintica (18,363 ft./5,597 m.) is a Holocene stratovolcano with no recorded eruptions in historic time.

Arjuno-Welirang (Java: 7.72S, 112.58E).

Arjuno-Welirang (10,954 ft./3,339 m.) is a stratovolcano whose sole recorded eruption to date occurred in 1952.

Asacha (Kamchatka, Russia: 52.35N, 157.83E).

Asacha (6,265 ft./1,910 m.) is a composite stratovolcano composed of several extinct cones. There is no indication of an eruption in historical time.

Asama (Honshu, Japan: 39.40N, 138.53E).

Asama-yama (8,364 ft./2,550 m.) is a complex stratovolcano composed of three overlapping bodies, Kurohu-yama, Kama-yama and Asama-yama. The earliest recorded eruption was in A.D. 685. There have been over 100 eruptions from 1108, with the most recent in 1990. Up to 800 people lost their lives in the 1598 eruption. They were religious pilgrims who had climbed to the summit and stayed there because it was an inauspicious day to descend. The eruption of 1783 reportedly killed 1,491 people. The Agatsuma River was dammed by mud flows and flooded, washing away 1,300 houses and up to 1,400 people. Suspended ash and dust reduced sunlight, causing cold and rainy weather with resultant famine. The eruption of 1900 killed 25 when a boulder swept through a village. Eleven died in a 1947 eruption while climbing the volcano.

Asavyo (Ethiopia: 13.07N, 41.60E).

Asavyo (3,937 ft./1,200 m.) is a Holocene shield volcano. There is no record of eruptions in historic time.

Ascension (Southern Atlantic: 7.95S, 14.37W).

Ascension Island (2,814 ft./858 m.) is a Holocene stratovolcano. There have been no known historic eruptions.

Askja (Iceland: 65.03N, 16.75W).

Askja (4,954 ft./1,510 m.) is a massive caldera in the mountain area known as Dyngjufjoll. The earliest recorded eruption was in 1875, which formed the lake Oeskjuvatn. Askja's most recent eruption occurred in 1961.

Asmara (Ethiopia: 11.27N, 41.52E).

Asmara (1,640 ft./500 m.) is a pyroclastic cone. There is no record of a historical eruption, though there have been eruptions in the past 10,000 years.

Aso (Kyushu, Japan: 32.88N, 131.10E).

Aso (5,222 ft./1,592 m.) is a caldera containing stratovolcanoes and cinder cones. The earliest recorded eruption occurred in A.D. 553. Aso is Japan's most prolific volcano, with over 150 eruptions since 1229, all from its cone, Naka-dake ("center peak"). The most recent eruption occurred in 1993. Many reportedly perished from ash suffocation in a 1827 eruption, while four sulfur miners lost their lives in the 1872 eruption, six tourists in that of 1953, and twelve ropeway workers in 1958. Three tourists died in a 1979 eruption near the ropeway station, northeast of the crater, and two tourists were killed by volcanic gases in November of 1997.

Assab Volcano Field (Ethiopia: 12.95N, 42.43E).

Assab Volcano Field (3,238 ft./987 m.) is a Holocene volcanic field. There is no record of any eruptions in historic time.

Asuncion (Mariana Is.: 19.67N, 145.40E).

Asuncion (2,811 ft./857 m.) is a stratovolcano whose earliest recorded eruption was in 1906.

Atacazo (Ecuador: 0.35S, 78.62W).

Atacazo (14,642 ft./4,463 m.) is a Holocene stratovolcano with no recorded eruptions in historic time.

Atitlán (Guatemala: 14.58N, 91.19W).

Atitlán (11,595 ft./3,535 m.), with the volcanoes San Pedro and Toliman, borders Lake Atitlan. The earliest recorded eruption occurred in 1469. The most recent eruption was in 1853.

Atka (Atka I., Aleutian Is., Alaska, USA: 52.38N, 174.15W).

Atka (5,030 ft./1,533 m.) is a central shield and caldera surrounded by several satellitic volcanoes. It is the largest volcanic center in the central Aleutians. The earliest recorded eruption occurred in 1812. The most recent eruption was from the Korovin vent in 1987. There was a possible small eruption reported in June of 1996.

Atlasova (Kamchatka, Russia: 57.97N, 160.65E).

Atlasova (5,787 ft./1,764 m.) is a Holocene shield volcano with no record of eruptions in historic time.

Atsonopuri (Kuril Is.: 44.80N, 147.13E).

Atsonopuri (3,952 ft./1,205 m.) is a stratovolcano located on Iturup Island in the southern Kuril Islands. The only recorded eruptions were small ones in 1812 and 1932.

Aucanquilcha, Cerro (Chile: 21.22S, 68.47W).

Cerro Aucanquilcha (20,262 ft./6,176 m.) is a Holocene stratovolcano with no eruptions recorded in historic time.

Auckland Field (New Zealand: 36.90S, 174.87E).

Auckland Field (853 ft./260 m.) is a volcanic field with evidence of volcanic activity in the past 2,000 years.

Augustine (named by Captain James Cook for St. Augustine on May 26, 1778) (Alaska, USA: 59.37N, 153.42W).

Augustine (4,205 ft./1,282 m.) is a lava dome that makes up part of an Aleutian volcanic arc in Cook Inlet, Alaska. The earliest recorded eruption was in 1812. An eruption in 1883 generated a giant wave that hit the community of English Bay, on Cook Inlet coast, 85 kilometers away. The tide was out when the wave struck, minimizing damage. Subsequent eruptions occurred in 1935, 1963, 1976 and 1986.

Avachinskaya Sopka (Kamchatka, Russia: 52.25N, 158.83E).

Avachinskaya Sopka (8,990 ft./2,741 m.) is Kamchatka's most active stratovolcano. Classified as a Somma volcano, the first recorded eruption occurred in 1737. There have been 16 known eruptions since, with a major explosive eruption in 1945. The most recent eruption in 1991 produced lava and mud flows and created a dome. Fumarolic activity was recorded in November of 1997.

Awu (Sangihe Is., Indonesia: 3.67N, 125.50E).

Awu (4,330 ft./1,320 m.) is a stratovolcano whose earliest recorded eruption occurred in 1640. About 3,000 people were killed in an eruption in 1711 when they were caught by flows of pumice and lava. Around 950 perished during an 1812 eruption. The largest number of casualties was 2,806 during the 1856 eruption, when eight villages were partly destroyed. Thirty-eight perished in pumice and lava flows, and one person drowned while swimming to a ship, during a 1966 eruption. Around 1,000 were also injured by the impact of fragments from the lava plug. The most recent eruption occurred in 1992.

Ayelu (Ethiopia: 10.08N, 40.70E).

Ayelu (7,035 ft./2,145 m.) is a stratovolcano located in Ethiopia's rift valley. There is no record of an historical eruption, though there is a likelihood of an eruption in the past 10,000 years.

Azufral, Volcán (Colombia: 1.08N, 77.68W).

Volcán Azufral (13,353 ft./4,070 ft.) is a stratovolcano located in Colombia. There have been no known historic eruptions.

Azufre, Cerro del (Chile: 21.78S, 68.23W).
Cerro del Azufre (17,998 ft./5,486 m.) is a Holocene stratovolcano with no record of eruptions in historic time.

Azul, Cerro 1 (Spanish, "blue peak") (Isabela I., Galápagos Is.: 0.90S, 91.42W).
Cerro Azul (5,545 ft./1,690 m.) is a stratovolcano with a steep summit caldera on the southwest end of Isabela Island. The earliest recorded eruption occurred in 1932. Cerro Azul has been one of the Galápagos' most active volcanoes since that time. In 1943 a P-39 fighter pilot from the Galápagos air base crashed when flying over the volcano at the time of an eruption. There have been subsequent eruptions in 1959 and 1979, and reports of volcanic activity in September of 1998.

Azul, Cerro 2 (Spanish, "blue peak") [**Quizapu**] (Chile: 35.65S, 70.76W).
Cerro Azul (12,427 ft./3,788 m.) is a stratovolcano whose earliest recorded eruption occurred in 1846. The most recent eruption took place in 1967.

Azuma (Honshu, Japan: 37.73N, 140.25E).
Azuma (6,640 ft./2,024 m.) is composed of overlapping stratovolcanoes and shield volcanoes. There were reports of eruptions in 1331 and 1711. The earliest recorded eruption was in 1889. Two geologists on the crater rim were killed by falling stones during an eruption in 1893. The most recent eruption in 1977 was rather small. All of the eruptions have been from cone Issaikyo.

B

Babuyan Claro (Philippines: 19.52N, 121.94E).
Babuyan Claro (3,870 ft./1,180 m.) is a stratovolcano that composes Babuyan Island, north of Luzon, in the Babuyan Channel. It is a stratovolcano that has erupted at least eight times since its earliest recorded eruption in 1652. Most of the eruptions have taken pace at the western vent, Smith Volcano, a symmetrical cinder cone. There was a major eruption in 1831, which caused extensive damage. The most recent eruption occurred in 1924.

Bachelor, Mount (mountain stands apart from Three Sisters) (Oregon, USA: 43.98N, 121.69W).
Mount Bachelor (9,064 ft./2,763 m.) is a shield volcano with a steep summit cone. There are no indications that there have been any eruptions since approximately 8,000 years ago.

Bagana (Bougainville: 6.14S, 155.19E).
Bagana (5,740 ft./1,750 m.) is one of seven volcanoes located on Bougainville Island in the Southwest Pacific. A lava cone, Bagana, has erupted over

20 times since its first known historical eruption in 1842. A major explosion in December of 1883 killed several people. Other major eruptions occurred in 1950, 1952 and 1966. There have been continuous eruptions since 1972, with lava flows documented as recently as August 1995.

Baitoushan (China/Korea: 41.98N, 128.08E).

Baitoushan (9,055 ft./2,744 m.) is a stratovolcano with a caldera located on the border of China and Korea. There have been five known eruptions in the past 1,000 years, with the most recent occurring in 1702. An eruption in 1050 was one of the largest known eruptions, with the volcano discharging nearly 150 cubic kilometers of pumice.

Bakening (Kamchatka, Russia: 53.90N, 158.07E).

Bakening (7,470 ft./2,277 m.) is a Holocene caldera with no record of eruptions in historic time.

Baker, Mt. (for Joseph Baker, officer in Vancouver's expedition) (Washington, USA: 48.79N, 121.82W).

Mount Baker (10,800 ft./3,285 m.) is a stratovolcano in northern Washington state. The volcano's summit is covered by glaciers, which caused the Indians to give it a name meaning "White Steep Mountain." There have been 13 recorded eruptions in historical time, with the earliest known occurring in 1792. A major eruption in 1843 caused a forest fire and dropped much volcanic ash. The most recent eruption occurred in 1880, though there was a steam release in 1975.

Balagan-Tas (Russia: 66.43N, 143.73E).

Balagan-Tas (3,258 ft./993 m.) is composed of cinder cones. The sole recorded eruption to date occurred in approximately 1775.

Balatocan (Mindanao, Philippines: 8.80N, 124.92E).

Balatocan (7,546 ft./2,300 m.) is a compound volcano with fumarolic activity. There have been no recorded eruptions in historic time.

Balbi (Bougainville: 5.83S, 154.98E).

Balbi (8.907 ft./2,715 m.) is a Holocene stratovolcano on Bougainville Island in the Solomon Island chain in the Southwest Pacific. There is no evidence of eruptions in historic time.

Bald Knoll (Utah, USA: 37.33N, 112.41W).

Bald Knoll (7,004 ft./2,135 m.) is composed of Holocene cinder cones. There is no record of eruptions in historic time.

Bal Haf, Harrat (Yemen: 14.05N, 48.33E).

Harrat Bal Haf (763 ft./233 m.) is a Holocene volcanic field with no record of eruptions in historic time.

Baluan (Admiralty Is.: 2.57S, 147.28E).

Baluan (833 ft./254 m.) is a Holocene stratovolcano with no record of eruptions in historic time.

Baluran (Java: 7.85S, 114.37E).

Baluran (4,091 ft./1,247 m.) is a Holocene stratovolcano with no record of eruptions in historic time.

Balut (Philippines: 5.40N, 125.37E).

Balut (2,795 ft./852 m.) is a Holocene stratovolcano 12 miles south of Mindanao. Balut has likely erupted in the past 10,000 years, but there are no recorded historic eruptions.

Bam (Papua New Guinea: 3.60S, 144.85E).

Bam (2,247 ft./685 m.) is a stratovolcano slightly northeast of Papua New Guinea. There have been 16 eruptions since the earliest recorded in 1872. During an eruption in 1954 the population of Bam was evacuated to Bogia on the mainland for six months. They found it hard to adapt to the new environment, resulting in the death of 25 people, with many more suffering serious illness. The most recent eruption occurred in 1960.

Bamus (New Britain, Papua New Guinea: 5.20S, 151.23E).

Bamus (7,375 ft./2,248 m.) is a stratovolcano on New Britain Island in the south Bismarck Sea. There have been four recorded explosive eruptions in historical time. The earliest was in 345 B.C. Others occurred in 270 B.C. and A.D. 1645. The most recent eruption was in 1886.

Banahaw (Luzon, Philippines: 14.07N, 121.48E).

Banahaw (7,142 ft./2,177 m.) is a Holocene volcanic complex with no record of eruptions in historic time.

Banda Api (Banda Sea, Indonesia: 4.52S, 129.87E).

Banda Api (2,100 ft./640 m.) is a caldera whose earliest recorded eruption occurred in 1586. The entire population of over 1,000 people at the foot of the volcano was reportedly killed in a 1694 eruption. During the most recent eruption in 1988, a lava flow overran a mosque in Batu Angus village, killing an elderly man who had sought refuge there. Two young men also died when their canoe was hit by a block of rock.

Bandai (Honshu, Japan: 37.60N, 140.08E).

Bandai (5,968 ft./1,819 m.) is a stratovolcano with a caldera located in northern Honshu. There have been four recorded eruptions since A.D. 806, including one in 1787. The most recent eruption occurred in 1888, when an avalanche of debris buried many villages, killing 461 people. Several lakes were formed where rivers were dammed by deposit. Some of these later burst, flooding downstream villages.

Banua Wuhu (Sangihe Is., Indonesia: 3.14N, 125.49E).
Banua Wuhu (-16 ft./-5 m.) is a submarine volcano whose earliest recorded submarine eruption occurred in 1835. The most recent eruption occurred in 1919.

Baransky (Kuril Is.: 45.10N, 148.02E).
Baransky (3,712 ft./1,132 m.) is a stratovolcano located on Iturup Island in the Southern Kuril Islands. The sole recorded eruption to date was a small explosive one in 1951.

Barcena (Mexico: 19.30N, 110.82W).
Barcena (1,089 ft./332 m.) is composed of cinder cones whose sole recorded eruption to date occurred in 1952.

Bárdharbunga (Iceland: 64.63N, 17.53W).
Bárdharbunga (6,560 ft./2,000 m.) is a stratovolcano whose earliest recorded eruption occurred in approximately A.D. 940, but ash layer datings indicate the earliest eruption at approximately 7050 B.C. The most recent eruption occurred in 1902. A fissure between Bárdhabunga and **Grímsvötn** in Vatnajökull, Europe's largest glacier, erupted in 1996 causing a flood that swept south, destroying roads, bridges, and power lines but causing no casualties, as the area of the flood had been evacuated.

Barkhatnaya Sopka (Kamchatka, Russia: 52.82N, 158.27E).
Barkhatnaya Sopka (2,854 ft./870 m.) is composed of Holocene lava domes. There is no record of eruptions in historic time.

Barren Island (Andaman Is.: 12.92N, 93.87E).
Barren Island (1,000 ft./305 m.) is a stratovolcano in the Andaman Islands in the Indian Ocean. The earliest recorded eruption occurred in 1787. There have been four moderate explosive eruptions since, including one in 1991 that lasted six months and caused damage. The most recent eruption occurred in 1994.

Barrier, The (Kenya: 2.32N, 36.57E).
The Barrier (3,358 ft./1,032 m.) is a complex shield volcano composed of four different volcanic centers. It is located near Lake Turkana and Lake Logipi in Kenya, forming a natural dam between the two lakes. There have been nine eruptions since the earliest recorded eruption in 1871. The most recent eruption was in 1921. Almost all the eruptions came from Teleki's Volcano (discovered in 1888 by Hungarian explorer Sámuel Teleki and named for him).

Baru (Panama: 8.80N, 82.56W).
Baru (11,371 ft./3,466 m.) is a volcanic complex whose earliest recorded eruption occurred in approximately 1550, although radiocarbon dating indicates an earlier eruption in approximately 600 B.C.

Barva (Costa Rica: 10.13N, 84.10W).

Barva (9,534 ft./2,906 m.) is a Holocene volcanic complex with no recorded eruptions in historic time.

Bas Dong Nai (Vietnam: 10.80N, 107.20E).

Bas Dong Nai (1,286 ft./392 m.) is a Holocene volcanic field with no record of eruptions in historic time.

Batur (Bali: 8.24S, 115.37E).

Batur (5,631 ft./1,717 m.) is a complex of coalesced volcanic cones within two nested calderas. It is located on the island of Bali. The earliest recorded eruption took place in 1804. There have been over 20 eruptions since. Two people were reportedly killed in the 1963 eruption, when three villages were partly destroyed as well as large areas of arable land. The most recent eruption occurred in 1974. Mild volcanic activity was reported in July of 1998.

Bayo, Cerro (Chile/Argentina: 25.42S, 68.58W).

Cerro Bayo (17,720 ft./5,401 m.) is a Holocene complex volcano with no record of eruptions in historic time.

Bayonnaise Rocks (Izu Is., Japan: 31.92N, 139.92E).

Bayonnaise Rocks (33 ft./10 m.) is a submarine volcano. The earliest recorded submarine eruption, 14 km. north of Bayonnaise Rocks, was recorded in 1896. The most recent eruption occurred in 1970. This and several unconfirmed later eruptions all came from the central dome Myojin-sho. The dome's 1952 eruption sank the research ship *Kaiyo-maru* with the loss of all 31 crew members.

Bayuda Volcanic Field (Sudan: 18.33N, 32.75E).

The Bayuda Volcanic Field is composed of cinder cones. There is evidence of volcanic activity in the past 2,000 years.

Bazman (Iran: 28.07N, 60.00E).

Bazman (11,447 ft./3,490 m.) is a stratovolcano in southeast Iran. There is no record of eruptions in historic times, though there are fumaroles.

Beerenberg (Norwegian, "bear mountain")(Jan Mayen I., Arctic Ocean: 71.08N, 8.17W).

Beerenberg (7,468 ft./2,277 m.) is the world's northernmost stratovolcano and forms the north end of Jan Mayen Island. Mostly covered by glaciers, Beerenberg has erupted six times since 1732. Following the 1970 eruption, all 39 inhabitants (men working on whaling stations) were obliged to evacuate. The most recent eruption occurred in January of 1985, with nearly 7 million cubic meters of lava discharged.

Belen'kaya (Russian, "whitish") (Kamchatka, Russia: 51.75N, 157.27E).
Belen'kaya (2,927 ft./892 m.) is a Holocene stratovolcano with no record of eruptions in historic time.

Belirang-Beriti (Sumatra: 2.82S, 102.18E).
Belirang-Beriti (6,424 ft./1,958 m.) is a compound volcano with fumarolic activity. There have been no recorded eruptions in historic time.

Belknap, Mt. (for R.S. Belknap, early settler) (Oregon, USA: 42.28N, 121.84W).
Mount Belknap (7,875 ft./2,096 m.) is a shield volcano on the crest of the High Cascades of Oregon. It likely began erupting approximately 3,000 years ago with the main shield forming nearly 1,700 years ago.

Bely (Russian, "white") (Kamchatka, Russia: 57.88N, 160.53E).
Bely (6,824 ft./2,080 m.) is a Holocene shield volcano with no record of eruptions in historic time.

Berg *see* **Kolokol Group.**

Berlin (Antarctica: 76.05S, 136.00W).
Berlin (11,410 ft./3,478 m.) is composed of shield volcanoes with fumarolic activity. There have been no known eruptions in historic time.

Beru (Ethiopia: 8.95N, 39.75E).
Beru (3,608 ft./1,100 m.) is an unknown type of Holocene volcano. There is no evidence of eruptions in historic time.

Berutarube (Kuril Is.: 44.47N, 146.93E).
Berutarube (4,001 ft./1,200 m.) is a Holocene stratovolcano located on Iturup Island in the Southern Kuril Islands. There have been no historic reports of an eruption. A suspected eruption in 1812 was likely only fumarolic activity.

Besar, Gunung (Sumatra: 4.43S, 103.67E).
Gunung Besar (6,230 ft./1,899 m.) is a stratovolcano whose sole recorded eruption to date occurred in 1940.

Bezymyanny (Russian, "nameless") (Kamchatka, Russia: 55.98N, 160.59E).
Bezymyanny (9,453 ft./2,882 m.), located on the Kamchatka Peninsula, is one of the most active stratovolcanoes on earth. The earliest recorded eruption was in 1956, when the distinctive new dome Novy (Russian, "new") arose on the site of the crater formed during the eruption. Ash deposits were 50 centimeters deep some 10 kilometers away, and mudflows extended 80 kilometers. Radiocarbon datings indicate earlier eruptions from approximately 7050 B.C, however. Since 1956 there have been over 30 eruptions, with the most recent in 1995–97,

when ashes were spewed five miles high, forcing U.S. airlines to change their flight paths. This eruption caused the formation of a lava dome.

Big Bunchgrass (Oregon, USA: 42.70N, 122.19W).
Big Bunchgrass (6,640 ft./2,024 m.) is a Holocene pyroclastic cone with no record of eruptions in historic time.

Big Cave (California, USA: 40.95N, 121.36W).
Big Cave (4,130 ft./1,259 m.) is a Holocene shield volcano with no record of eruptions in historic time.

Bilate River Field (Ethiopia: 7.07N, 38.10E).
The Bilate River Field (5,580 ft./1,700 m.) is a Holocene volcanic field with no record of eruptions in historic time.

Biliran (Philippines: 11.52N, 124.53E).
Biliran (3,895 ft./1,187 m.) is a compound volcano that composes a mountainous island north of the island of Leyte in the Philippines. The sole recorded eruption to date occurred in 1939.

Billy Mitchell (Bougainville: 9.09S, 155.22E).
Billy Mitchell (5,065 ft./1,544 m.) is a pyroclastic shield with likely volcanic activity in the past 500 years.

Binuluan (Luzon, Philippines: 17.31N, 121.09E).
Binuluan (7,641 ft./2,329 m.) is a compound volcano with fumarolic activity. The sole recorded eruption to date in 1952 was probably of steam only, but sulfur melted and flowed downhill, killing about 12 people.

Bir Borhut (Yemen: 15.55N, 50.63E).
Bir Borhut is a volcanic field with likely volcanic activity in the past 10,000 years.

Bishoftu Field (Ethiopia: 8.78N, 38.98E).
The Bishoftu Field (6,069 ft./1,850 m.) is a fissure vent with no known historic eruptions. There has been likely volcanic activity in the past 10,000 years.

Biu Plateau (Nigeria: 10.75N, 12.00E).
Biu Plateau is a volcanic field with possible volcanic activity in the past 10,000 years.

Black Peak (Alaska, USA: 56.53N, 158.80W).
Black Peak (3,386 ft./1,032 m.) is a Holocene stratovolcano with no record of eruptions in historic time.

Black Rock Desert (Utah, USA: 38.97N, 112.50W).
The Black Rock Desert (5,905 ft./1,800 m.) is a volcanic field with likely volcanic activity in the past 2,000 years.

Blanca, Loma (Chile: 36.29S, 71.01W).
Loma Blanca (7,441 ft./2,268 m.) is a Holocene stratovolcano with no record of eruptions in historic time.

Bliznets (Russian, "twin") (Kamchatka, Russia: 56.97N, 159.78E).
Bliznets (4,081 ft./1,244 m.) is a Holocene stratovolcano with no record of eruptions in historic time.

Blue Lake Crater (Oregon, USA: 44.42N, 121.77W).
Blue Lake Crater (4,035 ft./1,230 m.) is a Holocene Maar volcano with no record of eruptions in historic time.

Blue, Volcán (Nicaragua: 12.68N, 83.92W).
Volcán Blue (492 ft./150 m.) is composed of Holocene cinder cones. There have been no recorded eruptions in historic time.

Blup Blup (imitative) (Papua New Guinea: 3.51S, 144.62E).
Blup Blup (1,319 ft./402 m.) is a Holocene stratovolcano with no record of an historic eruption. An eruption of 1616 said to be of Blup Blup was actually of nearby **Manam**.

Bobrof (Aleutian Is., Alaska, USA: 51.90N, 177.43W).
Bobrof (2,421 ft./738 m.) is a stratovolcano with likely Holocene activity, but no recorded eruptions in historic time.

Bogatyr Ridge (Kuril Is.: 44.83N, 147.37E).
Bogatyr Ridge (5,359 ft./1,634 m.) is a Holocene stratovolcano located on Iturup Island in the Southern Kuril Islands. There is no record of any historic eruptions.

Bogoslof (Aleutian Is., Alaska, USA: 53.93N, 168.03W).
Bogoslof (331 ft./101 m.) is a submarine volcano whose earliest recorded submarine eruption, from its former dome, Old Bogoslof (Castle Rock), occurred in 1796. The most recent eruption took place in 1992.

Boina (Djibouti: 11.25N, 41.83E).
Boina (985 ft./300 m.) is a Quaternary fumarole field likely formed in the Pleistocene Era.

Boisa (Papua New Guinea: 3.99S, 144.97E).
Boisa (787 ft./240 m.) is a stratovolcano with no record of historic eruptions.

Bola (New Britain, Papua New Guinea: 5.15S, 150.03E).
Bola (3,789 ft./1,155 m.) is a Holocene stratovolcano with no record of historic eruptions.

Bolshe-Bannaya (Kamchatka, Russia: 52.90N, 157.78E).
Bolshe-Bannaya (3,937 ft./1,200 m.) is a Holocene volcano composed of lava domes. There is no record of eruptions in historic time.

Bolshoi Kekuknaysky (Kamchatka, Russia: 56.47N, 157.80E).
Bolshoi Kekuknaysky (4,596 ft./1,401 m.) are Holocene shield volcanoes with no record of eruptions in historic time.

Bolshoi Payalpan (Kamchatka, Russia: 55.88N, 157.78E).
Bolshoi Payalpan (6,253 ft./1,906 m.) are Holocene shield volcanoes with no record of eruptions in historic time.

Bolshoi Semiachik (Kamchatka, Russia: 54.32N, 160.02E).
Bolshoi Semiachik (5,642 ft./1,720 m.) is an extinct stratovolcano. There is evidence that the volcano has erupted at least twice, with the last eruption taking place near 4450 B.C.

Bombalai (Borneo: 4.40N, 117.88E).
Bombalai (1,742 ft./531 m.) is a Holocene volcanic cone with no record of eruptions in historic time.

Bona-Churchill (*Bona* for racing yacht; *Churchill* for British prime minister) (Alaska, USA: 61.38N, 141.75W).
Bona-Churchill (16,420 ft./5,005 m.) are Holocene stratovolcanoes with no record of eruptions in historic time.

Boquerón (El Salvador: 13.74N, 89.29W).
Boquerón (6,209 ft./1,893 m.) is a stratovolcano that grew within the collapsed caldera of an older volcano, San Salvador. There was volcanic activity on the northern side of Boquerón after the formation of the crater. The most recent eruption took place in June of 1917. A large earthquake with fissures releasing lava resulted.

Bora-Bericcio Complex (Ethiopia: 8.27N, 39.03E).
The Bora-Bericcio Complex (7,497 ft./2,285 m.) is composed of pumice cones. There have been no eruptions in historic time, though it is likely volcanic activity has occured in the past 10,000 years.

Borale Ale (Ethiopia: 13.72N, 40.60E).
Borale Ale (2,192 ft./668 m.) is a Holocene stratovolcano with no record of eruptions in historic time.

Borawli (Ethiopia: 13.30N, 40.98E).
Borawli (2,664 ft./812 m.) is a Holocene stratovolcano. There have been no recorded historical eruptions.

Borawli Complex (Ethiopia: 11.63N, 41.45E).
The Borawli Complex (2,871 ft./875 m.) is a lava dome likely formed in the past 10,000 years.

Boset-Bericha (Ethiopia: 8.56N, 39.47R).
Boset-Bericha (8,028 ft./2,447 m.) is a Holocene stratovolcano with no recorded eruptions in historic time.

Bouvet (Southern Atlantic: 54.42S, 3.35E).
Bouvet (2,559 ft./780 m.) is a Holocene shield volcano with no record of eruptions in historic time.

Bratan (Bali: 8.28S, 115.13E).
Bratan (7,467 ft./2,276 m.) is a Holocene caldera with no record of eruptions in historic time.

Brava (Cape Verde Is.: 14.85N, 24.72W).
Brava (2,950 ft./900 m.) is a Holocene stratovolcano creating a small island in the Cape Verde Islands. There are no known historic eruptions.

Bravo, Cerro (Spanish, "wild peak") (Colombia: 5.09N,75.30W).
Cerro Bravo (13,125 ft./4,000 m.) is a stratovolcano with evidence of volcanic activity in the past 300 years.

Brennisteinsfjöll (Icelandic, "burned stone mountain") (Iceland: 63.92N, 21.83W).
Brennisteinsfjöll (2,054 ft./626 m.) is composed of crater rows. The earliest recorded eruption occurred in approximately A.D. 1000. The most recent eruption took place in 1341.

Bridgeman I. (Antarctica: 62.05S, 56.75W).
Bridgeman Island (787 ft./240 m.) is a stratovolcano with no recorded eruptions in historic time.

Bridge River Cones (British Columbia, Canada: 50.80N, 123.40W).
The Bridge River Cones (8,200 ft./.2,500 m.) is a Holocene volcanic field with no record of eruptions in historic time.

Brimstone I. (Kermadec Is.: 30.23S, 178.92W).
Brimstone Island (-6,560 ft./-2000 m.) is a submarine volcano with no record of eruptions in historic time.

Bristol I. (South Sandwich Is.: 59.03S, 26.58W).

Bristol Island (3,600 ft./1,100 m.) is a compound stratovolcano in the South Sandwich Islands. It is largely covered in ice. There are reports of eruptions in 1823, 1935, 1936 and 1950. The most recent eruption occurred in 1956.

Broken Top (Oregon, USA: 44.1N, 121.7W).

Broken Top (9,185 ft./2,800 m.) is a complex stratovolcano. There is not evidence that the volcano has erupted in the past 10,000 years.

Bromo *see* **Tengger Caldera.**

Brushy Butte (California, USA: 41.18N, 121.44W).

Brushy Butte (3,852 ft./1,174 m.) is a Holocene shield volcano with no record of eruptions in historic time.

Bual Buali (Sumatra: 1.57N, 99.25E).

Bual Buali (5,968 ft./1,819 m.) is a stratovolcano with fumarolic activity. There is no record of eruptions in historic time.

Buckle I. (Balleny Is., Antarctica: 66.80S, 163.25E).

Buckle Island (4,065 ft./1,239 m.) is a stratovolcano whose earliest recorded eruption occurred in 1839. The most recent eruption took place in 1899.

Bud Dajo (Sulu Is., Philippines: 5.95N, 121.07E).

Bud Dajo (1,443 ft./440 m.) is a stratovolcano with pyroclastic cones composing the central portion of the island of Sulu in the Philippines. There were two small eruptions in 1641 and 1897.

Bufumbira (Uganda: 1.23S, 29.72E).

Bufumbira (8,025 ft./2,446 m.) is composed of Holocene cinder cones. There is no record of eruptions in historic time.

Buldir (for Stefan Buldirev, Russian sailor) (Aleutian Is., Alaska, USA: 52.37N, 175.98E).

Buldir (2,152 ft./656 m.) is a Holocene stratovolcano with no record of eruptions in historic time.

Bulusan (Luzon, Philippines: 12.77N, 124.05E).

Bulusan (5,133 ft./1,565 m.) is an active stratovolcano located on the southeast part of Luzon peninsula. There have at least 13 eruptions from Bulusan from 1886 through 1988.

Bunyaruguru Field (Uganda: 0.20S, 30.08E).

The Bunyaruguru Field (5,098 ft./1,554 m.) is composed of Holocene explosion craters. There is no record of eruptions in historic time.

Burney, Monte (Chile: 52.33S, 73.40W).

Monte Burney (5,768 ft./1,758 m.) is a stratovolcano whose sole recorded eruption to date took place in 1910.

Bus-Obo (Mongolia: 47.12N, 109.08E).

Bus-Obo (3,812 ft./1,162 m.) is a cinder cone with likely Holocene activity, but no recorded eruptions in historic time.

Butajiri (Ethiopia: 8.05N, 38.35E).

Butajiri (7,482 ft./2,281 m.), also known as Ara Shatan (meaning "Devil's Lake"), is a Holocene fissure vent located in the western portion of the Ethiopian Rift Valley. There is no record of historical eruptions.

Buzzard Creek (Alaska, USA: 64.07N, 148.42W).

Buzzard Creek (2,723 ft./830 m.) is composed of tuff rings with no record of eruptions in historic time.

C

Cabalian (Leyte, Philippines: 10.23N, 125.22E).

Cabalian (3,100 ft./945 m.) is a Holocene stratovolcano with no record of eruptions in historic time.

Caburgua (Chile: 39.20S, 71.83W).

Caburgua (3,264 ft./995 m.) is composed of Holocene cinder cones. There is no record of an eruption in historic time.

Cagua (Luzon, Philippines: 18.22N, 122.12E).

Cagua (3,717 ft./1,133 m.) is a Holocene stratovolcano with no record of eruptions in historic time.

Calabozos (Chile: 35.56S, 70.50W).

Calabozos (11,509 ft./3,508 m.) is a Holocene caldera with no record of eruptions in historic time.

Calayo (Mindanao, Philippines: 7.88N, 125.07E).

Calayo (2,119 ft./646 m.) is a tuff cone whose sole recorded eruption to date occurred in 1886.

Calbuco (Chile: 41.33S, 72.61W).

Calbuco (6,571 ft./2,003 m.) is an explosive Holocene andesitic stratovolcano near Lake Llanquihue in southern Chile. The earliest recorded eruption in 1893-94, was one of the largest historical eruptions in the region. An eruption in April of 1917 formed a lava dome in the crater. The last major eruption occurred in 1961. A minor eruption occurred in 1972. Calbuco remained inactive until August of 1996, when evidence of fumarolic activity was reported.

Callaqui (Chile: 37.92S, 71.45W).

Callaqui (10,380 ft./3,164 m.) is a stratovolcano in central Chile. The earliest recorded eruption occurred in 1751. There has been only one subsequent eruption in 1980. Continuous fumarolic activity from the main vent was reported in early 1997.

Cameroon, Mt. (Cameroon: 4.20N, 9.17E).

Mount Cameroon (13,435 ft./4,095 m.) is a stratovolcano towering above the coast of western Cameroon. The earliest recorded eruption occurred in approximately 450 B.C. (observed by a passing Carthaginian navigator). There have been numerous subsequent moderate explosive eruptions from the summit and flank vents. The most recent eruption occurred in 1982, causing the evacuation of over 300 people from their homes.

Camiguin de Babuyanes (north of Luzon, Philippines: 18.83N, 121.86E).

Camiguin de Babuyanes (2,335 ft./712 m.) is a stratovolcano that forms the southwestern portion of Camiguin Island. The only historic eruption recorded was a moderate phreatic eruption in 1857.

Campi Flegrei [Phlegraean Fields] (Greek *phleguros*, "burning," "scorching") (Italy: 40.83N, 14.14E).

Campi Flegrei (1,476 ft./458 m.) is a caldera whose earliest recorded eruption was in 1198. This eruption occurred at the Solfatara (Italian, "sulfur mine," from *solfo*, "sulfur") crater. (The crater's name gave the generic term for a volcanic area or vent that yields only hot vapors and gases, in part sulfurous.) The most recent eruption of Campi Flegrei in 1538 created Monte Nuovo, as the world's first documented "new mountain." Following this eruption, 24 people climbing the cone lost their footing in the dark and slid to their deaths on loose stones.

Campi Flegrei del Mar Sicilia [Phlegrean Fields] (*see* Campi Flegrei) (Sicily, Italy: 37.10N, 12.70E).

Campi Flegrei del Mar Sicilia (-26 ft./-8 m.) is a submarine volcano. The earliest recorded submarine eruption was in approximately 253 B.C. There were seven subsequent eruptions, most recently in 1911. Three of these eight eruptions created islands, but each was soon destroyed by Mediterranean waves. One was Graham Island (named for Sir James Graham, British first lord of admiralty), created in 1831, and vanished in 1832.

Candlemas I. (South Sandwich Is.: 57.08S, 26.72W).

Candlemas Island (1,804 ft./550 m.) is a stratovolcano whose earliest recorded eruption occurred in 1823 (from the aptly named Lucifer Hill), but ice core records suggests a previous eruption in approximately 1250 B.C. Subsequent eruptions of 1911 and 1953 have not been verified.

Canlaon (Negros, Philippines: 10.41N, 123.13E).
Canlaon (7,987 ft./2,435 m.) is a stratovolcano in the north central portion of the island of Negros in the Philippines. There have been 19 recorded eruptions, most moderate and explosive, between 1866 and 1993. A sudden phreatic explosion killed three hikers in August of 1996.

Capelinhos *see* Fayal.

Capital (Alaska, USA: 62.43N, 144.10W).
Capital Mountain (7,728 ft./2,356 m.) is a small shield volcano with a circular caldera.

Carlisle (Aleutian Is., Alaska, USA: 52.90N, 170.05W).
Carlisle (5,315 ft./1,620 m.) is a stratovolcano whose earliest recorded eruption took place in 1774. The second and most recent eruption occurred in 1828.

Carran-Los Venados (Chile: 40.35S, 72.07W).
Carran-Los Venados (3,658 ft./1,115 m.) is composed of pyroclastic cones. The earliest recorded eruption took place in 1907. Two persons were killed by gases during an eruption in 1955. The most recent eruption took place in 1979.

Carrizozo (from Spanish, "reed grass") (New Mexico, USA: 33.78N, 105.93W).
Carrizozo (5,679 ft./1,731 m.) is a Holocene cinder cone with no record of eruptions in historic time.

Casiri, Nevados (Peru: 17.47S, 69.82W).
Nevados Casiri (18,536 ft./5,650 m.) is a Holocene stratovolcano with no record of eruptions in historic time.

Catarman *see* Hibok-Hibok.

Catherine (Ethiopia: 13.92N, 40.42E).
Catherine (330 ft./100 m.) is a tuff ring. There is no record of an eruption in historic time, though it is likely volcanic activity has occured in the past 10,000 years.

Cayambe (Ecuador: 0.03N, 77.99W).
Cayambe (18,996 ft./5,790 m.) is a Holocene compound volcano in the Eastern Cordillera of the Ecuadorian Andes. There have been no eruptions in historical time.

Cayute-La Vigueria (Chile: 41.25S, 72.27W).

Cayute-La Vigueria (1,660 ft./506 m.) is composed of Holocene pyroclastic cones. There are no recorded eruptions in historic time.

Ceboruco, Volcán (Mexico: 21.12N, 104.50W).

Volcán Ceboruco (7,100 ft./2,164 m.) is a stratovolcano whose earliest recorded eruption took place in 1542. The most recent eruption occurred in 1875.

Cendres, Ile des (French, "isle of cinders") (Vietnam: 10.16N, 109.01E).

Ile des Cendres (-66 ft./-20 m.) is a submarine volcano whose sole recorded eruption to date occurred in 1823.

Central Island (L. Turkana, Kenya: 3.50N, 36.04E).

Central Island (1,804 ft./550 m.) is a Holocene stratovolcano with no record of eruptions in historic time.

Cerberus *see* **Semisopochnoi.**

Cereme (Java: 6.89S, 108.41E).

Cereme (10,098 ft./3,078 m.) is a stratovolcano whose earliest recorded eruption occurred in 1698. The most recent eruption occurred in 1951.

Chacana (Ecuador: 0.37S, 78.25W).

Chacana (15,232 ft./4,643 m.) is a caldera whose earliest recorded eruption occurred in 1760. The most recent eruption took place in 1773.

Chachani, Nevado (Peru: 16.19S, 71.53W).

Nevado Chachani (19,872 ft./6,057 m.) is a Holocene stratovolcano with no recorded eruptions in historic time.

Chagulak (Aleutian Is., Alaska, USA: 52.57N, 171.13W).

Chagulak (3,747 ft./1,142 m.) is a Holocene stratovolcano with no record of eruptions in historic time.

Chaîne des Puys (Latin *podium*, "height") (France: 45.50N, 2.75E).

Chaîne des Puys (4,800 ft./1,464 m.) are cinder cones in south-central France. The most recent volcanic eruption occurred at the Puy de Dome in approximately 5760 B.C.

Chaiten (Chile: 42.83S, 72.65W).

Chaiten (3,156 ft./962 m.) is a Holocene caldera with no recorded eruptions in historic time.

Chao (Chile: 22.12S, 68.15W).

Chao (16,732 ft./5,100 m.) is a Holocene lava dome with no record of an eruption in historic time.

Chapulul, Cerro (Chile: 38.37S, 71.08W).
Cerro Chapulul (7,031 ft./2,143 m.) is a Holocene cinder cone with no record of eruptions in historic time.

Chascon, Cerro (Bolivia: 21.88S, 67.90W).
Cerro Chascon (16,814 ft./5,125 m.) is a Holocene lava dome with no record of eruptions in historic time.

Cherny (Russian, "black") (Kamchatka, Russia: 56.82N, 159.67E).
Cherny (5,833 ft./1,778 m.) is a Holocene stratovolcano with no record of eruptions in historic time.

Chichinautzin (Mexico: 19.08N, 99.13W).
Chichinautzin (12,893 ft./3,930 m.) is a volcanic field with no record of eruptions in historic time.

Chichón, El (Spanish, "the lump") (Mexico: 17.36N, 93.23W).
El Chichón (3,478 ft./1,060 m.) is composed of lava domes. Its sole recorded eruption to date was in 1982, although radiocarbon dating indicates earlier eruptions from approximately A.D. 270. The catastrophic 1982 eruption caused an estimated 1,800 deaths, mainly in pumice and lava flows. Most of the casualties on the north side of the volcano resulted from fires started by red hot rock particles and by the collapse of buildings following earthquakes.

Chiginagak (Alaska, USA: 57.13N, 157.00W).
Chiginagak (6,780 ft./2,067 m.) is a symmetrical ice-covered stratovolcano composed mainly of andesite and dacite. Reported eruptions of 1852 and 1929 remain unverified. The sole recorded eruption to date occurred in 1971. There is an active fumarole on the northern slope.

Chikurachki (Kuril Is.: 50.32N, 155.46E).
Chikurachki (5,956 ft./1,816 m.) is a stratovolcano located on Paramushir in the Northern Kuril Islands. The first recorded eruption, from 1853 through 1859, was the largest. The most recent in 1986 was explosive and produced pyroclastic flows, lava flows and mudflows.

Chiliques (Chile: 23.58S, 67.70W).
Chiliques (18,957 ft./5,778 m.) is a Holocene stratovolcano with no record of eruptions in historic time.

Chillán, Nevados de (Chile: 36.86S, 71.38W).
Nevados de Chillán (10,538 ft./3,212 m.) is a stratovolcano whose earliest recorded eruption occurred in approximately 1650. The most recent eruption took place in 1987.

Chimborazo (Ecuador: 1.48S, 78.87W).
Chimborazo (20,700 ft./6,310 m.) is a Quaternary volcano in the Inter-Andean depression in Ecuador. There have been no eruptions in historic time.

Chinameca (El Salvador: 13.48N, 88.32W).
Chinameca (4,028 ft./1,228 m.) is a stratovolcano with fumarolic activity. There is no record of eruptions in historic time.

Chingo Volcanic Field (Guatemala: 14.12N, 89.73W).
The Chingo Volcanic Field (5,823 ft./1,775 m.) is a Holocene stratovolcano with no record of eruptions in historic time.

Chiquimula Volcanic Field (Guatemala: 14.83N, 89.55W).
The Chiquimula Volcanic Field (3,910 ft./1,192 m.) is composed of Holocene cinder cones with no record of eruptions in historic time.

Chiracha (Ethiopia: 6.65N, 38.12E).
Chiracha (5,413 ft./1,650 m.) is a Holocene stratovolcano with no record of historical eruptions.

Chirinkotan (Kuril Is.: 48.98N, 153.25E).
Chirinkotan (2375 ft./724 m.), on the Northern Kuril Islands, is a stratovolcano that has had at least five eruptions since the first recorded in 1884. The most recent, in 1986, lasted one day.

Chirip (Kuril Is.: 45.38N, 147.92E).
Chirip (5,212 ft./1,589 m.) is a stratovolcano located on Iturup Island in the Southern Kuril Islands. The earliest recorded eruption was a small explosive one in 1843. The second and most recent eruption occurred from a flank vent in 1860.

Chirpoi (Kuril Is.: 46.52N, 150.87E).
Chirpoi (2,434 ft./742 m.) is a caldera whose earliest recorded eruption occurred in 1712. The most recent eruption occurred in 1982.

Chokai (Honshu, Japan: 39.08N, 140.03E).
Chokai (7,316 ft./2,230 m.) is a stratovolcano whose earliest recorded eruption occurred in A.D. 573. An eruption in 1801 killed eight mountain climbers. There were also eruptions in 1821, 1834 and, most recently, in 1974.

Ch'uga-Ryong (Korea: 38.33N, 127.33E).
Ch'uga-Ryong (1,483 ft./452 m.) is a shield volcano with likely Holocene activity. There have been no recorded eruptions in historic time.

Chyulu Hills (Kenya: 2.68S, 37.88E).
Chyulu Hills (7,178 ft./2,188 m.) is a volcanic field with no evidence of eruptions in the past 300 years.

Cinnamon Butte (for color of rock) (Oregon, USA: 43.12N, 122.11W).
Cinnamon Butte (6,417 ft./1,956 m.) is composed of Holocene cinder cones. There is no record of an eruption in historic time.

Citlaltépetl *see* **Pico de Orizaba.**

Clear Lake (California, USA: 38.97N, 122.77W).
Clear Lake (4,721 ft./1,439 m.) is a Holocene volcanic field with no record of eruptions in historic time.

Cleveland (Aleutian Is., Alaska, USA: 52.82N, 169.95W).
Mount Cleveland (5,675 ft./1,730 m.) is a stratovolcano on Chuginadak Island's western side. It is one of the Aleutian Islands' most active volcanoes. There have been at least eight eruptions since 1893. In a 1944 eruption one man lost his life when he was crushed by falling rocks and subsequently covered by lava. There was an eruption in 1987 and a brief eruption in May of 1994.

Coatepeque (El Salvador: 13.87N, 89.55W).
Coatepeque (2,447 ft./746 m.) is a Holocene caldera. There has been no recorded volcanic activity in historic time.

Cochons, Ile aux (Indian Ocean: 46.10S, 50.23E).
Ile aux Cochons (2,543 ft./775 m.) is a Holocene stratovolcano with no record of eruptions in historic time.

Colachi (Chile: 23.23S, 67.65W).
Colachi (18,474 ft./5,631 m.) is a Holocene stratovolcano with no recorded eruptions in historic time.

Coleman Seamount (Solomon Is.: 8.83S, 157.17E).
Coleman Seamount is a Holocene submarine volcano with no recorded eruptions in historic time.

Colima Volcanic Complex (Mexico: 19.51N, 103.62W).
The Colima Volcanic Complex (13,448 ft./4,100 m.), located 75 miles south of Guadalajara, is Mexico's most active volcano. The complex consists of two main stratovolcanoes, Nevado de Colima and Volcán de Fuego. There have been over 50 eruptions since the earliest recorded one in 1560. The eruption of 1576 caused great destruction of land and an unknown number of fatalities. Deaths following the 1818 eruption probably resulted from starvation and disease. The most recent explosive eruptions occurred in 1987 and 1994.

Collumo, Cerro (Bolivia: 18.50S, 68.07W).
Cerro Collumo (12,716 ft./3,876 m.) is a Holocene Maar volcano with no record of eruptions in historic time.

Colo [Una Una] (Sulawesi, Indonesia: 0.17S, 121:61E).
Colo (1,663 ft./507 m.) is a stratovolcano whose earliest recorded eruption occurred in 1898. The most recent eruption occurred in 1983.

Concepción (Nicaragua: 11.54N, 85.62W).
Concepción (5,280 ft./1,610 m.) is a stratovolcano that composes the northwest part of the Isla de Ometepe in Nicaragua. There have been at least 24 eruptions since the earliest recorded in 1883. The most recent eruption occurred in 1986.

Conchagua (El Salvador: 13.28N, 87.85W).
Conchagua (4,101 ft./1,250 m.) is a stratovolcano with no record of eruptions in historic time.

Conchaguita (El Salvador: 13.22N, 87.76W).
Conchaguita (1,804 ft./550 m.) is a stratovolcano whose earliest recorded eruption took place in 1892.

Condor, Cerro el (Argentina: 26.62S, 68.35W).
Cerro el Condor (21,430 ft./6,532 m.) is a Holocene stratovolcano with no recorded eruptions in historic time.

Cook, Isla (Chile: 54.95S, 70.27W).
Isla Cook (492 ft./150 m.) is composed of Holocene lava domes with no recorded eruptions in historic time.

Copahue (Chile: 37.85S, 71.17W).
Copahue (9,728 ft./2,965 m.) is a composite cone with a summit crater containing a lake in central Chile. The earliest recorded eruption occurred in 1750. Copahue's most recent eruption occurred in 1992.

Copiapo (Chile: 27.30S, 69.13W).
Copiapo (19856 ft./6,052 m.) is a stratovolcano with no known eruptions in historic time.

Corbetti Caldera (Ethiopia: 7.18N, 38.43E).
Corbetti Caldera (7,612 ft./2,320 m.) is a Holocene caldera with no record of eruptions in historic time.

Corcovado (Spanish, "hunchbacked") (Chile: 43.18S, 72.80W).
Corcovado (7,546 ft./2,300 m.) is a stratovolcano whose earliest recorded eruption took place in 1834. The most recent eruption occurred in 1835.

Cordón Caulle (Chile: 40.52S, 72.20W).
Cordón Caulle (5,899 ft./1,798 m.) is composed of fissure vents whose earliest recorded eruption took place in 1921.

Cordón Chalviri (Chile: 23.85S, 67.62W).

Cordón Chalviri (18,448 ft./5,623 m.) is composed of Holocene stratovolcanoes with no record of eruptions in historic time.

Cordón del Azufre (Chile/Argentina: 25.33S, 68.52W).

Cordón del Azufre (17,923 ft./5,463 m.) is a Holocene complex volcano with no record of eruptions in historic time.

Cordón de Puntas Negras (Chile: 23.75S, 67.53W).

Cordón de Puntas Negras (19,199 ft./5,852 m.) is composed of Holocene stratovolcanoes with no record of eruptions in historic time.

Coronado (Mexico: 29.08N, 113.51W).

Coronado (1,509 ft./460 m.) is a stratovolcano with fumarolic activity. There have been no recorded eruptions in historic time.

Coropuna (Peru: 15.52S, 72.65W).

Coropuna (20,922 ft./6,377 m.) is a Holocene stratovolcano with no record of eruptions in historic time.

Coseguina (Nicaragua: 12.98N, 87.57W).

Coseguina (2,777 ft./847 m.) is a basaltic shield volcano in Nicaragua's northwest corner. The earliest recorded eruption occurred in 1809. A major eruption in January of 1835 produced a large central collapse crater, which contains a lake. There was another explosive eruption in 1852 that produced lava flows. The most recent eruption occurred in 1859, and Coseguina has been inactive since.

Coso Volcanic Field (Shoshonean, perhaps "fire") (California, USA: 36.03N, 117.82W).

The Coso Volcanic Field (7,874 ft./2,400 m.) is composed of Pleistocene lava domes with hot springs.

Cotopaxi (Quechua *kotto*, "mountain," *paksi*, "shining") (Ecuador: 0.68S, 78.44W).

Cotopaxi (19,000 ft./5,911 m.) is a stratovolcano. The earliest recorded eruption was in 1534. Over 50 eruptions have been recorded since then. Mud flows have caused deaths in various eruptions, but chiefly in that of 1877, when around 300 people in the Latacunga district perished. It is generally regarded as the world's highest active volcano, but some claim Nevado **Ojos del Salado** has this honor. The most recent eruption recorded was in 1904, though there are unconfirmed reports of an eruption in 1942. There was volcanic activity, including steam emissions and small earthquakes, in 1975.

Crater Flat (Nevada, USA: 36.77N, 116.55W).
Crater Flat (3,700 ft./1,128 m.) is a Holocene volcanic field with no record of eruptions in historic time.

Crater Lake [Mt. Mazama] (perhaps Nahuatl *mazama*, "deer") (Oregon, USA: 42.93N, 122.12W).
Crater Lake (8,106 ft./2,471 m.) occupies the crater of the extinct stratovolcano Mt. Mazama, which erupted in approximately 4895 B.C. The caldera is six miles wide. Crater Lake National Park was established in 1902.

Crater Mountain (New Guinea: 6.58S, 145.08E).
Crater Mountain (10,607 ft./3,233 m.) is a Holocene stratovolcano with no record of eruptions in historic time.

Craters of the Moon (Idaho, USA: 43.42N, 113.50W).
Craters of the Moon (6,576 ft./2,005 m.) is a large lava flow field composed of cinder cones, spatter cones and lava tubes, near the northern border of the Snake River Plain in Idaho. Radiocarbon dating indicates at least 10 eruptions from approximately 5890 B.C. (northwest of Echo Crater) to approximately 126 B.C. (south of Big Craters, near Broken Top). Its name, since 1924 that of the National Monument there, in Butte and Blaine counties, is for the fantastic shapes of lava flows.

Crow Lagoon (British Columbia, Canada: 54.70N, 130.23W).
Crow Lagoon (1,100 ft./335 m.) is a Holocene pyroclastic cone with no record of eruptions in historic time.

Cu-Lao Re Group (Vietnam: 15.38N, 109.12E).
The Cu-Lao Re Group (594 ft./181 m.) is composed of Holocene cones with no record of eruptions in historic time.

Cuicocha (Ecuador: 0.31N, 78.36W).
Cuicocha (10,650 ft./3,246 m.) is a Holocene caldera with no record of eruptions in historic time.

Cuilapa-Barbarena (Guatemala: 14.33N, 90.41W).
Cuilapa-Barbarena (4,770 ft./1,454 m.) is a Holocene volcanic field with no record of eruptions in historic time.

Cumbal (Colombia: 0.98N, 77.88W).
Cumbal (15,630 ft./4,764 m.) is a stratovolcano whose earliest recorded eruption occurred in 1877. A second and most recent eruption took place in 1926.

Curaçoa (Tonga Is.: 15.62S, 173.67W).
Curaçoa (-108 ft./-33 m.) is a submarine volcano. The earliest recorded

submarine eruption occurred in 1973. A second and most recent eruption occurred in 1979.

Curtis I. (Kermadec Is.: 30.54S, 178.57W).
Curtis Island (450 ft./137 m.) is a submarine volcano with no evidence of eruptions in historic time.

D

Dabbahu (Ethiopia: 12.60N, 40.48E).
Dabbahu (4,730 ft./1,442 m.) is a Holocene stratovolcano with no record of eruptions in historic time.

Dabbayra (Ethiopia: 12.38N, 40.07E).
Dabbayra (4,272 ft./1,302 m.) is a Holocene shield volcano with no recorded historical eruptions.

Dacht-i-Navar Group (Afghanistan: 33.95N, 67.92E).
The Dacht-i-Navar Group (12,470 ft./3,800 m.) consists of Holocene lava domes. There is no record of eruptions in historic time.

Dagit-Dagitan (Verde I., Philippines: 13.53N, 121.08E).
Dagit-Dagitan (1,194 ft./364 m.) is a Pleistocene stratovolcano with fumarolic activity. There is no record of eruptions in historic time.

Daisen (Honshu, Japan: 35.37N, 133.55E).
Daisen (5,679 ft./1,731 m.) is a Holocene stratovolcano with no record of eruptions in historic time.

Daisetsu (Hokkaido, Japan: 43.68N, 142.88E).
Daisetsu (7,513 ft./2,290 m.) is composed of overlapping stratovolcanoes and is Hokkaido's largest volcano. The only historic eruption took place around 1400. The Asahi-dake vent is the most recently active.

Dakataua (New Britain, Papua New Guinea: 5.06S, 150.11E).
Dakataua (1,310 ft./400 m.) is a caldera which likely experienced volcanic activity in the 1800s.

Dalaffilla (Ethiopia: 13.79N, 40.55E).
Dalaffilla (2,011 ft./613 m.) is a Holocene stratovolcano with no record of eruptions in historic time.

Dallol (Ethiopia: 14.24N, 40.30E).
Dallol (-157 ft./-48 m.) is an explosion crater that contains a salt lake. The sole recorded eruption to date occurred in 1926.

Dama Ali (Ethiopia: 11.28N, 41.63E).
Dama Ali (3,504 ft./1,068 m.) is a Holocene shield volcano. The sole recorded eruption to date occurred in 1631, when the village of Waraba was destroyed by an earthquake, killing around 50 people.

Damavand (Iran: 35.93N, 52.11E).
Damavand (18,602 ft./5,670 m.) is a Holocene stratovolcano with no evidence of eruptions in historic time.

Dana (Alaska, USA: 55.62N, 161.22W).
Dana (4,442 ft./1,354 m.) is a Holocene stratovolcano with no record of eruptions in historic time.

Danau Complex (Java: 6.20S, 105.97E).
The Danau Complex (5,833 ft./1,778 m.) is a Holocene caldera with no record of eruptions in historic time.

Dar-Alages (Armenia: 39.70N, 45.54E).
Dar-Alages (10,922 ft./3,329 m.) is a Holocene volcano with no recorded eruptions in historic time.

Dariganga Volcanic Field (Mongolia: 45.33N, 114.00E).
The Dariganga Volcanic Field (5,833 ft./1,778 m.) is composed of Holocene cinder cones with no record of eruptions in historic time.

Darwin, Volcán (Isabela I., Galápagos Is.: 0.18S, 91.28W).
Volcán Darwin (4,364 ft./1,330 m.) is a Holocene shield volcano whose sole recorded eruption to date occurred in 1813.

Datong (China: 40.00N, 113.28E).
Datong (6,175 ft./1,882 m.) is composed of cinder cones. Its sole recorded eruption to date occurred in approximately A.D. 450.

Datun Group (Taiwan: 25.17N, 121.52E).
The Datun Group (3,707 ft./1,130 m.) is a Pleistocene stratovolcano with fumarolic activity. There have been no recorded eruptions in historic time.

Davidof (Aleutian Is., Alaska, USA: 51.97N, 178.33E).
Davidof (1,043 ft./318 m.) is a stratovolcano with likely Holocene activity. There have been no recorded eruptions in historic time.

Davis Lake (Oregon, USA: 43.57N, 121.82W).
Davis Lake (7,096 ft./2,163 m.) is a Holocene volcanic field with no evidence of eruptions in historic time.

Dawson Strait Group (D'Entrecasteaux Is.: 9.62S, 150.88E).
The Dawson Strait Group (1,640 ft./500 m.) is a hydration rind volcanic field with likely volcanic activity in the past 2,000 years.

Deception I. (South Shetland Is., Antarctica: 62.97S, 60.95W).
Deception Island (1,890 ft./576 m.) is a volcanic island with a flooded caldera. The earliest recorded eruption occurred in approximately 1800. The most recent eruption took place in 1970. The island name refers to its deceptive shape: its central harbor is a breached, drowned volcanic crater. Fumarole Bay, on the west side of Port Foster, is named for its fumarole (vapor vent), the most active on the island. An Argentine research station here was closed to permanent occupation following a 1967 eruption.

Demon (Russian, "demon") (Kuril Is.: 45.50N, 148.85).
Demon (3,952 ft./1,205 m.) is a Holocene stratovolcano located on Iturup Island in the Southern Kuril Islands. There are no known historic eruptions.

Dempo (Sumatra: 4.03S,103.13E).
Dempo (10,410 ft./3,173 m.) is a stratovolcano whose earliest recorded eruption occurred in 1817. There have been over 20 eruptions since, most recently in 1974. Several eruptions have caused damage, but there have been no reported casualties.

Denison (Alaska, USA: 58.42N, 154.45W).
Denison (7,605 ft./2,318 m.) is a stratovolcano with likely volcanic activity in the past 10,000 years. There is no record of eruptions in historic time.

Descabezado Grande (Spanish, "great headless one") (Chile: 35.58S, 70.75W).
Descabezado Grande (12,969 ft./3,953 m.) is composed of stratovolcanoes whose sole recorded eruption to date occurred in 1932.

Devils Desk (Alaska, USA: 58.48N, 154.30W).
Devils Desk (6,409 ft./1,954 m.) is a volcanic neck of a former stratovolcano. It is uncertain if Devils Desk has erupted in the past 10,000 years.

Devils Garden (Oregon, USA: 43.51N, 120.86W).
Devils Garden (5,000 ft./1,525 m.) is a lava flow field covering 45 square miles. It is reportedly between 50,000 and 10,000 years old.

Devils Tower (Wyoming, USA: 44.6N, 104.7W).
Devils Tower (5,112 ft./1,558 m.) is possibly the eroded remnant of a volcanic neck. Located near the Belle Fouche River, it is made of magma and is approximately 40 million years old. It is the focal point of the Devils Tower National Monument.

Dgida Basin (Russia: 50.52N, 103.25E).

Dgida Basin (4,920 ft./1,500 m.) is composed of Holocene cinder cones with no record of eruptions in historic time.

Dhamar, Harrat (Yemen: 14.57N, 44.67E).

Harrat Dhamar (11,480 ft./3,500 m.) is a volcanic field whose sole recorded eruption to date occurred in 1937.

Diable, Morne au (French, "devil's hill") (Dominica, West Indies: 15.62N, 61.45W).

Morne au Diable (2,825 ft./861 m.) is a stratovolcano with fumarolic activity. There is no evidence of eruptions in historic time.

Diablotins, Morne (French "hill of the imps") (Dominica, West Indies: 15.50N, 61.42W).

Morne Diablotins (4,691 ft./1,430 m.) is a stratovolcano with fumarolic activity. There is no evidence of eruptions in historic time.

Diamond Craters (for John Diamond, early settler) (Oregon, USA: 43.10N, 118.75W).

Diamond Craters (4,200–4,750 ft./1,280–1,450 m.) is a monogenetic Quaternary volcanic field in southeast Oregon.

Didicas (north of Luzon, Philippines: 19.08N, 122.02E).

Didicas (800 ft./244 m.) is a compound volcano whose earliest recorded eruption occurred in 1773. An eruption in 1969 caused the deaths of three people, who drowned while fishing. A submarine explosion at Didicas, 70 km. away, generated a giant wave. The most recent eruption occurred in 1978.

Dieng Volcanic Complex (Java: 7.20S, 109.92E).

The Dieng Volcanic Complex (8,400 ft./2,565 m.) is a complex volcano located on central Java in Indonesia. The earliest recorded eruption occurred in 1375. In 1786 a ground fissure opened and 38 people died in the collapse that destroyed the village of Jampang. Approximately 40 people were reportedly killed at Butak in a 1928 eruption, while over 100 perished in each of the 1944 and 1964 eruptions. Most fatalities were in the 1979 eruption, when inhabitants of Kaputjukan fled along a trail to Batur. Over 150 were later found dead on the track, seemingly asleep, in single file as when walking. The most recent eruption occurred in 1993 and seismic and volcanic activity was reported in June of 1998.

Discovery, Mt. (Antarctica: 78.2S, 165.2E).

Mount Discovery (8,794 ft./2,681 mt.) is a central volcano that was formed approximately 5.3 million years ago. There are several volcanic domes on the mountain's north side and a summit made of lava flows.

Dofen (Ethiopia: 9.35N, 40.13E).
Dofen (3,776 ft./1,151 m.) is a Holocene stratovolcano with no record of any historic eruptions.

Dolomieu *see* Piton de la Fournaise.

Doma Peaks (New Guinea: 5.90S, 143.15E).
Doma Peaks (11,706 ft./3,568 m.) is a Holocene stratovolcano with no record of eruptions in historic time.

Domuyo, Volcán (Argentina: 36.63S, 70.42W).
Volcán Domuyo (15,715 ft./4,790 m.) is a Holocene stratovolcano with no record of eruptions in historic time.

Dona Juana (Colombia: 1.47N, 76.92W).
Dona Juana (13,615 ft./4,150 m.) is a stratovolcano whose sole recorded eruption to date occurred in 1897. This lasted nine years and caused the deaths of around 50 people who were burned by hot rocks and ash in avalanches. At least 200 animals were also killed.

Don João de Castro Bank (Azores: 38.23N, 26.63W).
Don João de Castro Bank (-46 ft./-14 m.) is a large submarine volcano between Terceira and San Miguel Islands. The sole recorded eruption to date occurred in 1720.

Dotsero (perhaps Ute personal name) (Colorado, USA: 39.65N, 107.03W).
Dotsero (7,382 ft./2,250 m.) is a Holocene explosion crater. There is no record of eruptions in historic time.

Douglas (for English cleric, John Douglas) (Alaska, USA: 58.87N, 153.55W).
Douglas (7,021 ft./2,140 m.) is a stratovolcano with fumarolic activity. There is no record of eruptions in historic time.

Drum (Alaska, USA: 62.12 N, 144.64W).
Drum (11,508 ft./3,661 m.) is a stratovolcano in Alaska's Wrangell Mountains. There have been no historical eruptions on Mount Drum.

Dubbi (Ethiopia: 13.58N, 41.81E).
Dubbi (5,330 ft./1,625 m.) is a towering stratovolcano near the coast of the Red Sea. The volcano is also known as Edd, Gebel Dubbey and Djebel Dubbeth. The earliest recorded eruption occurred in 1400. A second and most recent eruption occurred in 1861, when two villages were destroyed and large herds of cattle killed. Over 100 people perished. There were unconfirmed reports of eruptions in 1863 and 1900.

Dukono (Halmahera, Indonesia: 1.70N, 127.87E).

Dukono (3,566 ft./1,087 m.) is a complex volcano and one of Indonesia's most active volcanoes. The earliest recorded eruption occurred in 1550, causing an unknown amount of destruction and death. There were smaller eruptions in 1719, 1868 and 1901. There have been continuous eruptions from Dukono since 1933.

Duncan Canal (Alaska, USA: 56.50N, 133.10W).

Duncan Canal (50 ft./15 m.) is a Holocene volcano with no record of eruptions in historic time.

Durango Volcanic Field (Mexico: 24.15N, 104.45W).

The Durango Volcanic Field (6,808 ft./2,075 m.) is composed of Holocene cinder cones. There is no record of eruptions in historic time.

Dutton (Alaska, USA: 55.18N, 162.27W).

Dutton (4,833 ft./1,473 m.) is a Holocene stratovolcano with no record of eruptions in historic time

Dzenzursky (Kamchatka, Russia: 53.64N, 158.92E).

Dzenzursky (7,070 ft./2,155 m.) is a Holocene compound volcano with no record of eruptions in historic time.

E

Eagle Lake Field (California, USA: 40.63N, 121.83W).

The Eagle Lake Field (4,520 ft./1,652 m.) is composed of Holocene fissure vents. There have been no recorded eruptions in historic time.

East Epi (Vanuatu: 16.68S, 168.37E).

East Epi (-111 ft./-34 m.) is a submarine caldera. The earliest recorded eruption occurred in 1920. There have been five more confirmed eruptions and an additional six suspected. An explosive eruption in 1953 created a new island. The most recent eruption likely occurred in 1988.

Easter I. (Central Pacific: 27.12S, 109.45W).

Easter Island (1,739 ft./530 m.) is composed of Holocene shield volcanoes. There is no record of eruptions in historic time.

Ebeko (Kuril Is.: 50.68N, 156.02E).

Ebeko (3,791 ft./1,156 m.) is located on Paramushir in the Northern Kuril Islands. It is a somma volcano and one of the most active in the region. There have been eleven eruptions, mostly small phreatic and explosive eruptions, from the earliest recorded in 1793 through the most recent in 1991.

Ebulobo (Flores I., Indonesia: 8.81S, 121.18E).
Ebulobo (6,968 ft./2,124 m.) is a stratovolcano whose earliest recorded eruption occurred in 1830. The most recent eruption to date occurred in 1969.

Eburru, Ol Doinyo (Kenya: 0.63S, 36.23E).
Ol Doinyo Eburru (9,370 ft./2,856 m.) is a Holocene volcanic complex with no record of an eruption in historic time.

Ecuador, Volcán (Isabela I., Galápagos Is.: 0.02N, 91.55W).
Volcán Ecuador (2,592 ft./790 m.) is a Holocene shield volcano with no recorded eruptions in historic time.

Edgecumbe (for Lord Edgecumbe [1721–1795]) (Alaska, USA: 57.05N, 135.75W).
Edgecumbe (3,202 ft./976 m.) are Holocene stratovolcanoes with no record of eruptions in historic time.

Edziza (British Columbia, Canada: 57.72N, 130.63W).
Edziza (9,140 ft./2,786 m.) is a Holocene stratovolcano with no record of eruptions in historic time.

Eggella (Kamchatka, Russia: 56.57N, 158.52E).
Eggella (3,432 ft./1,046 m.) is a Holocene shield volcano with no record of eruptions in historic time.

Egmont, Mt. (for John Percival, Second Earl of Egmont [1711-1770]) (New Zealand: 39.30S, 174.07E).
Mount Egmont (8,261 ft./2,518 m.), also known as Taranaki, is a stratovolcano that began forming over 70,000 years ago. Radiocarbon dating indicates eruptions from at least 3050 B.C. to 1500, with tree rings dating more recent eruptions in approximately 1655 and 1755.

Egon (Flores I., Indonesia: 8.67S, 122.45E).
Egon (5,585 ft./1,703 m.) is a stratovolcano on Flores Island in Indonesia. There are unconfirmed reports of an eruption in 1888. The sole recorded eruption to date occurred in 1907.

Ekarma (Kuril Is.: 48.96N, 153.93E).
Ekarma (3,837 ft./1,170 m.) is a stratovolcano which has formed an island in the northern Kurils. The earliest recorded eruption in 1767 formed a summit dome. The most recent eruption occurred in 1980.

Elbrus (Old Persian name *Harburz*, "high mountain") (Russia: 43.33N, 42.45E).
Mount Elbrus (18,476 ft./5,633 m.) is a stratovolcano in southwestern Russia. The only eruption in recorded history occurred in A.D. 50.

Eldfell ("fire mountain" in Icelandic) (Iceland: 63.43N, 20.28W).

Eldfell (915 ft./279 m.) is a volcano on Heimaey Island in the Vestman-naeyjar archipelago. The earliest recorded submarine eruption occurred in 1637. The island of Surtsey was created in the 1963 eruption, and the most recent eruption in January of 1973 partly destroyed the port of Heimaey.

Elmenteita Badlands (Kenya: 0.52S, 36.27E).

The Elmenteita Badlands (6,975 ft./2,126 m.) is a Holocene pyroclastic cone with no record of eruptions in historic time.

Elovsky (Kamchatka, Russia: 57.53N, 160.53E).

Elovsky (4,531 ft./1,381 m.) is a Holocene shield volcano with no record of eruptions in historic time.

Emmons Lake (Alaska, USA: 55.33N, 162.07W).

Emmons Lake (4,806 ft./1,465 m.) is a Holocene caldera with no record of eruptions in historic time.

Emperor of China (Banda Sea, Indonesia: 6.62S, 124.22E).

The Emperor of China (-9,350 ft./-2,850 m.) is a likely submarine volcano with no recorded eruptions in historic time.

Empung *see* **Lokon-Empung**.

Emuruangogolak (Kenya: 1.50N, 36.33E).

Emuruangogolak (4,357 ft./1,328 m.) is a shield volcano with likely eruptions in the twentieth century.

Erciyes Dagi (Turkey: 38.52N, 35.48E).

Erciyes Dagi (12,848 ft./3,916 m.) is a Holocene stratovolcano with no record of any eruptions in historic time.

Erebus, Mt. (Greek god of darkness and Underworld) (Ross I., Antarctica: 77.53S, 167.17E).

Mount Erebus (12,444 ft./3,794 m.)is a shield volcano and is the world's southernmost active volcano. The earliest recorded eruption took place in 1841. The most recent eruption occurred in 1995 and is still active. Ross Island was discovered by British naval officer James Ross on board HMS *Erebus* during his Antarctic expedition of 1839–43 and the volcano is named as much for his ship as for the Greek god. However, the name is apt for a volcano with its "hellish" depths. Ross's other ship gave its name to Mt. **Terror**.

Erta Ale (Ethiopia: 13.60N, 40.67E).

Erta Ale (2,001 ft./613 m.) is located in the Afar region of Ethiopia. It is one of the world's most active volcanoes. The earliest recorded eruption was in

1906. Subsequent eruptions occurred in 1940 and 1960. Erta Ale most recently erupted in 1967, and is still ongoing.

E-San (Hokkaido, Japan: 41.80N, 141.17E).
E-San (2,028 ft./618 m.) is a stratovolcano whose earliest recorded eruption took place in 1846, when many were killed by mud flows. The most recent eruption occurred in 1874.

Escala (Bolivia: 21.50S, 66.88W).
Escala (13,120 ft./4,000 m.) is a Holocene lava dome with no record of eruptions in historic time.

Escorial, Cerro (Chile/Argentina: 25.08S, 68.37W).
Cerro Escorial (17,870 ft./5,447 m.) is a Holocene stratovolcano with no record of eruptions in historic time.

Esjufjöll (Iceland: 64.27N, 16.65W).
Esjufjöll (5,774 ft./1,760 m.) is a stratovolcano whose sole recorded eruption to date occurred in 1927.

Esmeralda Bank (Mariana Is.: 15.00N, 145.25E).
The Esmeralda Bank (-141 ft./-43 m.) is a submarine volcano with fumarolic activity, but no recorded eruptions.

Espenberg (for Karl Espenberg, a surgeon) (Alaska, USA: 66.35N, 164.33).
Espenberg (797 ft./243 m.) is a volcanic field with no record of eruptions in historic time.

Es-Safa (Syria: 33.08N, 37.15E).
Es-Safa is a volcanic field whose sole recorded eruption to date occurred in approximately 1850.

Etna (Phoenician *attuna*, "furnace") [**Mongibello**] (Italian *monte bello*, "beautiful mountain") (Sicily, Italy: 37.73N, 15.00E).
Mount Etna (10,991 ft./3,350 m.), a shield volcano, has the world's longest recorded eruption record, from approximately 1500 B.C., with radiocarbon datings indicating earlier eruptions going back to approximately 6190 B.C. There have been around 200 eruptions since then, the most recent in 1995. Some 40 people died in an eruption of 140 B.C. Several were killed in 1832, when the front of the lava flow exploded. In 1843 inhabitants of the town of Bronte at the foot of Etna were watching the lava's advance when the flow front suddenly exploded, killing 36. A further 20 survived only a few hours. Nine died in a 1979 eruption with at least 20 seriously injured. Around 200 tourists were in the area at the time. Two tourists were killed and seven injured in the 1987

eruption. Lava flow down the southeastern slopes in early 1998 raised fears of an impending major eruption.

Eyjafjöll (Icelandic, "island mountain") (Iceland: 63.63N, 19.62W).

Eyjafjöll (5,466 ft./1,666 m.) is a stratovolcano whose sole recorded eruption to date occurred in 1821.

F

Falcon I. (Tonga Is.: 20.32S, 175.42W).

Falcon Island (476 ft./145 m.) is a submarine volcano whose earliest recorded eruption occurred in 1877. The most recent eruption occurred in 1970.

Falso Azufre (Chile/Argentina: 26.80S, 68.37W).

Falso Azufre (19,324 ft./5,890 m.) is a Holocene complex volcano with no recorded eruptions in historic time.

Fantale (Ethiopia: 8.975N, 39.93S).

Fantale (6,584 ft./2,007 m.) is a stratovolcano located on the floor of the Ethiopian Rift Valley. There is no recorded evidence of an historical eruption, though small fumaroles have occurred.

Farallón de Pajaros (Mariana Is.: 20.53N, 144.90E).

Farallón de Pajaros (1,181 ft./360 m.) is a stratovolcano whose earliest recorded eruption occurred in 1864. The most recent eruption, recorded hydrophonically, was noted in 1967.

Fayal (Azores: 38.60N, 28.73W).

Fayal (3,421 ft./1,043 m.) is a single basaltic stratovolcano. There was a Strombolian eruption in 1672 which produced lava flows and small cones on the island's western part. A Vulcanian eruption in 1957 of Capelinhos, the dome on Fayal's western flank, created a new island which ultimately fused to the mainland.

Fedotych (Kamchatka, Russia: 57.13N, 160.40E).

Fedotych (3,166 ft./965 m.) is a Holocene stratovolcano with no record of eruptions in historic time.

Fentale (Ethiopia: 8.97N, 39.93E).

Fentale (6,585 ft./2,007 m.) is a stratovolcano. The earliest recorded eruption was in 1250. The second and most recent eruption occurred in 1820.

Fernandina (Galápagos Is.: 0.37S, 91.55W).

Fernandina (4,904 ft./1,495 m.) is a volcanic island in the Galápagos. The earliest recorded eruption occurred in 1813. There have been over 20 eruptions since. During a 1968 eruption, a large part of the crater floor subsided by approximately 300 meters. There were major eruptions in 1991 and, most recently, in January of 1995, when lava entering the sea killed numerous fish and birds.

Firura, Nevados (Peru: 15.23S, 72.63W).
Nevados Firura (18.038 ft./5,498 m.) is composed of Holocene stratovolcanoes with no record of eruptions in historic time.

Fisher (Unimak I., Aleutian Is., Alaska, USA: 54.67N, 164.35W).
Fisher (3,589 ft./1,094 m.) is a stratovolcano whose earliest recorded eruption occurred in 1795. The most recent eruption took place in 1830.

Floreana (Galápagos Is.: 1.30S, 90.45W).
Floreana (2,100 ft./640 m.) is a Holocene shield volcano with no record of eruptions in historic time.

Flores (Azores: 39.40N, 31.17W).
Flores (3,002 ft./915 m.) is a Holocene stratovolcano with no recorded eruptions in historic time.

Flores, Volcán de (Guatemala: 14.30N, 90.00W).
Volcán de Flores (5,249 ft./1,600 m.) is a Holocene volcanic field with no record of eruptions in historic time.

Fogo (Portuguese, "fire") (Cape Verde Is.: 14.95N, 24.35W).
Fogo (9,279 ft./2,829 m.) is a stratovolcano capped by a Cha caldera five miles in diameter. There have been 10 recorded eruptions since the earliest in 1500. An eruption and earthquakes in 1847 caused some fatalities. There were subsequent eruptions in 1951 and, most recently, in April of 1995, forcing the evacuation of numerous inhabitants of the island.

Fonualei (Tonga Is.: 18.02S, 174.52W).
Fonualei (656 ft./200 m.) is a stratovolcano whose earliest recorded eruption occurred in 1791. The most recent eruption occurred in 1957.

Fort Portal Field (Uganda: 0.70N, 30.25E).
The Fort Portal Field (5,000 ft./1,524 m.) is composed of tuff cones with evidence of eruptions in the past 10,000 years. There have been no eruptions in historic time.

Fort Selkirk (Yukon, Canada: 62.93N, 137.38W).
Fort Selkirk (4,065 ft./1,239 m.) is a Holocene volcanic field with no record of eruptions in historic time.

Four Craters Lava Field (Oregon, USA: 43.36N, 120.67W).
The Four Craters Lava Field (4,925 ft./1,501 m.) is a Holocene volcanic field with no recorded eruptions in historic time.

Fournaise, Piton de la (French, "furnace peak") (Réunion: 21.23S, 55.71E).

Piton de la Fournaise (8,632 ft./2,631 m.) is a basaltic shield volcano on Réunion Island in the western Indian Ocean. One of the most active volcanoes on Earth, the earliest recorded eruption occurred in 1640. There have been over 150 eruptions since then, mostly from crater Dolomieu (named for French geologist Dieudonné Dolomieu [1750–1801], who gave his name to the mineral dolomite, and so to Italian mountain group Dolomites.). Three visitors died in a 1972 eruption after spending 48 hours in cold mists on lava fields. The most recent eruption occurred in 1992.

Fourpeaked (Alaska, USA: 58.77N, 153.68W).

Fourpeaked (6,903 ft./2,104 m.) is a stratovolcano with likely volcanic activity in the past 10,000 years. There is no record of eruptions in historic time.

Fremrinamur (Iceland: 65.43N, 16.65W).

Fremrinamur (3,081 ft./939 m.) is a Holocene stratovolcano with no recorded eruptions in historic time.

Frosty (Alaska, USA: 55.07N, 162.82W).

Frosty (6,299 ft./1,920 m.) is a Holocene stratovolcano near Unimak Island in the Aleutian island chain of Alaska. There are no records of eruptions in historical time.

Fuego (Spanish, "fire") (Guatemala: 14.47N, 90.88W).

Fuego (12,342 ft./3,763 m.), overlooking Antigua, Guatemala's former capital, is one of Central America's most active stratovolcanoes. The earliest recorded eruption occurred in 1524. There have been over 50 eruptions since then, primarily Vulcanian producing pyroclastic flows. Seven died in a 1963 eruption and 10 in 1971. Many houses were destroyed by weight of ash in an October 1974 eruption, with two or three persons reportedly killed by "hot water and mud." The most recent eruption occurred in 1987. There are still active fumaroles in the summit crater.

Fuerteventura (Canary Is.: 28.36N, 14.02W).

Fuerteventura (1,735 ft./529 m.) is composed of fissure vents. There are indications of eruptions in the last 10,000 years, but no recorded historical eruptions.

Fuji (perhaps Ainu, "spitfire") (Honshu, Japan: 35.35N, 138.73E).

Fuji (12,388 ft./3,776 m.) is one of the world's best known stratovolcanoes. The earliest recorded eruption occurred in A.D. 781, while radiocarbon dating indicates the earliest eruption could have been in approximately 8050 B.C. There have been over 50 eruptions since then, most recently in 1708. Five of the known eruptions have caused damage, but there are no records of fatalities. The mountain is Japan's highest peak and its sacred symbol. (Its alternate name, Fujiyama, adds Japanese *yama*, "mountain." The Japanese themselves call it *Fujisan*, with *san* also meaning "mountain.").

Fukujin (Volcano Is., Japan: 21.92N, 143.44E).
Fukujin (-712 ft./-217 m.) is a submarine volcano whose earliest recorded eruption occurred in 1951.

Fukutoku-okanoba *see* **Shin-Iwo-jima.**

Furnas (San Miguel, Azores: 37.77N, 25.32W).
Furnas (2,640 ft./805 m.) is a stratovolcano with a four-mile in diameter summit caldera. There is a large lake near the caldera's west side. The sole recorded eruption to date was in 1630, although radiocarbon dating indicates four earlier eruptions from approximately 4570 B.C. At least 200 people were killed in a 1630 eruption when a violent pumice explosion caused mud flows in Ribeira Quente on the south coast.

Fuss Peak (Kuril Is.: 50.27N, 155.25E).
Fuss Peak (5,812 ft./1,772 m.) is a stratovolcano on Paramushir in the Northern Kuril Islands. Still active, the only recorded eruption occurred in 1854.

G

Gabillema (Ethiopia: 11.08N, 41.27E).
Gabillema (4,787 ft./1,459 m.) is a Holocene stratovolcano with no record of eruptions in historic time.

Gade Ale (Ethiopia: 13.97N, 40.41E).
Gade Ale (942 ft./287 m.) is a Holocene stratovolcano with no record of eruptions in historic time.

Galápagos Rift (Eastern Pacific: 0.79N, 86.15W).
The Galápagos Rift (-8,200 ft./-2,500 m.) is a Holocene submarine volcano with no record of eruptions in historic time.

Galeras (Colombia: 1.22N, 77.37W).
Galeras (14,029 ft./4,276 m.) is a complex volcano in southern Colombia. The earliest recorded eruption occurred in 1535, with radiocarbon dating indicating the earliest eruption in approximately 2570 B.C. There have been over 25 eruptions since then, most recently in 1993, when a sudden explosion killed nine, among them six volcanologists in (and on rim of) the inner crater.

Gallego (Solomon Is.: 9.35S, 159.73E).
Gallego (3,280 ft./1,000 m.) is a Holocene volcanic field with no record of eruptions in historic time.

Galunggung (Java: 7.25S, 108.05E).
Galunggung (7,111 ft./2,168 m.) is a stratovolcano on the west part of the island of Java. The earliest recorded eruption occurred in 1822, when over 4,000 people were killed and 144 villages were destroyed. Up to around 70 also lost their lives in a 1982 Vulcanian-type eruption, when the *Washington Post* reported three killed by falling rocks. Others died in traffic accidents and from exposure to cold, ash, and hunger. (The main victims were elderly and infants.). The most recent eruption was phreatic and occurred in 1984.

Gamalama (Halmahera, Indonesia: 0.80N, 127.32E).
Gamalama (5,625 ft./1,715 m.), also known as the Peak of Ternate, is a stratovolcano with multiple craters forming an island 11 kilometers in diameter. The earliest recorded eruption occurred in 1538. Since then Gamalama has erupted over 50 times. During the 1772 eruption, around 30 slaves working at the foot of the volcano were killed by glowing ash and rock, and several drowned in 1773 when fleeing an eruption on overloaded boats. An eruption of 1775 killed over 1,000; some drowned when escaping by boat. Five died and five were injured in a 1962 eruption. The most recent eruption occurred in 1993.

Gambier, Mt. (Australia: 37.77S, 142.50E).
Mount Gambier (3,316 ft./1,011 m.) is a volcanic complex of Maar volcanoes in the Newer Volcanic Province in South Australia. It was formed about 4,900 years ago and is the youngest group of volcanoes on the Australian continent.

Gamchen (Kamchatka, Russia: 54.97N, 160.70E).
Gamchen (8,449 ft./2,576 m.) is a nested Holocene volcano located in the caldera of an older volcano on the east coast of Kamchatka. There is no record of an eruption in historical time.

Gamkonora (Halmahera, Indonesia: 1.37N, 127.52E).
Gamkonora (5,364 ft./1,635 m.) is a stratovolcano. The earliest recorded eruption occurred in 1564. There was a major eruption in 1673 that caused fatalities and produced a tsunami. Recent eruptions occurred in 1981 and 1987.

Garat, Mt. *see* **Gaua.**

Garbes (Djibouti: 11.42N, 42.20E).
Garbes (3,280 ft./1,000 m.) is a Quaternary fumarole field formed in the Pleistocene Era.

Garbuna Group (New Britain, Papua New Guinea: 5.45S, 150.03E).
The Garbuna Group (1,850 ft./564 m.) are Holocene stratovolcanoes with no record of eruptions in historic time.

Gareloi (Russian, "burning") (Aleutian Is., Alaska, USA: 51.78N, 178.80W).
Gareloi (5,159 ft./1,573 m.) is a small conical stratovolcano with two summits in the Aleutian Islands. There have been nearly 15 eruptions since the earliest recorded in 1760. An explosive eruption in 1929 produced 12 craters along a 2.5 mile fissure reaching from the summit to the ocean. The most recent eruption occurred in 1989.

Garibaldi, Mt. (British Columbia, Canada: 49.85N, 123.00W).
Mount Garibaldi (8,786 ft./2,678 m.) is a Holocene stratovolcano with no record of eruptions in historic time.

Garibaldi Lake (British Columbia, Canada: 49.92N, 123.03W).
Garibaldi Lake (7,598 ft./2,316 m.) is a Holocene volcanic field with no record of eruptions in historic time.

Gariboldi *see* **Kone.**

Garove (New Britain, Papua New Guinea: 4.69S, 149.50E).
Garove (1,207 ft./368 m.) is a Holocene stratovolcano with no record of eruptions in historic time.

Garua Harbour (New Britain, Papua New Guinea: 5.27S, 150.09E).
Garua Harbour (1,854 ft./565 m.) is a Holocene volcanic field with no record of eruptions in historic time.

Gaua (Santa María I., Vanuatu: 14.27S, 167.50E).
Gaua (2,614 ft./797 m.) is a stratovolcano which forms Santa Maria Island. There have been 13 eruptions, all from Mt. Gharat, a secondary cone and summit of the volcano, since 1963. Most of the eruptions were small and the most recent occurred in April of 1982. Fumarolic activity was reported in July of 1996.

Gayolesten (Sumatra: 3.87N, 97.60E).
Gaylesten (4,921 ft./1,500 m.) is a fumarole field with no recorded eruptions in historic time.

Gedamsa Caldera (Ethiopia: 8.35N, 39.18E).
Gedamsa Caldera (6,509 ft./1,984 m.) is a Holocene caldera with no record of eruptions in historic time.

Gede (Java: 6.78S, 106.98E).
Gede (9,705 ft./2,958 m.) is a stratovolcano whose earliest recorded eruption occurred in 1747. Gede has erupted 20 times since then, most recently in 1957.

Genovesa (Galápagos Is.: 0.32N, 89.96W).
Genovesa (210 ft./64 m.) is a Holocene shield volcano with no record of eruptions in historic time.

Geodesistoy (Kamchatka, Russia: 56.33N, 158.67E).
Geodesistoy (3,839 ft./1,170 m.) is a Holocene shield volcano with no record of eruptions in historic time.

Geureudong, Bur Ni (Sumatra: 4.82N, 96.80E).
Bur Ni Geureudong (8,497 ft./2,590 m.) is a stratovolcano with fumarolic activity. There have been no recorded eruptions in historic time.

Gilibanta (Indonesia: 8.52S, 119.35E).
Gilibanta is a submarine volcano with no recorded eruptions.

Girekol (Turkey: 39.17N, 43.33E).
Girekol, in eastern Turkey, is a Holocene volcano with no record of historic eruptions.

Glacier Peak (Washington, USA: 48.11N, 121.11W).
Glacier Peak (10,539 ft./3,213 m.) is a small stratovolcano in Washington state's Cascade Range. Most of the eruptions from Glacier Peak have been tephra eruptions, occurring over 11,000 years ago.

Golaya (Russian, "bare") (Kamchatka, Russia: 52.26N, 157.79E).
Golaya (2,792 ft./851 m.) is a stratovolcano with no record of eruptions in historic time.

Golden Trout Creek (California, USA: 36.36N, 118.32W).
Golden Trout Creek (9,468 ft./2,886 m.) is a Holocene volcanic field with no recorded eruptions in historic time.

Golets-Tornyi Group (Kuril Is.: 45.25N, 148.35E).
Golets-Tornyi Group (1,450 ft./442 m.) consists of pyroclastic cones and is located on Iturup Island in the southern Kuril Islands. There are suspected, but unconfirmed, eruptions in the past 10,000 years.

Gollu Dag (Turkey: 38.25N, 34.57E).
Gollu Dag (7,031 ft./2,143 m.) is a Holocene lava dome with no record of historic eruptions.

Golovnin (Kuril Is.: 43.85N, 145.53E).
Golovnin (1,774 ft./541 m.) is a caldera on Kunashir Island in the southern Kuril Islands. There was a small recorded eruption in 1848.

Goodenough, Mt. (D'Entrecasteaux Is.: 9.48S, 150.35E).
Mount Goodenough (722 ft./220 m.) is a Holocene volcanic field with no record of an historic eruption.

Goosenest (Oregon, USA: 42.79N, 122.15W).
Goosenest (7,260 ft./2,213 m.) is a Holocene shield volcano with no record of eruptions in historic time.

Gordo, Cerro (Mexico: 19.75N, 98.81W).
Cerro Gordo (9,993 ft./3,046 m.) is a Holocene cinder cone with no recorded eruptions in historic time.

Gordon (Alaska, USA: 62.13N, 143.08W).
Gordon (9,039 ft./2,755 m.) is composed of Holocene cinder cones with no record of eruptions in historic time.

Gorelaya Sopka (Russian, "burning volcano") (Kamchatka, Russia: 52.56N, 158.03E).
Gorelaya Sopka (6,000 ft./1,829 m.) is an active caldera volcano with five small overlapping stratovolcanoes. The earliest recorded eruption occurred in 1828, but datings of ash layers indicate at least 30 earlier eruptions going back as early as approximately 7250 B.C. There have been recent eruptions in 1980-81 and 1984–86.

Gorny Institut (Russian, "mining institute") (Kamchatka, Russia: 57.33N, 160.20E).
Gorny Institut (6,972 ft./2,125 m.) is a Holocene stratovolcano with no record of eruptions in historic time.

Goryashchaya Sopka (Russian, "burning volcano") (Shimushir I., Kuril Is.: 46.83N, 151.75E).
Goryashchaya Sopka (2,922 ft./891 m.) is an active stratovolcano on Shimushir Island in the central Kuril Islands. There have been five recorded eruptions since the earliest in 1842, with the most recent in 1914. There are unconfirmed reports of an eruption in 1944.

Graciosa (Azores: 39.02N, 27.97W).
Graciosa (1,318 ft./402 m.) is a Holocene stratovolcano with a caldera in the Azore Islands. There is a 600 feet wide cave with a lake within near the bottom of the caldera. There are no records of historic eruptions.

Gran Canaria (Canary Is.: 28.00N, 15.58W).
Gran Canaria (6,398 ft./1,950 m.) is a shield volcano with fissure vents which makes up one of the largest islands in the Canary Islands.

Great Sitkin (Aleutian Is., Alaska, USA: 52.08N, 176.13W).
Great Sitkin (5,707 ft./1,740 m.) is a stratovolcano within a caldera at the summit of a shield volcano. There is evidence of an eruption in 1760, and possibly as many as a dozen eruptions since. The last recorded eruption occurred in 1974, though an unconfirmed eruption may have taken place in 1987.

Griggs (Alaska, USA: 58.3N, 155.10W).
Griggs (8,000 ft./2,317 m.) is a Holocene stratovolcano on the Alaska Peninsula. Griggs has not erupted in historic times, though there are active fumaroles near the summit.

Grille, La (Indian Ocean: 11.47S, 43.33E).
La Grille (3,566 ft./1,087 m.) is a Holocene shield volcano with no record of eruptions in historic time.

Grímsnes (Iceland: 64.03N, 20.87W).
Grímsnes (702 ft./214 m.) is composed of crater rows. There is no record of eruptions in historic time.

Grímsvötn (Iceland: 64.42N, 17.33W).
Grímsvötn (5,658 ft./1,724 m.) is a central volcano in Iceland's Grímsvötn volcanic system. The earliest recorded eruption occurred in A.D. 905, but ash rings indicate eruption as early as 4550 B.C. Grímsvötn has erupted 45 times. Following an eruption in 1706 a third of Iceland's population died of smallpox. An eruption of 1783–5 destroyed summer crops and poisoned livestock, causing widespread famine and an estimated death toll of 9,350, one in five members of the population. Lava flow from the 27-km-long Laki (Lakagigar) crater row extended 65–70 km, a world record. A fissure between Grímsvötn and **Bárdhabunga** in Vatnajökull ("water glacier"), Europe's largest glacier, erupted in 1996, causing a *jökulhlaup* (glacier burst) that swept south, destroying roads, bridges, and power lines but causing no casualties, as the area of the flood had been evacuated.

Groppo (Ethiopia: 11.73N, 40.25E).
Groppo (3,051 ft./930 m.) is a Holocene stratovolcano with no record of eruptions in historic time.

Grozny Group (Kuril Is.: 45.02N, 147.87E).
The Grozny Group (3,972 ft./1,211 m.) is a complex of volcanoes located on Iturup Island in the southern Kuril Islands. There have been five reported eruptions of small to moderate size between 1968 and 1989.

Guadelupe (Mexico: 29.07N, 118.28W).
Guadelupe (3,609 ft./1,100 m.) is a Holocene shield volcano with no record of eruptions in historic time.

Guagua Pichincha (Ecuador: 0.17S, 78.56W).

Guagua Pichincha (15,692 ft./4,784 m.) is a stratovolcano overlooking Ecuador's capital, Quito. The city has been badly damaged by eruptions on several occasions. The earliest recorded eruption occurred in 1566. During an eruption in 1660 ten inches of ash and volcanic residue covered the city of Quito. The most recent eruption occurred in 1993, when two volcanologists were killed.

Guallatir (Chile: 18.42S, 69.17W).

Guallatir (19,913 ft./6,071 m.) is a stratovolcano in the Andes in northern Chile. It is the highest active volcano in the world. The earliest recorded eruption occurred in 1825. There have been four eruptions since, most recently in 1993.

Guayaques (Chile/Bolivia: 22.88S, 67.58W).

Guayaques (18,038 ft./5,498 m.) is composed of Holocene lava domes. There are no recorded eruptions in historic time.

Guazapa (El Salvador: 13.90N, 89.12W).

Guazapa (4,718 ft./1,438 m.) is a Holocene stratovolcano with no record of eruptions in historic time.

Gufa (Ethiopia: 12.55N, 4253E).

Gufa (1,968 ft./600 m.) is a Holocene volcanic field with no record of eruptions in historic time.

Guguan (Mariana Is.: 17.32N, 145.85E).

Guguan (942 ft./287 m.) is a stratovolcano and part of the Mariana Islands volcanic arc. The sole recorded eruption to date was in 1883, which produced pyroclastic flows and lava.

Guntur (Java: 7.13S, 107.83E).

Guntur (7,379 ft./2,249 m.) is a complex volcano whose earliest recorded eruption occurred in 1690. Many perished in an 1800 eruption. A river, carrying sulfurous mud, poured down the valley bearing carcasses of people and animals, covering the countryside with a thick coat of mud. The most recent eruption occurred in 1847.

Gunungapi Wetar (Banda Sea, Indonesia: 6.64S, 126.65E).

Gunungapi Wetar (925 ft./282 m.) is a stratovolcano whose earliest recorded eruption occurred in 1512. The only subsequent eruption took place in 1699.

H

Hachijo-jima (Izu Is., Japan: 33.13N, 139.77E).

Hachijo-jima (2,802 ft./854 m.) is a stratovolcano whose earliest recorded eruption occurred in 1487. The most recent eruption occurred in 1606.

Hachimantai (Honshu, Japan: 39.95N, 140.85E).
   Hachimantai (5,295 ft./1,614 m.) is a Holocene stratovolcano with no record of eruptions in historic time.

Hakkoda Group (Honshu, Japan: 40.65N, 140.88E).
   The Hakkoda Group (5,200 ft./1,585 m.), located near Aomori City in northeastern Honshu, is composed of Holocene stratocones and lava domes. The highest peak is O-take, which has no evidence of historical eruptions. Gases from a volcanic hot spring killed three Japanese rangers, and poisoned 18 others during a 1997 training exercise.

Hakone (Honshu, Japan: 35.22N, 139.02E).
   Hakone (4,720 ft./1,439 m.) is a volcanic complex composed of seven central cones inside double calderas. One of the cones is a stratovolcano and the other six are steep lava domes. The main body of Hakone is a massive stratovolcano with a central caldera 6.8 miles across. There have been two eruptions of Hakone in historic times, the most recent occurring in 950 B.C. Although there was no eruption, ten people were killed in 1953 in a landslide.

Haku-San (Honshu, Japan: 36.15N, 136.78E).
   Haku-San (8,865 ft./2,702 m.) is a stratovolcano whose earliest recorded eruption occurred in A.D. 706, but radiocarbon dating indicates at least 12 previous eruptions from approximately 7050 B.C. The most recent eruption occurred in 1659.

Haleakala (Hawaiian, "house of the sun") (Maui, Hawaii, USA: 20.71N, 156.25W).
   Haleakala (10,023 ft./3,055 m.), also known as East Maui, is one of two shield volcanoes that compose the island of Maui. It is the third largest shield volcano in the Hawaiian islands. The sole recorded eruption to date occurred in 1790, although radiocarbon datings indicate 10 earlier eruptions going back to approximately 7450 B.C. The name derives from a legend that the demigod Maui imprisoned the sun here in order to lengthen the day.

Halemaumau *see* **Kilauea.**

Halla (Korea: 33.37N, 126.53E).
   Halla (6,398 ft./1,950 m.) is a shield volcano with only two recorded eruptions, in 1002 and A.D. 1007.

Hamman Demt, Jabal (Yemen: 14.05N, 44.75E).
   Jabal Hamman Demt is a Holocene cone with no record of eruptions in historic time.

Hangar *see* **Khangar.**

Hararo Manda (Ethiopia: 12.17N, 40.82E).
Hararo Manda (1,968 ft./600 m.) consists of fissure vents which have not erupted in historic time. There was likely volcanic activity in the past 10,000 years.

Harcourt, Mt. (Victorialand, Antarctica: 72.3S, 1701E).
Mount Harcourt (5,153 ft./1,571 m.) is a stratovolcano, which with three overlapping shield volcanoes composes Hallett Peninsula, which extends into the Ross Sea.

Hargy (New Britain, Papua New Guinea: 5.33S, 151.10E).
Hargy (3,766 ft./1,148 m.) is a stratovolcano on New Britain Island in the south Bismarck Sea. There were eruptions from the Galloseulo vent in 5050 B.C. and in A.D. 950.

Harimkotan (Kuril Is.: 49.12N, 154.51E).
Harimkotan (3,755 ft./1,145 m.) is a stratovolcano on Shiashkotan in the northern Kuril Islands. There were six recorded eruptions from 1713 through 1933. During the most recent eruption in 1933, a giant tidal wave, reportedly over 60 feet high, caused by the collapse of the Severgin volcano cone, reached Onekotan and Paramushir Islands, killing two people.

Haruj (Libya: 27.25N, 17.50E).
Haruj (3,937 ft./1,200 m.) is composed of Holocene scoria cones with no record of eruptions in historic time.

Haruna (Honshu, Japan: 36.47N, 138.88E).
Haruna (4,754 ft./1,449 m.) is a stratovolcano. Ash rings date the earliest eruption in approximately A.D. 450. Two eruptions in the sixth century buried an agricultural community, which was unearthed by archaeologists only in the twentieth century.

Hasan Dagi (Turkey: 38.13N, 34.17E).
Hasan Dagi (10,673 ft./3,253 m.) is a Holocene stratovolcano with no record of eruptions in historic time.

Haut Dong Nai (Vietnam: 10.80N, 107.20E).
Haut Dong Nai (3,280 m./1,000 m.) is a Holocene volcanic field with no record of eruptions in historic time.

Hayes (for Charles W. Hayes [1858–1916], geologist) (Alaska, USA: 61.62N, 152.48W).
Hayes (9,147 ft./2,788 m.) is a Holocene stratovolcano with no record of eruptions in historic time.

Haylan, Jabal (Yemen: 15.43N, 44.78E).
Jabal Haylan (5,085 ft./1,550 m.) is a Holocene volcanic field with no record of eruptions in historic time.

Hayli Gubbi (Ethiopia: 13.50N, 40.72E).
Hayli Gubbi (1,709 ft./521 m.) is a Holocene shield volcano with no record of eruptions in historic time.

Heard I. (Indian Ocean: 53.11S, 73.51E).
Heard Island (9,000 ft./2,745 m.) is an active stratovolcano in the south Indian Ocean. The earliest recorded eruption occurred in 1910 from Mawson Peak (named for the Australian Antarctic explorer). There were seven known subsequent eruptions, including an eruption that lasted from January of 1985 until January of 1987. The most recent eruption occurred in 1993.

Heart Peaks (British Columbia, Canada: 58.60N, 131.97W).
Heart Peaks (6,601 ft./2,012 m.) is a Holocene shield volcano with no record of eruptions in historic time.

Heimaey *see* **Eldfell**.

Hekla (Old Icelandic, "cloak," referring to covering of smoke) (Iceland: 63.98N, 19.70W).
Hekla (4,890 ft./1,491 m.) is a stratovolcano, and Iceland's most active volcano. The earliest recorded eruption occurred in A.D. 1104, but radiocarbon datings indicate at least 20 earlier eruptions going back to 5850 B.C. An eruption in 1766 caused widespread fatalities, with around 600 deaths from famine the following winter. A scientist filming the 1947 eruption was killed by a glowing block rolling off in front of a lava flow. The most recent eruption was in 1991.

Helatoba-Taratung (Sumatra: 2.03N, 98.93E).
Helatoba-Taratung (3,609 ft./1,100 m.) is a fumarole field with no record of eruptions in historic time.

Hell's Half Acre (Idaho, USA: 43.50N, 112.45W).
Hell's Half Acre (5,351 ft./1,631 m.) is a Holocene shield volcano with no record of eruptions in historic time.

Hengill (Iceland: 64.18N, 21.33W).
Hengill (2,635 ft./803 m.) is composed of crater rows. There is no record of eruptions in historic time.

Herbert (for Hilary A. Herbert [1834–1919], lawyer, Confederate Army officer) (Aleutian Is., Alaska, USA: 52.75N, 170.12W).
Herbert (4,232 ft./1,290 m.) is a Holocene stratovolcano with no record of eruptions in historic time.

Hertali (Ethiopia: 9.78N, 40.33E).
Hertali (2,952 ft./900 m.) is a fissure vent that has likely erupted in the past 10,000 years.

Hibok-Hibok (Camiguin, Philippines: 9.20N, 124.67E).
Hibok-Hibok (4,369 ft./1,332 m.) is a stratovolcano composing the island of Camiguin, 12 miles north of Mindanao, in the Philippines. Also known as Catarman, the earliest recorded eruption was in 1827. Over three hundred deaths reportedly occurred during an eruption in 1861. Some fatalities occurred during the 1871-75 eruption, which also formed the Mount Vulcan lava dome. *Time* reported 68 deaths in pumice and lava flows from the 1950 eruption. The same journal reported 500 were killed in a 1951 eruption, with 266 bodies found and around 1,500 people unaccounted for. The most recent eruption occurred in 1953.

Hierro (Canary Is.: 27.73N, 18.03W).
Hierro (4,920 ft./1,500 m.) is a shield volcano in the Canary Islands. The only known historic eruption, in 1793, was from the Volcán de Lomo Negro vent and produced lava flows.

Hijiori (Honshu, Japan: 38.60N, 140.18E).
Hijiori (1,693 ft./516 m.) is a caldera with no recorded eruptions in historic time.

Hiuchi (Honshu, Japan: 36.95N, 139.28E).
Hiuchi (7,697 ft./2,346 m.) is a Holocene stratovolcano with no record of eruptions in historic time.

Hobicha Caldera (Ethiopia: 6.78N, 37.83E).
The Hobicha Caldera (5,905 ft./1,800 m.) is a caldera in Ethiopia with a likelihood of volcanic activity in the past 10,000 years.

Hodson (South Sandwich Is.: 56.70S, 27.15W).
Hodson (5,266 ft./1,605 m.) is a Holocene stratovolcano with no recorded eruptions in historic time.

Hofsjökull (Iceland: 64.78N, 18.92W).
Hofsjökull (5,846 ft./1,782 m.) is a Holocene subglacial volcano. There have been no recorded eruptions in historic time.

Hohnel Island *see* **South Island.**

Holotepec (Mexico: 19.08N, 99.48W).
Holotepec (9,842 ft./3,000 m.) is a Holocene volcanic field with no record of eruptions in historic time.

Homa Mountain (Kenya: 0.38S, 34.50E).

Homa Mountain (5,745 ft./1,751 m.) is a Holocene volcanic complex with no record of eruptions in historic time.

Home Reef (Tonga Is.: 18.99S, 174.77W).

Home Reef (-7 ft./-2 m.) is a submarine volcano in the southwest Pacific Ocean. The earliest recorded eruption occurred in 1852. The most recent eruption occurred in 1984.

Honggeertu (China: 41.47N, 113.00E).

Honggeertu (5,577 ft./1,700 m.) is composed of Holocene cinder cones. There are no recorded eruptions in historic time.

Hood, Mt. (for Lord Samuel Hood [1724–1816], English admiral) (Oregon, USA: 45.37N, 121.69W).

Mount Hood (11,237 ft./3,426 m.) is a stratovolcano composed of lava flows, domes and volcaniclastic deposits. It is the tallest mountain in Oregon and a popular attraction for skiers and hikers. Mount Hood's main cone was formed approximately 500,000 years ago. The earliest recorded eruption was in 1859. The most recent eruption occurred in 1866.

Hoodoo Mountain (British Columbia, Canada: 56.78N, 131.28W).

Hoodoo Mountain (5,971 ft./1,820 m.) is a Holocene subglacial volcano with no record of eruptions in historic time.

Hornitos, Los (Chile: 35.72S, 70.81W).

Los Hornitos (6,562 ft./2,000 m.) is composed of Holocene cinder cones. There have been no recorded eruptions in historic time.

Hornopiren, Volcán (Chile: 41.87S, 72.43W).

Volcán Hornopiren (5,157 ft./1,572 m.) is a Holocene stratovolcano with no record of eruptions in historic time.

Hualalai (Hawaii, USA: 19.69N, 155.87W).

Hualalai (8,278 ft./2,523 ft.) is Hawaii's westernmost shield volcano. The sole recorded eruption occurred in 1800, but radiocarbon dating shows around 20 earlier eruptions from approximately 7540 B.C. Two persons were killed in the 1800 eruption when lava flows surrounded a hut at night.

Huanquihue Group (Argentina: 39.87S, 71.55W).

The Huanquihue Group (4,265 ft./1,300 m.) is a pyroclastic cone with no record of eruptions in historic time.

Huaynaputina (Peru: 16.61S, 70.85W).

Huaynaputina (15,912 ft./4,850 m.) is a stratovolcano whose earliest recorded eruption occurred in 1600, killing around 1,400 inhabitants of at least 11 villages. The most recent eruption took place in 1667.

Hudson, Cerro (Chile: 45.90S, 72.97W).
Cerro Hudson (6,250 ft./1,905 m.) is a stratovolcano whose earliest recorded eruption took place in 1891. Three people were killed during a 1971 eruption. The most recent eruption occurred in 1991, when meltwater flooded down the Huemules River valley, and blocks of ice up to 5 meters in diameter washed almost to the Pacific coast, 35 kilometers away.

Hudson Mountains (Antarctica: 74.33S, 99.42W).
The Hudson Mountains (2,457 ft./749 m.) are likely composed of stratovolcanoes with no evidence of eruptions in historic time.

Huelemolle (Chile: 39.30S, 71.82W).
Huelemolle (2,657 ft./810 m.) is composed of Holocene cinder cones with no recorded eruptions in historic time.

Huequi (Chile: 42.38S, 72.58W).
Huequi (4,324 ft./1,318 m.) is a stratovolcano whose earliest recorded eruption occurred in 1890.

Huila (Colombia: 2.92N, 76.05W).
Huila (17,602 ft./5,365 m.) is a volcanic complex composed of three major peaks — Pico Norte, Pico Central and Pico Sur. The sole recorded eruption to date occurred in approximately 1555.

Hulubelu (Sumatra: 5.35S, 104.60E).
Hulubelu (3,412 ft./1,040 m.) is a caldera with fumarolic activity. There is no record of eruptions in historic time.

Hunter I. (Southwestern Pacific: 22.40S, 172.05E).
Hunter Island (974 ft./297 m.) is a stratovolcano whose earliest recorded eruption occurred in 1835. The most recent eruption took place in 1903.

Hutapanjang (Sumatra: 2.27S, 101.60E).
Hutapanjang is a Holocene stratovolcano with no record of eruptions in historic time.

Hydrographers Range (New Guinea: 9.00S, 148.37E).
Hydrographers Range (6,283 ft./1,915 m.) is a Holocene stratovolcano with no record of eruptions in historic time.

I

Iamelele (D'Entrecasteaux Is.: 9.52S, 150.53E).
Iamelele (656 ft./200 m.) is composed of Holocene lava domes. There have been no historic eruptions.

Ibu (Halmahera, Indonesia: 1.48N, 127.63E).

Ibu (4,347 ft./1,325 m.) is a stratovolcano. The sole recorded eruption was an explosive one in 1911

Ibusuki Volcanic Field (Kyushu, Japan: 31.22N, 130.57E).

The Ibusuki Volcanic Field (3,025 ft./922 m.) is composed of calderas. The earliest recorded eruption occurred in A.D. 874, although datings of ash layers indicate at least 20 previous eruptions from approximately 5050 B.C. The most recent eruption occurred in A.D. 885. Almost all eruptions have been from volcano Kaimon.

Ichinskaya Sopka Kamchatka, Russia: 55.68N, 157.73E).

Ichinskaya Sopka (11,880 ft./3,621 m.) is a Holocene stratovolcano with no record of eruptions in historic time.

Iettunup (Kamchatka, Russia: 58.40N, 161.08E).

Iettunup (4,396 ft./1,340 m.) is a Holocene shield volcano with no record of eruptions in historic time.

Igwisi Hills (Tanzania: 4.87S, 31.92E).

The Igwisi Hills are Holocene tuff cones with no record of volcanic activity in historic time.

Iizuna (Honshu, Japan: 36.73N, 138.13E).

Iizuna (6,289 ft./1,917 m.) is a Holocene stratovolcano with no record of eruptions in historic time.

Ijen (Java: 8.06S, 114.24E).

Ijen (7,826 ft./2,386 m.) is a stratovolcano with a summit caldera ten miles in diameter. The earliest recorded eruption was in 1796 from Kawah Ijen, the active vent. Many houses were destroyed in the 1817 eruption, with about 400 cattle killed. The number of human casualties remains uncertain. The most recent eruption occurred in 1993.

Iktunup (Kamchatka, Russia: 58.08N, 160.77E).

Iktunup (7,546 ft./2,300 m.) is a Holocene shield volcano with no record of eruptions in historic time.

Iliamna (Alaska, USA: 60.03N, 153.08W).

Iliamna (10,013 ft./3,053 m.) is a stratovolcano west of the Cook Inlet in Alaska. The earliest recorded eruption was in 1778. There were recorded subsequent eruptions in 1867 and 1876, and several other reported, but unconfirmed eruptions. The most recent eruption occurred in 1953.

Iliboleng (Adonara I., Indonesia: 8.34S, 123.26E).

Iliboleng (5,442 ft./1,659 m.) is a stratovolcano on Adonara Island in the

Nusa Tengarra Island chain of Indonesia. The earliest recorded eruption occurred in 1885. There have been 20 subsequent eruptions. A major eruption in 1973–74 caused much damage to vegetation along the slope. The most recent eruption occurred in 1993.

Ililabalekan (Lomblen I., Indonesia: 8.53S, 123.42E).

Ililabalekan (3,340 ft./1,018 m.) is a stratovolcano with fumarolic activity. There have been no recorded eruptions in historic time.

Ilimuda (Flores I., Indonesia: 8.48S, 122.67E).

Ilimuda (3,608 ft./1,100 m.) is a stratovolcano on Flores Island in Indonesia. There are fumaroles present, but no record of eruptions in historic time.

Iliniza (Ecuador: 0.66S, 78.71W).

Iliniza (17,218 ft./5,248 m.) is a Holocene stratovolcano in the Western Cordillera of the Andes. There is no record of an eruption in historical time.

Iliwerung (Lomblen I., Indonesia: 8.54S, 123.59E).

Iliwerung (3,340 ft./1,018 m.) is a volcanic complex whose earliest recorded eruption occurred in 1870. Around 300 cattle were killed in a 1948 eruption, and two fisherman were swept away in a giant wave resulting from the eruption of 1973. A massive landslide in a 1979 eruption caused a wave up to nine meters high, devastating four villages. The death toll on Lomblen Island was given as 539 (175 bodies recovered, 364 missing). The most recent eruption occurred in 1993.

Ilopango (El Salvador: 13.67N, 89.05W).

Ilopango (1,475 ft./450 m.) is a caldera in central El Salvador. The sole recorded eruption to date was in 1879, although radiocarbon dating indicates an earlier eruption in A.D. 260. This was a major catastrophe, destroying many early Mayan cities, with possibly thousands killed. The volcano is an island in a lake that formed in its crater.

Ilyinsky (Kamchatka, Russia: 51.49N, 157.20E).

Ilyinsky (5,176 ft./1,578 m.) is a stratovolcano located on the northeast portion of Kamchatka's Paushetka caldera fault boundary. The sole recorded eruption to date was from a crater on the northwest slope in 1901.

Imagination Peak (Oregon, USA: 42.55N, 122.20W).

Imagination Peak (6,516 ft./1,986 m.) is a Holocene pyroclastic cone with no record of eruptions in historic time.

Imuruk Lake (Inuit [Eskimo], meaning unknown) (Alaska, USA: 65.60N, 163.92W).

Imuruk Lake (2,001 ft./610 m.) is composed of shield volcanoes with no record of eruptions in historic time.

Indian Heaven (Washington, USA: 45.93N, 121.82W).
Indian Heaven (4,964 ft./1,513 m.) is composed of Holocene shield volcanoes with no record of eruptions in historic time.

Ingakslugwat Hills (Alaska, USA: 61.43N, 164.47W).
The Ingakslugwat Hills (623 ft./190 m.) are Holocene cinder cones with no record of eruptions in historic time.

Inielika (Flores I., Indonesia: 8.73S, 120.98E).
Inielika (5,115 ft./1,559 m.) is a complex volcano whose sole recorded eruption to date occurred in 1905.

Inierie (Flores I., Indonesia: 8.87S, 120.95E).
Inierie (7,365 ft./2,245 m.) is a stratovolcano with fumarolic activity. There is no record of eruptions in historic time.

Inyo Craters (for Native American word said to mean "place where great spirit dwells") (California, USA: 37.69N, 119.02W).
Inyo Craters (8,625 ft./2,629 m.) is composed of lava domes with evidence of volcanic activity in the past 2,000 years.

Ipala Volcanic Field (Guatemala: 14.55N, 89.63W).
The Ipala Volcanic Field (5,413 ft./1,650 m.) is a Holocene stratovolcano with no record of eruptions in historic time.

Iraya (north of Luzon, Philippines: 20.47N, 122.01E).
Iraya (3,310 ft./1,009 m.) is a stratovolcano, forming the north end of Batan Island. The sole recorded eruption to date was in 1464.

Irazú, Mt. (Costa Rica: 9.98N, 83.85W).
Mount Irazú (11,257 ft./3,432 m.) is Costa Rica's highest stratovolcano. The earliest recorded eruption was in 1723, and there have been at least 23 eruptions since. The most recent two-year eruption beginning in 1963 caused the deaths of at least 20 people in mud flows. Ash dammed a nearby river, flooding the city of Cartago and seriously damaging coffee crops.

Iriga (Luzon, Philippines: 13.46N, 123.46E).
Iriga (3,924 ft./1,196 m.) is a Holocene stratovolcano. The sole recorded eruption to date occurred in approximately 1628, when an avalanche devastated villages at the foot of the volcano. The number of fatalities remains uncertain.

Iriomote-jima (Ryukyu Is., Japan: 24.56N, 124.00E).
Iriomote-jima (-656 ft./-200m.) is a submarine volcano whose sole recorded submarine eruption to date occurred in 1924.

Irruputuncu (Chile/Bolivia: 20.73S, 68.55W).
Irruputuncu (16,939 ft./5,163 m.) is a stratovolcano in northern Chile. There was no record of documented historical eruptions until a minor eruption was reported in late 1995.

Isanotski (Unimak I., Aleutian Is., Alaska, USA: 54.75N, 163.73W).
Isanotski (8,025 ft./2,446 m.) is a stratovolcano in the Aleutian Island chain. Also known as "Ragged Jack," Isanotski's earliest recorded eruption was in 1795. The most recent eruption occurred in 1831.

Isarog (Luzon, Philippines: 13.66N, 123.37E).
Isarog (6,450 ft./1,966 m.) is a Holocene stratovolcano with no record of eruptions in historic time.

Ischia (Italy: 40.73N, 13.90E).
Ischia (2,589 ft./789 m.) is a complex volcano forming a main island off the Bay of Naples. The earliest recorded eruption was in 500 B.C., although potassium-argon dating indicates likely eruptions as early as 7550 B.C. The most recent eruption occurred in 1302, when several people and animals were reportedly killed. Many fled to neighboring islands and the mainland.

Iskut-Unuk River Cones (British Columbia, Canada: 56.58N, 130.55W).
The Iskut-Unuk River Cones (6,168 ft./1,880 m.) are cinder cones with likely volcanic activity in the past 200 years.

Isluga (Chile: 19.15S, 68.83W).
Isluga (16,568 ft./5,050 m.) is a stratovolcano whose earliest recorded eruption took place in 1863. The most recent eruption occurred in 1913.

Issaikyo *see* **Azuma.**

Itasy Volcanic Field (Madagascar: 19.00S, 46.77E).
The Itasy Volcanic Field (5,905 ft./1,800 m.) is composed of Holocene scoria cones with no record of eruptions in historic time.

Ithnayn, Harrat (Saudi Arabia: 26.58N, 40.20E).
Harrat Ithnayn (5,331 ft./1,625 m.) is a Holocene volcanic field with no record of eruptions in historic time.

Iult (Kamchatka, Russia: 55.23N, 160.59E).
Iult (6,092 ft./1,857 m.) is a Holocene stratovolcano with no record of eruptions in historic time.

Ivan Grozny *see* **Grozny Group.**

Ivao Group (Kuril Is.: 45.77N, 149.68E).

The Ivao Group (4,677 ft./1,426 m.) is a Holocene cinder cone field located on Urup Island in the southern Kuril Islands. There are no known historic eruptions.

Iwaki (Honshu, Japan: 40.65N, 140.30E).

Iwaki (5,331 ft./1,625 m.) is a stratovolcano whose earliest recorded eruption occurred in 1597. The most recent eruption occurred in 1863.

Iwaonupuri (Hokkaido, Japan: 42.88N, 140.63E).

Iwaonupuri (3,786 ft./1,154 m.) is a Holocene stratovolcano with no record of eruptions in historic time.

Iwate (Honshu, Japan: 39.85N, 141.00E).

Iwate (6,696 ft./2,041 m.), in northern Honshu, is a volcanic complex consisting of a breached caldera and pyroclastic cones. The earliest recorded eruption occurred in 1686. There was a small eruption reported in 1919 and fumarolic activity was noted in 1934.

Iwo-jima (meaning "Sulfur Island") (Volcano Is., Japan: 24.75N, 141.33E).

Iwo-jima (528 ft./161 m.) is a submarine caldera. Iwo-jima's cone is called Mount Suribachi. The earliest recorded eruption was in 1922. There have been at least nine other eruptions since, most recently in 1982.

Ixtepeque, Volcán (Guatemala: 14.42N, 89.68W).

Volcán Ixtepeque (4,239 ft./1,292 m.) is composed of Holocene lava domes with no record of eruptions in historic time.

Iya (Flores I., Indonesia: 8.88S, 121.63E).

Iya (2,090 ft./637 m.) is a stratovolcano whose earliest recorded eruption occurred in 1844. The most recent eruption occurred in 1969, when two people were killed and 10 injured. One village was completely destroyed and seven partly destroyed.

Iyang-Argapura (Java: 7.97S, 113.57E).

Iyang-Argapura (10,131 ft./3,088 m.) is a Holocene complex volcano with no record of eruptions in historic time.

Izalco (for Native American people) (El Salvador: 13.81N, 89.63W).

Izalco (6,396 ft./1,950 m.) is a small stratovolcano composed of basalt. The earliest recorded eruption occurred in 1770. Over 50 eruptions have occurred since then, most recently a small flank eruption in 1966. An eruption of 1926 caused several deaths. Izalco's continuous glow enabled nineteenth-century sailors to steer a course by it and so they nicknamed it the "Lighthouse of the Pacific." (*Cf.* **Stromboli**.)

Iztaccíhuatl (Nahuatl, "white woman") (Mexico: 19.18N, 98.64W).
Iztaccíhuatl (17,338 ft./5,286 m.) is an extinct stratovolcano with three summits but no crater. Three snowy peaks resemble the head, breast, and feet of a sleeping woman, hence the name. It is joined by a ridge to **Popocatépetl.**

Izumbwe-Mpoli (Tanzania: 8.93S, 33.40E).
Izumbwe-Mpoli (5,144 ft./1,568 m.) is a Holocene pyroclastic cone with no record of an eruption in historic time.

Izu-Tobu (Honshu, Japan: 34.92N, 139.12E).
Izu-Tobu (4,613 ft./1,406 m.) is a volcanic field composed of pyroclastic beds, a lava platform, shield volcanoes, stratovolcanoes and lava domes. The sole recorded eruption to date was in 1989, although ash layer datings indicate at least four previous eruptions, the earliest being approximately 8050 B.C.

J

Jackies Butte (Oregon, USA: 43.61N, 117.59W).
Jackies Butte (4,659 ft./1,420 m.) is a Holocene volcanic field with no record of eruptions in historic time.

Jailolo (Halmahera, Indonesia: 1.17N, 127.32E).
Jailolo (3,707 ft./1,130m.) is a Holocene stratovolcano. There have been no reported eruptions in historic time.

Jalajala (Luzon, Philippines: 14.35N, 121.33E).
Jalajala (2,438 ft./743 m.) is a fumarolic field with no record of eruptions in historic time.

Jalua (Ethiopia: 15.04N, 39.82E).
Jalua (2,339 ft./713 m.) is a Holocene stratovolcano with no record of eruptions in historic time.

Jan Mayen *see* **Beerenberg.**

Jaraquay Volcanic Field (Mexico: 29.33N, 114.50W).
The Jaraquay Volcanic Field (3,150 ft./960 m.) is composed of Holocene cinder cones with no evidence of eruptions in historic time.

Jefferson, Mt. (for Thomas Jefferson [1743–1826], US president) (Oregon, USA: 44.69N, 121.80W).
Mount Jefferson (10,492 ft./3,199 m.) is a stratovolcano composed of andesite and dacite. There have been no reported eruptions in historical time. There was an eruption at the Forked Butte vent, south of the main

volcano, in 4500 B.C. and a suspected eruption at South Cinder Peak in A.D. 950.

Jingpohu (China: 44.08N, 128.83E).

Jingpohu (1,640 ft./500 m.) is a Holocene volcanic field with no record of eruptions in historic time.

Jocotitlán (Mexico: 19.72N, 99.76W).

Jocotitlán (12,959 ft./3,950 m.) is a stratovolcano with likely volcanic activity in the past 2,000 years.

Jordan Craters (Oregon, USA: 43.03N, 117.42W).

The Jordan Craters (3,900–4,600 ft./1,200–1,400 m.) is a monogenetic volcanic field in southeast Oregon with three main vents.

Jorullo (Mexico: 19.48N, 102.25W).

Jorullo (10,397 ft./3,170 m.) is a cinder cone volcano in Mexico's Michoacan-Guanajuato volcanic field. Jorullo was created during an eruption on September 29, 1759. It continued to erupt for the next 15 years, becoming the longest cinder cone eruption recorded. There have been no subsequent eruptions.

K

Kaba (Sumatra: 3.52S, 102.62E).

Kaba (6,404 ft./1,952 m.) is a stratovolcano whose earliest recorded eruption occurred in 1833, when 126 people lost their lives in a mud flow from the crater lake. The most recent eruption occurred in 1956.

Kabargin Oth (Georgia: 42.55N, 44.00E).

The Kabargin Oth Group (11,975 ft./3,650 m.) is composed of cinder cones from the Holocene period. There is no record of eruptions in recorded history.

Kadovar (Papua New Guinea: 3.62S, 144.62E).

Kadovar (1,197 ft./365 m.) is a Holocene stratovolcano. There was an unconfirmed eruption in 1700.

Kagamil (Aleutian I., Alaska, USA: 52.97N, 169.72W).

Kagamil (2,929 ft./893 m.) is a stratovolcano whose sole recorded eruption to date occurred in 1929.

Kaguyak (Alaska, USA: 58.62N, 154.05W).

Kaguyak (2,955 ft./904 m.) is a Holocene stratovolcano in the Katmai National Park on the Alaska Peninsula. A major eruption in A.D. 325 is one of the largest known historic eruptions in North America. The eruption created a caldera, which contains a crater lake.

Kahoolawe (south of Maui, Hawaii, USA: 20.57N, 156.57W).
Kahoolawe (1,475 ft./450 m.) is a single shield volcano consisting of theolitic and alkalic basalt. It is 12 miles across and creates one of the smallest of the major Hawaiian Islands. There have been no known historic eruptions.

Kaikone (New Zealand: 35.30S, 173.90E).
Kaikone — Bay of Islands (1,273 ft./388 m.) is a volcanic field with indication of volcanic activity in the past 2,000 years.

Kaileney (Kamchatka, Russia: 57.70N, 160.58E).
Kaileney (5,190 ft./1,582 m.) is a Holocene shield volcano with no record of eruptions in historic time.

Kaimon *see* **Ibusuki Volcanic Field.**

Kaitoku Seamount (Volcano Is., Japan: 26.12N, 141.10E).
The Kaitoku Seamount (-33 ft./-10 m.) is a submarine volcano whose earliest recorded eruption occurred in 1543. The most recent eruption occurred in 1984.

Kalatungan (Mindanao, Philippines: 7.95N, 124.80E).
Kalatungan (9,265 ft./2,824 m.) is a Holocene stratovolcano with no record of eruptions in historic time.

Kambal'naya Sopka (Kamchatka, Russia: 51.30N, 156.87E).
Kambal'naya Sopka (7,072 ft./2,156 m.) is a compound stratovolcano. There is a crater lake at Kambal'naya's summit. There is no record of historic eruptions.

Kamen' (Russian, "rock") (Kamchatka, Russia: 56.02N, 160.59E).
Kamen' (1,591 ft./485 m.) is a Holocene stratovolcano with no record of eruptions in historic time.

Kanaga (Aleut, meaning uncertain) (Aleutian Is., Alaska, USA: 51.92N, 177.17W).
Kanaga (4,287 ft./1,307 m.) is a stratovolcano in the southernmost portion of the Aleutian arc. It resides in an older caldera known as Mount Kanaton. There have been seven known eruptions since the earliest in 1763. The most recent eruption occurred in 1994.

Kana Keoki (Solomon Is.: 8.75S, 157.03E).
Kana Keoki (2,297 ft./-700 m.) is a Holocene submarine volcano with no reported volcanic eruptions.

Kannabe (Honshu, Japan: 35.50N, 134.68E).
Kannabe (1,509 ft./460 m.) is a Holocene shield volcano with no record of eruptions in historic time.

Kanpu (Honshu, Japan: 39.93N, 139.88E).
Kanpu (1,165 ft/355 m.) is composed of Holocene lava domes with no record of eruptions in historic time.

Kaokohe–Bay of Islands (New Zealand: 35.30S,173.90E).

Karacalidag (Turkey: 37.67N, 39.83E).
Karacalidag (6,420 ft./1,957 m.) is a Holocene shield volcano with no record of eruptions in historic time.

Karang (Java: 6.27S, 106.04E).
Karang (5,833 ft./1,778 m.) is a stratovolcano with fumarolic activity. There have been no eruptions in historic time.

Karangetang [Api Siau] (Siau I., Indonesia: 2.78N, 125.48E).
Karangetang (5,853 ft./1,784 m.) is an active volcano on the northern end of Siau Island. The earliest recorded eruption occurred in 1675. There have been over 40 subsequent eruptions reported. Four people lost their lives in earthquakes caused by a 1974 eruption, while in 1992 seven farmers perished when burned by lava and pumice flows. Volcanic activity has been present since 1993 and three people were killed by pyroclastic flows in June of 1997. The most recent eruption was reported in July of 1998.

Karapinar Field (Turkey: 37.67N, 33.65E).
The Karapinar Field (4,272 ft./1,302 m.) is composed of cinder cones and was formed in the Holocene period. There has been no record of eruptions in the past 2,000 years.

Karisimbi (Dem. Rep. of Congo [Zaire]/Rwanda: 1.50S, 29.45E).
Karisimbi (14,787 ft./4,507 m.) is a stratovolcano in the Bufumbira field, forming part of the Virunga field in Rwanda's East African rift valley. It is the highest, and one of the most recent, of the eight major volcanoes in the area.

Karkar (Papua New Guinea: 4.65S, 145.96E).
Karkar (6,033 ft./1,839 m.) is an island stratovolcano off the north coast of New Guinea. The earliest recorded eruption occurred in 1643. There have been nine subsequent eruptions, usually from the Bengiai Cone in the summit caldera. An eruption in 1895 resulted in the deaths of about 20 children and elderly people from starvation or disease. The most recent eruption occurred in 1979, killing two volcanologists at an observation camp near the crater rim.

Karpinsky Group (for A.P. Karpinsky [1846–1936], Russian geologist) (Kuril Is.: 50.13N, 155.37E).

The Karpinsky Group (4,411 ft./1,345 m.), on Paramushir in the northern Kuril Islands, is made of cones. A small explosive eruption occurred in 1952.

Kars Plateau (Turkey: 40.75N, 42.90E).

The Kars Plateau (9,842 ft./3,000 m.) is a volcanic field with no record of eruptions in historic time. There was likely volcanic activity in the past 10,000 years.

Karthala (Indian Ocean: 11.75S, 43.38E).

Karthala (7,746 ft./2,361 m.) is an active shield volcano which, with Massif de la Grille, composes Grande Comore, the largest island in the Comores Archipelago. The earliest recorded eruption was in 1050. In the summer of 1903 emanation of suffocating gases killed 17 people, although no actual eruption occurred. The most recent eruption was a phreatic explosion and took place in 1991.

Karua *see* **Kuwae.**

Karymskaya Sopka (Kamchatka, Russia: 54.05N, 159.43E).

Karymskaya Sopka (4,874 ft./1,486 m.) is a stratovolcano within a caldera in southeast Kamchatka. The earliest recorded eruption occurred in 1771. There have been over 30 eruptions since including moderately large eruptions in 1960–64, 1965–67 and 1970–82. There have been explosive eruptions from 1996–98.

Kasatochi (Aleutian Is., Alaska, USA: 52.18N, 175.50W).

Kasatochi (4,311 ft./1,314 m.) is a stratovolcano whose sole recorded eruption to date occurred in 1760.

Kasbek *see* **Kazbek.**

Kasuga Seamount (Volcano Is., Japan: 21.77N, 143.72E).

The Kasuga Seamount (-1,831 ft./-558 m.) is a likely submarine volcano with no recorded eruptions.

Katla (Iceland: 63.63N, 19.05W).

Katla (4,961 ft./1,512 m.) is a subglacial volcano beneath the Myrdalsjokull icecap. The earliest recorded eruption occurred in approximately A.D. 935. The most recent eruption in 1918 triggered *jökulhlaup* (glacier burst), a great flood that carried one 400 meter boulder 14 kmilometers and huge icebergs three kilometers.

Katmai (Inuit [Eskimo], meaning uncertain) (Alaska, USA: 58.27N, 154.98W).

Katmai (6,714 ft./2,047 m.) was once a cluster of several small stratovolcanoes. The sole recorded eruption to date was in 1912, and was the world's largest (simultaneously with neighboring **Novarupta**) in the twentieth century.

Ash lay 60 centimeters thick in the streets of Kodiak, and the Ukak River valley to the northwest was covered by incandescent sand. The National Geographic Society's 1916 expedition to the valley discovered countless steam jets, so they named it the Valley of Ten Thousand Smokes.

Katunga (Uganda: 0.47S, 30.18E).
Katunga (5,600 ft./1,707 m.) is a Holocene tuff cone with no record of eruptions in historic time.

Katwe-Kikorongo Field (Uganda: 0.08S, 29.92E).
Katwe-Kikorongo (3,500 ft./1,067 m.) is a Holocene volcanic field with an area of 80 square miles, consisting of nearly 80 explosion craters, or Maars.

Kavachi (Solomon Is.: 9.02S, 157.95E).
Kavachi (-66 ft./-20 m.) is a submarine volcano in the Solomon Island chain. The earliest recorded eruption was in 1939, and there have been at least 24 eruptions since. Eight of the eruptions formed short-lived islands that were eroded by the sea. The most recent eruption occurred in January of 1997.

Kawahkamojang (Java: 7.12S, 107.80E).
Kawahkamojang (5,676 ft./1,730 m.) is a fumarolic field with no recorded eruptions in historic time.

Kawahkaraha (Java: 7.17S, 108.08E).
Kawahkaraha (3,789 ft./1,155 m.) is a fumarolic field with no recorded eruptions in historic time.

Kawahmanuk (Java: 7.23S, 107.72E).
Kawahmanuk (8,556 ft./2,608 m.) is a fumarolic field with no recorded eruptions in historic time.

Kawi-Butak (Java: 7.92S, 112.45E).
Kawi-Butak (8,697 ft./2,651 m.) is a Holocene stratovolcano with no record of eruptions in historic time.

Kazbek (Georgia: 42.70N, 44.50E).
Kazbek (16,568 ft./5,050 m.) is a stratovolcano that is thought to have erupted in the past 2,000-3,000 years.

Kebeney (Kamchatka, Russia: 57.10N, 159.93E).
Kebeney (5,010 ft./1,527 m.) is a Holocene shield volcano with no record of eruptions in historic time.

Kekurny (Kamchatka, Russia: 56.40N, 158.85E).
Kekurny (4,518 ft./1,377 m.) is a Holocene shield volcano with no record of eruptions in historic time.

Kelimutu (Flores I., Indonesia: 8.76S, 121.83E).
Kelimutu (5,380 ft./1,640 m.) is a complex volcano whose earliest recorded eruption occurred in approximately 1865. The most recent eruption occurred in 1968.

Kell (Kamchatka, Russia: 51.65N, 157.35E).
Kell (2,952 ft./900 m.) is an extinct stratovolcano within the large Prizrak caldera. There is no evidence of an eruption in historic time.

Keluo Group (China: 49.37N, 125.92E).
The Keluo Group (2,198 ft./670 m.) is composed of Holocene pyroclastic cones with no record of eruptions in historic time.

Kelut (Java: 7.93S, 112.31E).
Kelut (5,679 ft./1,731 m.) is an active stratovolcano on the island of Java's eastern side. The earliest recorded eruption occurred in A.D. 1000. An eruption in 1586 reportedly killed 10,000 people. The exact cause of the deaths is unknown, although accounts tell of an eruption of "flaming sulfur," ejection of large stones into a city, and ash that blotted out the sun for three days. There have been at least 15 eruptions in the past 200 years. An eruption in 1919 cost the lives of 5,110 people, mostly in mud flows. An eruption in 1966 killed 215 similarly. Roof collapses under the weight of ash in the most recent eruption in 1990 caused the deaths of 32.

Kenya, Mt. (Kenya: 0.15S, 37.15E).
Mount Kenya is a dome-shaped central volcano and the largest mountain in Kenya. Most of the volcano's activity occurred during Pleistocene times. There have been no eruptions in historic time.

Kerguelen Is. (Indian Ocean: 49.58S, 69.50E).
Kerguelen Island (1,840 m.) is a Holocene stratovolcano with no record of eruptions in historic time.

Kerinci (Sumatra: 1.69S, 101.27E).
Kerinci (12,480 ft./3,805 m.) is a stratovolcano on the western portion of the Indonesian island of Sumatra. Also known as Gadang, Berapi Kurinci, and Peak of Indrapura, it is Indonesia's highest volcano. There have been at least 20 eruptions since the earliest recorded in 1838. The most recent occurred in 1960–70. There was some volcanic activity reported in August of 1996.

Kerlingarfjöll (Iceland: 64.63N, 19.32W).
Kerlingarfjöll (4,881 ft./1,488 m.) is a Holocene stratovolcano with no record of eruptions in historic time.

Ketoi (Kuril Is.: 47.35N, 152.47E).
Ketoi (3,845 ft./1,172 m.) is a stratovolcano in the central Kuril Islands.

There were three explosive eruptions from the Pallas Peak vent in 1843, 1924 and 1960.

Khangar (Kamchatka, Russia: 54.75N, 157.38E).
Khangar (6,562 ft./2,000 m.) is a Holocene stratovolcano with no record of eruptions in historic time.

Khanuy Gol (Mongolia: 48.67N, 102.75E).
Khanuy Gol (6,188 ft./1,886 m.) is a Holocene volcanic field with no record of eruptions in historic time.

Khaybar, Harrat (Saudi Arabia: 25.00N, 39.92E).
Harrat Khaybar (6,867 ft./2,093 m.) is a volcanic field whose sole recorded eruption to date occurred in approximately A.D. 650.

Khodutka (Kamchatka, Russia: 52.06N, 157.70E).
Khodutka (6,855 ft./2,090 m.) is a conical stratovolcano within a caldera. There is no evidence of an eruption in historical time.

Kialagvik (Alaska, USA: 57.38N, 156.75W).
Kialagvik (5,166 ft./1,575 m.) is a small central Holocene stratovolcano consisting of andesite and dacite. It is mostly covered with ice and snow. There is no record of historic eruptions.

Kiaraberes-Gagak (Java: 6.73S, 106.65E).
Kiaraberes-Gagak (4,957 ft./1,511 m.) is a stratovolcano whose earliest recorded eruption occurred in 1923. The most recent eruption took place in 1939.

Kibo *see* **Kilimanjaro.**

Kick-'em-Jenny (north of Grenada, West Indies: 12.30N, 61.63W).
Kick-'em-Jenny (-525 ft./-160 m.) is a submarine volcano located six miles north of the island of Granada. It is the most active volcano in the Lesser Antilles volcanic arc. Kick-'em-Jenny is known to have erupted ten times between 1939 and, most recently, 1990.

Kieyo (Tanzania: 9.23S, 33.78E).
Kieyo (7,136 ft./2,175 m.) is a stratovolcano whose sole recorded eruption to date occurred in 1800. Local accounts say many perished when lava engulfed villages while the inhabitants were asleep.

Kikai (Ryukyu Is., Japan: 30.78N, 130.28E).
Kikai (2,352 ft./717 m.) is a submarine caldera with three small islands. An eruption 6,300 years ago was the largest in the Holocene period. The earliest

recorded historic eruption was in 1934 and volcanic activity was detected most recently in 1988.

Kikhpinych (Kamchatka, Russia: 54.49N, 160.25E).

Kikhpinych (5,091 ft./1,552 m.) is a stratovolcano with three summits. Most of Kikhpinych's volcanic activity has occurred at Savich, the northern cone. Radiocarbon dating indicates the earliest eruption approximately 2850 B.C. There is evidence of at least eight subsequent eruptions, most recently, by dating of ash layers, in A.D. 1550.

Kilauea (Hawaiian, "much spreading") (Hawaii, USA: 19.42N, 155.29W).

Kilauea (4,009 ft./1,222 m.) is a subaerial shield volcano on the Island of Hawaii. The earliest recorded eruption was in 1750, although radiocarbon dating indicates eruptions as far back as approximately 4650 B.C. An eruption in 1790 which formed the present caldera, caused around 100 deaths, mainly in lava and pumice flows. The volcano is the most continuously active in the world, with lava streaming into the ocean at a steady rate of nearly five meters every three seconds for years on end, since 1983 from vent Puu Oo. (*Puu* is Hawaiian for "peak." *Oo* said to have been named by a helicopter pilot because the vent broke out near the letter "O" in the word "south" printed on his map.) Most eruptions in the first half of the twentieth century were from the pit crater Halemaumau. See also **Loihi Seamount.**

Kilimanjaro (Tanzania: 3.07S, 37.35E).

Kilimanjaro (19,335.6 ft./5,895 m.) is a huge stratovolcano that includes three cones (Kibo, Mawensi, and Shira) that have not erupted in historic times. Kilimanjaro is also known as Kilima Dschara, Oldoinyo Oibor ("white mountain" in Masai) and Kiliman Njaro ("shining mountain" in Swahili). The youngest cone, Kibo, still emits steam and sulfur.

Kinrara (Queensland, Australia: 18.4S, 144.9E).

Kinrara is the youngest volcano in the McBride Volcanic Province, having erupted in the last 20,000 years.

Kirishima (Kyushu, Japan: 31.93N, 130.87E).

Kirishima (5,576 ft./1,700 m.) is a shield volcano with over 20 eruptive centers. The earliest recorded eruption occurred in A.D. 742 with ash layer datings showing previous eruptions going back to approximately 7050 B.C. There have been over 70 eruptions since then, chiefly from crater Ohachi. The most recent eruption, at Shinmoe-dake, occurred in 1992.

Kishb, Harrat (Saudi Arabia: 22.80N, 41.38E).

Harrat Kishb (4,839 ft./1,475 m.) is a Holocene volcanic field with no record of eruptions in historic time.

Kiska (Aleutian Is., Alaska, USA: 52.10N, 177.60E).
Kiska (4,003 ft./1,220 m.) is a stratovolcano whose earliest recorded eruption occurred in 1962. The most recent eruption took place in 1990.

Kita-dake *see* **Sakura-jima.**

Kita-Iwo-jima (Volcano Is., Japan: 25.43N, 141.23E).
Kita-Iwo-jima (2,598 ft./792 m.) is a stratovolcano whose earliest recorded eruption took place in 1780. The most recent eruption occurred in 1945.

Kizimen (Kamchatka, Russia: 55.13N, 160.32E).
Kizimen (8,153 ft./2,485 m.) is a stratovolcano whose sole recorded eruption to date occurred in 1927, although radiocarbon datings indicate four earlier eruptions, the first in approximately 7800 B.C.

Klabat (Sulawesi, Indonesia: 1.47N, 125.03E).
Klabat (6,545 ft./1,995 m.) is a stratovolcano with fumarolic activity. There have been no recorded eruptions in historic time.

Klyuchevskaya Sopka (for nearby village of Klyuchi, "spring") (Kamchatka, Russia: 56.06N, 160.64E).
Klyuchevskaya (or Kliuchevskoi) Sopka (15,584 ft./4,835 m.) is an active stratovolcano on the Kamchatka Peninsula. The first recorded eruption was in 1697, although ash layer datings indicate the earliest to be in approximately 5050 B.C. There have been over 80 eruptions since then, most recently in 1995. Smoke continuously billows above the summit. The volcano is one of most vigorous in the Pacific's "Ring of Fire" and is the highest of active volcanoes on Kamchatka Peninsula. An unspecified number of casualties occurred in the 1762 eruption, and one death each in 1978 and 1983. There has been fumarolic and seismic activity recorded in 1998.

Kohala (Hawaii: 20.12N, 155.7W).
Kohala (5,577 ft./1,700 m.) is the oldest subaerial volcano composing the Island of Hawaii. It is considered extinct, as there is no evidence of an eruption in the past 60,000 years.

Kolbeinsey Ridge (north of Iceland: 66.67N, 18.50W).
Kolbeinsey Ridge is a submarine volcano whose earliest recorded submarine eruption occurred in 1372. The only eruption certainly recorded since then took place in 1755.

Kolkhozny (Kamchatka, Russia: 55.07N, 160.77E).
Kolkhozny (7,090 ft./2,161 m.) is a Holocene stratovolcano with no record of eruptions in historic time.

Kolob (for Kolob, star in Mormon cosmography) (Utah, USA: 37.33N, 113.12W).
Kolob (8,947 ft./2,727 m.) is a volcanic field with no record of eruptions in historic time.

Kolokol Group (Russian, "bell") (Kuril Is.: 46.04N, 150.05E).
The Kolokol Group (4,356 ft./1,328 m.) is a somma volcano located on Urup Island in the southern Kuril Islands. The Berg and Trezubetz vents have been responsible for nine recorded eruptions between 1780 and 1973. An eruption in 1940 produced a dome of Berg.

Komaga-Take (Hokkaido, Japan: 42.07N, 140.68E).
Komaga-Take (3,740 ft./1,140 m.) is an andesitic stratovolcano near the city of Hakodate. The earliest recorded eruption occurred in 1640, when an avalanche caused a giant wave that killed 700 people. Many ships were also destroyed. There were major eruptions recorded in 1856 and 1929, the latter being one of the largest eruptions in Japan during the twentieth century. The most recent eruption occurred in 1942.

Komarov (Kamchatka, Russia: 55.03N, 160.72E).
Komarov (6,791 ft./2,070 m.) is a Holocene stratovolcano with no record of eruptions in historic time.

Kone (Ethiopia: 8.80N, 39.69E).
Kone (5,312 ft./1,619 m.), also known as Gariboldi (after the Italian engineer who built a road near the mountain during the occupation of Ethiopia in the 1930s), is a caldera. The sole recorded eruption to date occurred in 1820 according to local legend.

Koniuji (Aleutian Is., Alaska, USA: 52.22N, 175.13W).
Koniuji (892 ft./272 m.) is a stratovolcano with no known volcanic eruptions.

Kookooligit Mountains (Alaska, USA: 63.60N, 170.43W).
Kookooligit Mountains are composed of a Holocene shield volcano with no record of eruptions in historic time.

Koolau (Oahu, Hawaii, USA: 21.37N, 157.80W).
Koolau (3,087 ft./941 m.) is a Holocene shield volcano with no record of eruptions in historic time.

Koranga (New Guinea: 7.33S, 146.71E).
Koranga is a Holocene explosion crater with no recorded information on volcanic activity.

Korath Range (Ethiopia: 5.10N, 35.88E).
The Korath Range (2,992 ft./912 m.) is composed of tuff cones. There is likely volcanic activity in the past 10,000 years.

Koro (Fiji Is.: 17.32S, 179.40W).
Koro (1,713 ft./522 m.) is composed of Holocene cinder cones with no record of eruptions in historic time.

Korosi (Kenya: 0.77N, 36.12E).
Korosi (4,744 ft./1,446 m.) is a Holocene shield volcano with no record of eruptions in historic time.

Korovin *see* **Atka.**

Koryakskaya Sopka (Kamchatka, Russia: 53.32N, 158.69E).
Koryakskaya Sopka (11,335 ft./3,456 m.) is a stratovolcano on the Kamchatka peninsula. The earliest recorded eruption occurred in 1895. There were subsequent eruptions in 1926 and, most recently, an explosive eruption in 1956 that produced pyroclastic flows.

Kos (Greece: 36.83N, 27.26E).
Kos (1,410 ft./430 m.) consists of solfatara fields and hot springs. There have been no eruptions in the past 10,000 years.

Koshelev (Kamchatka, Russia: 51.36N, 156.75E).
Koshelev (5,943 ft./1,812 m.) is a compound stratovolcano with a large caldera. Also known as Chaokhch, the sole recorded eruption to date occurred in approximately 1690.

Koussi, Emi (Chad: 19.80N, 18.53E).
Emi Koussi (11,204 ft./3,415 m.) is a high Holocene stratovolcano located between Lake Chad and the Gulf of Syrte. There have been no reported eruptions in historic time.

Kozu-shima (Izu Is., Japan: 34.22N, 139.15E).
Kozu-shima (1,883 ft./574 m.) is composed of lava domes with only two early recorded eruptions, in A.D. 832 and A.D. 838.

Kozyrevsky (Kamchatka, Russia: 55.58N, 158.38E).
Kozyrevsky (6,614 ft./2,016 m.) is a Holocene shield volcano with no record of eruptions in historic time.

Krafla (Iceland: 65.73N, 16.78W).
Krafla (2,133 ft./650 m.) is a caldera with a high temperature geothermal field. The earliest recorded eruption was in 1724, but ash layer counts indicate

over 15 previous eruptions dating from approximately 8050 B.C. The 1724 eruption lasted five years and was known as "The Myvatn Fires" (named for the nearby farming district of Myvatn). The most recent eruption ended in 1984.

Krainy (Russian, "farthest") (Kamchatka, Russia: 56.37N, 159.03E).
Krainy (5,098 ft./1,554 m.) is a Holocene shield volcano with no record of eruptions in historic time.

Krakatau (Javanese *rekatak*, "to split") (Sunda Strait, Indonesia: 6.10S, 105.42E).
Krakatau (2,667 ft./813 m.) is a caldera that lies between the islands of Java and Sumatra in the Sunda strait. The earliest recorded eruption occurred in approximately A.D. 250. There have been over 40 eruptions since then, most recently in 1995. A major eruption in 1883 was the greatest in historic times and destroyed much of Krakatau island. The top of the volcano blew off, causing a giant wave 20 meters high that destroyed 165 villages, killing a total of 36,380. The explosion was heard four hours later on Rodrigues Island, 4,776 kilometers away, as distinctly as "the roar of heavy guns." There have been frequent small explosions since 1927, and a new island, Anak Krakatau (Child of Krakatau) has been formed. Steaming and fumarolic activity was reported in 1996 and 1997.

Krasheninnikov (for S.P. Krasheninnikov [1711–1755], Russian explorer of Kamchatka) (Kamchatka, Russia: 54.59N, 160.27E).
Krasheninnikov (6,091 ft./1,857 m.) is two connected cones located in a caldera of an older volcano. Radiocarbon datings indicate over 30 eruptions from approximately 8050 B.C., with the most recent occurring in A.D. 1550.

Krísuvík (Iceland: 63.93N, 22.20W).
Krísuvík (1,243 ft./379 m.) is composed of crater rows. The earliest recorded eruption took place in 1151. The most recent eruption occurred in 1340.

Kronotskaya Sopka (Kamchatka, Russia: 54.75N, 160.53E).
Kronotskaya Sopka (11,572 ft./3,528 m.) is a stratovolcano located to the east of Kronotskoe Lake. It is cone-shaped with a summit crater filled with lava and capped with ice. Though the volcano was long considered extinct, there were local reports of an eruption in November of 1922.

Ksudach (Kamchatka, Russia: 51.80N, 157.53E).
Ksudach (3,539 ft./1,079 m.) is a shield caldera which stands above the lakes Bolshoe ("big" in Russian) and Kraternoe ("cratered" in Russian). The sole recorded eruption to date occurred in 1907, although radiocarbon and ash layer datings indicate at least a dozen earlier eruptions from approximately 6850 B.C. The 1907 eruption was a major one venting from the Stubel stratocone.

Kuchinoerabu-jima (Ryukyu Is., Japan: 30.43N, 130.22E).
Kuchinoerabu-jima (2,129 ft./649 m.) is a stratovolcano forming an island. There have been over 13 eruptions recorded since the earliest known in 1840. The most recent eruption was explosive and short-lived in September of 1980.

Kuchino-shima (Ryukyu Is., Japan: 29.97N, 129.93E).
Kuchino-shima (2,057 ft./627 m.) is a Holocene stratovolcano with no record of eruptions in historic time.

Kudryavy *see* **Medvezhya.**

Kuei-Shan-Tao (Taiwan: 24.85N, 121.92E).
Kuei-Shan-Tao (1,316 ft./401 m.) is a Pleistocene stratovolcano with fumarolic activity. There are no recorded volcanic eruptions.

Kuju Group (Kyushu, Japan: 33.08N, 131.25E).
The Kuju Group (5,866 ft./1,788 m.) consists of 10 stratovolcanoes and lava domes near the Aso caldera. The earliest recorded eruption occurred in 1662. Subsequent eruptions occurred in 1675 and 1738. Volcanic activity was also reported in 1996.

Kukak (Alaska, USA: 58.47N, 154.35W).
Kukak (6,693 ft./2,040 m.) is a stratovolcano on the Alaskan Peninsula. There are no known eruptions in the past 10,000 years, though it often steams from fumaroles at the summit.

Kula (Turkey: 36.58N, 28.52E).
Kula (2,460 ft./750 m.) is composed of cinder cones formed in the Holocene Era. There is no record of volcanic activity in historic time.

Kul'kev (Kamchatka, Russia: 56.37N, 158.37E).
Kul'kev (3,002 ft./915 m.) is a Holocene shield volcano with no record of volcanic activity in historic time.

Kunlun Volcanic Group (China: 35.52N, 80.20E).
The Kunlun Volcanic Group (19,055 ft./5,808 m.) is composed of pyroclastic cones. The sole recorded eruption to date occurred in 1951.

Kuntomintar (Kuril Is.: 48.77N, 154.02E).
Kuntomintar (2,716 ft./828 m.) is a Pleistocene hydrothermal field near Sinarka on Shiashkotan in the northern Kuril Islands. There have been no recorded eruptions of Kuntomintar.

Kunyit (Sumatra: 2.59S, 101.63E).
Kunyit (7,057 ft./2,151 m.) is a stratovolcano with fumarolic activity. There have been no recorded eruptions in historic time.

Kupreanof (for I.A. Kupreyanov, governor of Russian America, 1836–40) (Alaska, USA: 56.02N, 159.80W).
Kupreanof (6,217 ft./1,895 m.) is a stratovolcano whose sole recorded eruption to date occurred in 1987.

Kurikoma (Honshu, Japan: 38.95N, 140.78E).
Kurikoma (5,341 ft./1,628 m.) is a stratovolcano whose earliest recorded eruption occurred in approximately 1726. The most recent eruption took place in 1950.

Kurohime (Honshu, Japan: 36.80N, 138.13E).
Kurohime (6,736 ft./2,053 m.) is a Holocene stratovolcano with no record of eruptions in historic time.

Kurose Hole (Izu Is., Japan: 33.40N, 139.68E).
The Kurose Hole (-351 ft./-107 m.) is a Holocene submarine volcano with no known eruptions in historic time.

Kurub (Ethiopia: 11.88N, 41.21E).
Kurub (2,050 ft./625 m.) is a Holocene stratovolcano with no record of eruptions in historic time.

Kusatsu-Shirane (Honshu, Japan: 36.62N, 138.55E).
Kusatsu-Shirane (7,139 ft./2,176 m.) is a stratovolcano consisting of overlapping cones and three crater lakes. The earliest recorded eruption occurred in 1805, but radiocarbon datings indicate five before that, from approximately 6270 B.C. The most recent eruption occurred from the Yu-gama vent in 1983.

Kutali, Tavani (Vanuatu: 16.73S, 168.28E).
Tavani Kutali (2,733 ft./833 m.) is a likely Holocene stratovolcano with no record of eruptions in historic time.

Kutcharo (Hokkaido, Japan: 43.55N, 144.43E).
Kutcharo (or Kuttyaro) (3,280 ft./1,000 m.) is a caldera formed approximately 30,000 years ago. It is now largely filled by Kutcharo Lake with Nakajima, a post-caldera stratovolcano, forming an island in the lake. The eastern half of the caldera is filled with Atosanupuri, a younger volcanic complex. The most recent eruption there was dated at A.D. 1000. Another stratovolcano, Mashu, grew on the caldera's eastern rim.

Kuttara (Hokkaido, Japan: 42.50N, 141.18E).
Kuttara (1,906 ft./581 m.) is a stratovolcano that had only one known historic eruption. There was small phreatic eruption from a flank vent in 1820.

Kuttyaro *see* **Kutcharo.**

Kutum Volcanic Field (Sudan: 14.50N, 25.80E).
The Kutum Volcanic Field is composed of Holocene scoria cones with no record of eruptions in historic time.

Kuwae (Vanuatu: 16.83S, 168.54E).
Kuwae (or Karua) (-6 ft./-2 m.) is a submarine stratovolcano with a summit caldera. There have been over a dozen reported eruptions since 1452. The most recent eruption occurred in 1974. There were unconfirmed eruptions in 1977, 1979 and 1980.

Kverkfjöll (Iceland: 64.65N, 16.72W).
Kverkfjöll (6,299 ft./1,920 m.) is a stratovolcano whose earliest recorded eruption took place in 1655. The most recent eruption occurred in 1968.

Kyatwa Volcanic Field (Uganda: 0.45N, 30.25E).
The Kyatwa Volcanic Field (4,691 ft./1,430 m.) consists of Holocene tuff cones with no record of eruptions in historic time.

L

La Palma (Canary Is.: 28.58N, 17.83W).
La Palma (7,957 ft./2,426 m.) is stratovolcano with two large volcanic centers in the western Canary Islands. There have been seven known historic eruptions since 1435, including major eruptions in 1585, 1646, and the most recent in 1971, from the Teneguia vent.

Labo (Luzon, Philippines: 14.02N, 122.79E).
Labo (5,066 ft./1,544 m.) is a Holocene compound volcano with no record of eruptions in historic time.

Laguna Volcanic Field (Luzon, Philippines: 14.12N, 121.30E).
The Laguna Volcanic Field (2,146 ft./654 m.) is composed of scoria cones with likely volcanic activity in the past 2,000 years.

Laki *see* **Grímsvötn.**

Lamington, Mt. (for Baron Lamington [1860–1940], governor of Queensland, Australia) (New Guinea: 8.95S, 148.15E).
Mount Lamington (5,510 ft./1,680 m.) is a stratovolcano. The sole recorded eruption to date was in 1951, but radiocarbon datings indicate two earlier eruptions, in approximately 5980 and 4850 B.C. About 3,000 died in the 1951 eruption, caught in lava and pumice flows through villages on the volcano's northern flank. (Local authorities did not realize Lamington actually was a volcano.)

Lamongan (Java: 8.00S, 113.34E).

Lamongan (5.417 ft./1,651 m.) is a stratovolcano whose earliest recorded eruption occurred in 1799. Over 40 eruptions have followed, the most recent in 1898.

Langila (New Britain, Papua New Guinea: 5.25S, 148.42E).

Langila (4,364 ft./1,330 m.), consisting of four small overlapping composite cones, is one of the most active stratovolcanoes in New Britain. The earliest recorded eruption was in 1878. The most recent eruption occurred in 1993. Volcanic activity has been recorded from 1996–98.

Langjökull (Icelandic, "long glacier") (Iceland: 64.75N, 19.98W).

Langjökull (4.462 ft./1,360 m.) is a stratovolcano with evidence of volcanic activity in the past 2,000 years.

Lanin (Chile/Argentina: 39.63S, 71.50W).

Lanin (12,293 ft./3,747 m.) is a Holocene stratovolcano with no record of eruptions in historic time.

Lanzarote (Canary Is.: 29.03N, 13.63W).

Lanzarote (2,060 ft./670 m.) is a shield volcano with four main calderas and numerous cones. There were eruptions in 1730 and 1824, which covered much of the island in basalt.

Larderello (Italy: 43.25N, 10.87E).

Larderello (1,640 ft./500 m.) is composed of explosion craters. The sole recorded eruption to date occurred in 1282.

Lascar (Chile: 23.37S, 67.73W).

Lascar (18,346 ft./5,592 m.) is a stratovolcano with six overlapping summit craters in the northern Chilean Andes. It is one of the most active volcanoes in the region. The earliest recorded eruption occurred in 1848. The most recent eruption took place in 1993.

Lassen Volcanic Center (for Peter Lassen, Danish immigrant pioneer) (California, USA: 40.49N, 121.51W).

The Lassen Volcanic Center (10,456 ft./3,187 m.) is a stratovolcano whose sole recorded eruption to date occurred in 1917, from Lassen Peak itself, but radiocarbon datings show at least four earlier eruptions from Chaos Crags, the earliest in approximately A.D. 800.

Lastarria (Chile/Argentina: 25.17S, 68.50W).

Lastarria (18,691 ft./5,697 m.) is a Holocene stratovolcano that is noted for sulfur deposits remaining from its lava flows.

Late (Tonga Is.: 18.81S, 174.65W).
Late (1,699 ft./518 m.) is a stratovolcano whose earliest recorded eruption occurred in 1790. There was only one later eruption recorded in 1854.

Latukan (Mindanao, Philippines: 7.65N, 124.47E).
Latukan (7,080 ft./2,158 m.) is a Holocene stratovolcano with no record of eruptions in historic time.

Lautaro (Chile: 49.02S, 73.55W).
Lautaro (11,089 ft./3,380 m.) is a stratovolcano whose earliest recorded eruption, between Lakes San Martin and Viedma, was in 1879. The most recent, observed from the air, occurred in 1961.

Lavic Lake (adjectivel form of *lava*) (California, USA: 34.75N, 116.62W).
Lavic Lake (4,905 ft./1,495 m.) is a Holocene volcanic field with no record of eruptions in historic time.

Lawu (Java: 7.62S, 111.92E).
Lawu (10,712 ft./3,265 m.) is a Holocene stratovolcano with no record of eruptions in historic time.

Leizhou Bandao (China: 20.83N, 109.78E).
Leizhou Bandao (850 ft./259 m.) is a Holocene volcanic field with no recorded eruptions in historic time.

Lengai, Ol Doinyo (Tanzania: 2.75S, 35.90E).
Ol Doinyo Lengai (9,479 ft./2,890 m.) is a stratovolcano whose earliest recorded eruption occurred in 1880. The most recent eruption occurred in 1993. It is the world's only active carbonatite volcano, *i.e.* with rocks composed of carbonates rather than silicates. Its lavas consist largely of sodium carbonate (washing soda), and it supplies nearby caustic Lake Natron with alkali.

Leonard Range (Mindanao, Philippines: 7.39N, 126.40E).
The Leonard Range (2,625 ft./800 m.) is a Holocene stratovolcano with no recorded eruptions in historic time.

Lereboleng (Flores I., Indonesia: 8.36S, 122.84E).
Lereboleng (3,663 ft./1,117 m.) is a complex volcano on Flores Island in Indonesia. There were eruptions from the Burak vent in 1873, 1876 and 1881.

Leskov I. (South Sandwich Is.: 56.67S, 28.13W).
Leskov Island (623 ft./190 m.) is a stratovolcano with fumarolic activity. There is no record of eruptions in historic time.

Leutongey (Kamchatka, Russia: 57.30N, 159.83E).
Leutongey (4,373 ft./1,333 m.) is a Holocene shield volcano with no recorded eruptions in historic time.

Level Mountain (British Columbia, Canada: 58.42N, 131.35W).
Level Mountain (7,185 ft./2,190 m.) is a Holocene shield volcano with no record of eruptions in historic time.

Lewotobi (Flores I., Indonesia: 8.53S, 122.77E).
Lewotobi (5,587 ft./1,703 m.) is a stratovolcano on Flores Islands in Indonesia. There have been at least 19 eruptions since the earliest recorded in 1675. Most have occurred at the Lewotobi Lakilaki vent. Major eruptions in 1869 and 1907 were responsible for several deaths. The most recent eruption occurred in 1991.

Lewotolo (Lomblen I., Indonesia: 8.27S, 123.50E).
Lewotolo (4,669 ft./1,423 m.) is a stratovolcano whose earliest recorded eruption occurred in 1660. The most recent eruption took place in 1951.

Lexone (Chile: 17.87S, 69.48W).
Lexone (17,520 ft./5,340 m.) is composed of Holocene lava domes. There is no record of eruptions in historic time.

Liado Hayk Field (Ethiopia: 9.57N, 40.28E).
The Liado Hayk Field (2,880 ft./878 m.) is a Maars volcanic field likely formed in the Holocene Era. There is no historic record of volcanic eruptions.

Liamuiga (St. Kitts, West Indies: 17.37N, 62.80W).
Liamuiga (3,793 ft./1,156 m.), formerly known as Mount Misery, is an andesitic stratovolcano with an open summit crater. There are unconfirmed reports of historical eruptions in 1692 and 1843.

Licancábur (Chile/Bolivia: 22.83S, 67.88W).
Licancábur (19,409 ft./5,916 m.) is a Holocene stratovolcano. A small lake in the volcano's summit crater may be the world's highest, at a height of almost 6,000 meters.

Lihir (New Ireland: 3.12S, 152.64E).
Lihir (2,297 ft./700 m.) is a Holocene volcanic complex with no evidence of eruptions in historic time.

Lipari (Lipari Is., Italy: 38.48N, 14.95E).
Lipari (2,000 ft./600 m.) is a stratovolcano in the Aeolian archipelago in the Tyrrhenian Sea. The sole recorded eruption to date was in A.D. 729, but tracks left by uranium fission particles indicate early eruption in approximately 7900 B.C.

Little Sitkin (Aleutian Is., Alaska, USA: 51.95N, 178.53E).
Little Sitkin (3,942 ft./1,202 m.) is a stratovolcano on Little Sitkin Island in the Aleutians. The first recorded historical eruption was explosive and occurred in 1776. A second, and most recent, eruption occurred in 1828.

Ljósufjöll (Icelandic, "bald mountain") (Iceland: 64.87N, 22.23W).
Ljósufjöll (3,241 ft./988 m.) is a fissure vent with no record of eruptions in historic time.

Llaima (Chile: 38.69S, 71.73W).
Llaima (10,253 ft./3,125 m.) is one of the largest and most active volcanoes in central Chile. The earliest recorded eruption occurred in 1640, with radiocarbon datings showing three earlier eruptions from approximately 7410 B.C. There have been over 40 eruptions since then, most recently in 1992. Volcanic activity, including fumarolic activity at the summit vent and small explosions and ash output continued in 1997 and 1998.

Llullaillaco (Chile/Argentina: 24.72S, 68.53W).
Llullaillaco (22,109 ft./6,739 m.) is a stratovolcano, reportedly the second highest in the world. There have been recorded eruptions in 1854, 1868 and 1877.

Loihi Seamount (Hawaii, USA: 18.92N, 155.27W).
Loihi Seamount (-3,178 ft./-969 m.) is a submarine volcano, and the youngest in the Hawaiian chain, being discovered in 1954. The latest eruption occurred in 1996, when cone Pele's Vents converted into a crater, now called Pele's Pit. (The name, not to be confused with Mt. **Pelée**, is that of Hawaiian volcano goddess.) The growing volcano is expected to merge with the island of Hawaii to become a successor to **Mauna Loa** and **Kilauea**, which would become extinct. Possible earlier eruptions were reported 1971, 1975, 1984 and 1986.

Loki-Fogrufjöll (Iceland: 64.48N, 17.80W).
Loki-Fogrufjöll (5,151 ft./1,570 m.) is a subglacial volcanic system. The sole recorded eruption to date occurred in 1910. Possible eruptions in 1986 and 1991 are unverified.

Lokon-Empung (Sulawesi, Indonesia: 1.36N, 124.79E).
Lokon-Empung (5,200 ft./1,580 m.) is a stratovolcano on northern Sulawesi. The earliest recorded eruption occurred in approximately 1375. There have been at least 21 further eruptions in historic times. The most recent eruption occurred in 1992, which forced the evacuation of over 10,000 people.

Lolo (New Britain, Papua New Guinea: 5.47S, 150.50E).
Lolo (2,641 ft./805 m.) is a stratovolcano on New Britain Island in the south Bismarck Sea. There is likelihood of an eruption in the past 10,000, years but no evidence to prove it.

Lolobau (New Britain, Papua New Guinea: 4.92S, 151.16E).
Lolobau (2,815 ft./858 m.) is a caldera capping a stratovolcano located on New Britain Island in the South Bismarck Sea. The earliest recorded eruption occurred in 1100. A subsequent eruption in 1904-05 produced a Plinian eruption column. Another eruption occurred in 1908 and a large eruption happened in 1911-12. There was major solfatara activity in Lolobau Crater from 1937 until 1950, and the activity stopped completely in 1969.

Loloru (Bougainville: 6.52S, 155.62E).
Loloru (6,191 ft./1,887 m.) is a pyroclastic shield on Bougainville Island in the Solomon Islands chain. There have been six explosive Holocene eruptions, with the most recent occurring approximately 1,050 years ago.

Lomonosov Group (Kuril Is.: 50.25N, 155.43E).
Lomonosov Group (5,513 ft./1,681 m.), on Paramushir in the Northern Kuril Islands, is composed of Holocene cinder cones. There have been no historic eruptions.

Longavi, Nevado de (Chile: 36.19S, 71.16W).
Nevado de Longavi (10,636 ft./3,242 m.) is a Holocene stratovolcano with no record of eruptions in historic time.

Longgang Group (China: 42.33N, 126.50E).
The Longgang Group (3,280 ft./1,000 m.) is composed of Holocene cinder cones with no record of eruptions in historic time.

Long I. (Papua New Guinea: 5.36S, 147.12E).
Long Island (4,189 ft./1,280 m.) is a complex volcano located along the Bismarck Volcanic Arc, northeast of New Guinea. The earliest recorded eruption was in 1933, with radiocarbon dating indicating two before this, in approximately 2040 B.C. and 1660. Legends tell of hundreds of deaths in the latter through flows of lava and pumice and giant waves. The most recent eruption occurred in 1993.

Long Valley (California, USA: 37.70N, 118.87W).
The Long Valley caldera (11,122 ft./3,390 m.) is located between the Sierra Nevada mountains and the Basin and Range Province. It is one of North America's largest Quaternary rhyolitic volcanic centers. The caldera was produced by a catastrophic eruption approximately 730,000 years ago.

Longonot (Kenya: 0.92S, 36.45E).
Longonot (9,108 ft./2,776 m.) is a young shield volcano in Kenya's rift valley. There is no record of an historical eruption, though local legend tells of one in the 1860s.

Lonquimay (Chile: 38.38S, 71.58W).
Lonquimay (9,400 ft./2,865 m.) is a small symmetrical stratovolcano in central Chile. The earliest recorded eruption occurred in 1853. The most recent eruption occurred from 1988–90, producing lava flows.

Lopevi (Vanuatu: 16.51S, 168.35E).
Lopevi (4,747 ft./1,447 m.) is a stratovolcano which forms a small island in Vanuatu. The earliest recorded eruption occurred in 1863. There has been almost continuous volcanic activity since then. A Plinian explosion in July of 1960 forced the evacuation of the island. There was another major eruption from the summit crater lasting from July of 1963 until 1965, producing lava flows that reached the sea. The most recent eruption occurred in October of 1982.

Lower Chindwin (Myanmar: 22.28N, 95.10E).
Lower Chindwin (1,263 ft./385 m.) is a Holocene volcanic field with no record of eruptions in historic time.

Lumut Balai, Bukit (Sumatra: 4.22S, 103.62E).
Bukit Lumut Balai (6,742 ft./2,055 m.) is a stratovolcano with fumarolic activity. There is no record of eruptions in historic time.

Lumutdun, Bukit (Sumatra: 3.38S, 102.37E).
Bukit Lumutdun (8,094 ft/2,467 m.) is a stratovolcano with fumarolic activity. There is no record of eruptions in historic time.

Lunar Crater Field (Nevada, USA: 38.48N, 115.97W).
The Lunar Crater Field (7,398 ft./2,255 m.) is composed of Holocene cinder cones. There is no record of eruptions in historic time.

Lunayyir, Harrat (Saudi Arabia: 25.17N, 37.75E).
Harrat Lunayyir (4,495 ft./1,370 m.) is a volcanic field whose sole recorded eruption to date occurred in approximately 1000.

Lurus (Java: 7.70S, 113.58E).
Lurus (1,768 ft./539 m.) is a Holocene complex volcano with no record of eruptions in historic time.

L'vinaya Past' (Russian, "lion's maw") (Kuril Is.: 44.62N, 147.00E).
L'vinaya Past' (1,732 ft./528 m.) is a stratovolcano located on Iturup Island in the southern Kuril Islands. There was a major explosive eruption in approximately 7480 B.C.

Lysuholl (Iceland: 64.87N, 23.25W).
Lysuholl (1,772 ft./540 m.) is composed of Holocene pyroclastic cones. There are no recorded eruptions in historic time.

M

Ma Alalta (Ethiopia: 13.02N, 40.20E).
Ma Alalta (5,955 ft./1,815 m.) is a Holocene stratovolcano with no record of eruptions in historic time.

Maca (Chile: 45.10S, 73.20W).
Maca (10,098 ft./3,078 m.) is a Holocene stratovolcano with no record of eruptions in historic time.

Macauley I. (Kermadec Is.: 30.20S, 178.47W).
Macauley Island (781 ft./238 m.) is a Holocene caldera with no record of eruptions in historic time.

Macdonald (Australian Is., Central Pacific: 28.98S, 140.25W).
Macdonald (-164 ft./-50 m.) is a submarine volcano whose earliest recorded submarine eruption occurred in 1928. The most recent eruption took place in 1989.

Machín, Cerro (Colombia: 4.48N, 75.40W).
Cerro Machín (8,695 ft./2,650 m.) is a Holocene stratovolcano with no record of eruptions in historic time.

Macizo de Larancagua (Bolivia: 18.25S, 68.53W).
Macizo de Larancagua (18,110 ft./5,520 m.) is a Holocene stratovolcano with no recorded eruptions in historic time.

Macizo de Pacuni (Bolivia: 18.32S, 68.80W).
Macizo de Pacuni (17,716 ft./5,400 m.) is a Holocene stratovolcano with no recorded eruptions in historic time.

Madera, La (Nicaragua: 11.45N, 85.51W).
La Madera (4,572 ft./1,394 m.) is a Holocene stratovolcano that forms the southeastern portion of Isla de Ometepe in Lake Nicaragua. There have been no known eruptions in historic times.

Madilogo (New Guinea: 9.20S, 147.57E).
Madilogo (2,788 ft./850 m.) is a Holocene pyroclastic cone with no record of eruptions in historic time.

Magaso (Negros, Philippines: 9.26N, 123.17E).
Magaso (6,247 ft./1,904 m.) is a Holocene stratovolcano with no record of eruptions in historic time.

Mageik (Alaska, USA: 58.20N, 155.08W).
Mageik (7,103 ft./2,165 m.) is a stratovolcano with only two definite eruptions recorded, in 1927 and 1936.

Mahagnoa (Leyte, Philippines: 11.52N, 124.85E).
Mahagnoa (2,625 ft./800 m.) is a stratovolcano with fumarolic activity. There is no record of eruptions in historic time.

Mahawu (Sulawesi, Indonesia: 1.36N, 124.86E).
Mahawu (4,343 ft./1,324 m.) is a stratovolcano. The earliest recorded eruption was in 1788. The most recent eruption occurred in 1977.

Mahukona (Hawaii: 20.1N, 156.1W).
Mahukona (-3,600 ft./-1,110 m.) is a submarine volcano northwest of the Island of Hawaii. The volcano's summit once stood 800 feet above sea level. It subsided under the sea between 435,000 and 365,000 years ago.

Maipo (Chile/Argentina: 34.16S, 69.83W).
Maipo (17,271 ft./5,264 m.) is a caldera whose earliest recorded eruption took place in 1826. The most recent eruption occurred in 1912.

Makaturing (Mindanao, Philippines: 7.65N, 124.47E).
Makaturing (6,365 ft./1,940 m.) is a Holocene stratovolcano with no record of eruptions in historic time.

Makian (Halmahera, Indonesia: 0.32N, 127.40E).
Makian (4,452 ft./1,357 m.) is a stratovolcano forming a small volcanic island. The earliest recorded eruption occurred in 1550. Many died during the 1646 eruption, and perhaps as many as 2,000 in that of 1760. An eruption in 1861 caused 326 deaths, either in ash flows or when drowned while fleeing by boat. The most recent eruption occurred in 1988.

Makushin (perhaps Russian *makushka*, "head," "top," as island's highest peak) (Unalaska I., Aleutian Is., Alaska, USA: 53.90N, 166.93W).
Makushin (6,680 ft./2,036 m.) is a stratovolcano whose earliest recorded eruption occurred in 1768. The most recent eruption took place in 1987.

Malang Plain (Java: 8.02S, 112.68E).
The Malang Plain (2,231 ft./680 m.) is a Holocene Maars volcano with no record of eruptions in historic time.

Malinao (Luzon, Philippines: 13.42N, 123.58E).
Malinao (5,079 ft./1,548 m.) is a stratovolcano with evidence of fumarolic activity. There is no record of eruptions in historic time.

Malinche, La (Mexico: 19.23N, 98.03W).
La Malinche (14,502 ft./4,420 m.) is a Holocene stratovolcano with no record of eruptions in historic time.

Malindang (Mindanao, Philippines: 8.22N, 123.63E).
Malindang (7,989 ft./2,435 m.) is a Holocene stratovolcano with no record of eruptions in historic time.

Malindig (Marinduque I., Philippines: 13.24N, 122.02E).
Malindig (3,796 ft./1,157 m.) is a stratovolcano with hot springs.

Mallahle (Ethiopia: 13.27N, 41.65E).
Mallahle (2,871 ft./875 m.) is a Holocene stratovolcano with no record of eruptions in historic time.

Maly Payalpan (Kamchatka, Russia: 55.82N, 157.98E).
Maly Payalpan (5,912 ft./1,802 m.) is a Holocene shield volcano with no record of eruptions in historic time.

Maly Semlyachik (Kamchatka, Russia: 54.13N, 159.67E).
Maly Semlyachik (5,117 ft./1,560 m.) is a caldera in the northeast part of the Sena-Soboliny caldera. The earliest recorded eruption in 1804 was also the largest. There have been over 20 subsequent eruptions, most recently in 1952.

Managlase Plateau (New Guinea: 9.08S, 148.33E).
The Managlase Plateau (4,403 ft./1,342 m.) is a volcanic field with no record of historical eruptions.

Manam (northeast of New Guinea: 4.10S, 145.06E).
Manam (5,927 ft./1,807 m.) is a basaltic stratovolcano north of Papua New Guinea. The earliest recorded eruption occurred in 1616. There have been over 30 eruptions since then. The most recent, in 1996, caused an avalanche which destroyed the village of Budua, killing 12 people.

Manda-Inakir (Ethiopia: 12.38N, 42.20E).
Manda-Inakir (1,970 ft./600 m.) is a fissure vent whose sole recorded eruption to date occurred in 1928.

Mandalagan (Negros, Philippines: 10.61N, 123.22E).
Mandalagan (6,165 ft./1,879 m.) is a Holocene stratovolcano with no recorded eruptions in historic time.

Manengouba (Cameroon: 5.03N, 9.83E).
Manengouba (7,910 ft./2,411 m.) is a Holocene stratovolcano with no record of eruptions in historic time.

Manuk (Banda Sea, Indonesia: 5.53S, 130.29E).
Manuk (925 ft./282 m.) is a stratovolcano with fumarolic activity. There is no evidence of an eruption in historic time.

Maquiling (Luzon, Philippines: 14.13N, 121.20E).

Maquiling (3,576 ft./1,090 m.) is a Holocene stratovolcano with no recorded eruptions in historic time.

Marapi (Sumatra: 0.38S, 100.47E).

Marapi (9,485 ft./2,891 m.) is a complex volcano whose earliest recorded eruption occurred in 1770. There have been over 50 eruptions since then, most recently in 1987, which was still ongoing in 1993. During an eruption in 1979 approximately 80 people were killed when a landslide traveled down slope, hitting five villages and farmland. In 1992 one person was killed and five injured while climbing to the summit.

Marchena (Galápagos Is.: 0.33N, 90.47W).

Marchena (1,125 ft./343 m.) is a shield volcano whose sole recorded eruption to date occurred in 1991.

Marha, Jabal el-(Yemen: 15.28N, 44.22E).

Jabal el-Marha (8,695 ft./2,650 m.) is composed of Holocene tuff cones with no record of eruptions in historic time.

Marion I. (Indian Ocean: 46.90S, 37.75E).

Marion Island is composed of shield volcanoes whose sole recorded eruption to date occurred in 1980.

Mariveles (Luzon, Philippines: 14.50N, 120.50E).

Mariveles (4,659 ft./1,420 m.) is a Holocene stratovolcano with no evidence of eruptions in historic time.

Markagunt Plateau (Paiute, "highland of trees") (Utah, USA: 37.58N, 112.67W).

The Markagunt Plateau (9,318 ft./2,840 m.) is a volcanic field with no record of eruptions in historic time.

Maroa (New Zealand: 38.42S, 176.08E).

Maroa (3,793 ft./1,156 m.) is composed of calderas which have likely experienced volcanic activity in the past 2,000 years.

Marra, Jebel (Sudan: 12.95N, 24.27E).

Jebel Mara (9,980 ft./3,042 m.) is a volcanic field with likely volcanic activity in the past 5,000 years.

Marsabit (Kenya: 2.32N, 37.97E).

Marsabit (5,599 ft./1,701 m.) is a Holocene shield volcano with no record of eruptions in historic time.

Martin (Alaska, USA: 58.17N, 155.35W).
Martin (6,102 ft./1,860 m.) is a stratovolcano with two eruptions recorded in 1951 and 1953.

Más a Tierra see Robinson Crusoe I.

Masaraga (Luzon, Philippines: 13.32N, 123.60E).
Masaraga (4,357 ft./1,328 m.) is a Holocene stratovolcano with no record of eruptions in historic time.

Masaya (Nicaragua: 11.98N, 86.16W).
Masaya (2,083 ft./635 m.) is a caldera containing 13 vents. There are three major cones, Masaya, Nindiri, and Santiago, the latter of which was formed in 1853. An eruption in 4550 B.C. was one of the Earth's largest in the Holocene period. The earliest recorded historic eruption occurred in 1524. There have been nearly 20 subsequent eruptions, most recently in 1993.

Mascota Volcanic Field (Mexico: 20.62N, 104.83W).
The Mascota Volcanic Field (8,334 ft./2,540 m.) is composed of Holocene shield volcanoes. There is no record of eruptions in historic time.

Mashkovtsev (Kamchatka, Russia: 51.10N, 156.72E).
Mashkovtsev (1,650 ft./503 m.) is a small extinct Holocene stratovolcano near the Cape of Lopatka. Mashkovtsev was formed during the post-glacial era. There have been no historic eruptions.

Mashu (Hokkaido, Japan: 43.57N, 144.57E).
Mashu (2,805 ft./855 m.) is a caldera overlooking Lake Mashu. There was a major eruption from the central vent in 4875 B.C. The most recent eruption, from a flank vent, occurred in A.D. 970.

Mat Ala (Ethiopia: 13.10N, 41.15E).
Mat Ala (1,716 ft./523 m.) is a Holocene shield volcano with no record of eruptions in historic time.

Matthew I. (Southwestern Pacific: 22.33S, 171.32E).
Matthew Island (580 ft./177 m.) is a stratovolcano whose earliest recorded eruption occurred in approximately 1949. The most recent eruption took place in 1956.

Matutum (Mindanao, Philippines: 6.37N, 125.11E).
Matutum (7,523 ft./2,293 m.) is a Holocene stratovolcano with no record of eruptions in historic time.

Maui, East see Haleakala.

Maule, Laguna del (Chile: 36.02S, 70.58W).

Laguna del Maule (10,144 ft./3,092 m.) is composed of Holocene strato-volcanoes. There is no record of eruptions in historic time.

Mauna Kea (Hawaiian *mauna*, "mountain," *kea*, "white") (Hawaii, USA: 19.82N, 55.47W).

Mauna Kea (13,792 ft./4,205 m.) is considered a dormant shield volcano and is the tallest on the island of Hawaii. The last eruption occurred in approximately 1650 B.C. It is the only Hawaiian volcano known to be glaciated. Mauna Kea is the site of the world's largest cluster of astronomical observatories, including a huge 10-meter Keck I telescope.

Mauna Loa (Hawaiian *mauna*, "mountain," *loa*, "big") (Hawaii, USA: 19.47N, 155.61W).

Mauna Loa (13,681 ft./4,170 m.) is the largest, and one of the most active, volcanoes on the planet. The earliest recorded eruption occurred in 1750, but radiocarbon datings indicate many before this, going back to approximately 8050 B.C. From 1843 through 1984 Mauna Loa erupted on an average of once every 4½ years. Mauna Ulu ("growing mountain") was formed as a volcanic shield in 1969 and most volcanic activity was centered there through 1974, with lava covering almost 45 square kilometers. An earthquake produced by the 1868 eruption generated giant waves that killed 46 people, while another 31 perished in mud flows resulting from heavy rains. Mauna Loa's dome is 120 kilometers long and 50 kilometers wide. Its crater, Mokuaweoweo, covers 10.5 square kilometers and descends to a depth of 150–180 meters. The Hawaii Volcanoes National Park, embracing Mauna Loa and **Kilauea**, was established in 1916. See also **Loihi Seamount**.

Mauna Ulu *see* **Mauna Loa**.

Mawensi *see* **Kilimanjaro**.

Mawson Peak *see* **Heard I.**

Mayon (Luzon, Philippines: 13.26N, 123.68E).

Mayon (5,153 ft./1,571 m.) is a conical-shaped stratovolcano and the most active in the Philippines. The earliest recorded eruption occurred in 1616. Since then Mayon has erupted over 40 times. Mud flows from typhoon rains following the 1766 eruption caused the deaths of 49 people, while around 1,200 perished in the 1814 eruption, most of them in lava and pumice flows. Although there was no eruption in 1873, about 1,500 died in mud flows set off by rain. Rock and ash flows burned 350 to death in the 1897 eruption, and the 1981 eruption saw the deaths of around 200 in a mud flow caused by a typhoon. The flow of lava and pumice killed 75 in the most recent eruption in 1993.

Mayor I. (New Zealand: 37.28S, 176.25E).
Mayor Island (1,165 ft./355 m.) is a Holocene shield volcano with no record of eruptions in historic time.

May-Ya-Moto (Dem. Rep. of Congo [Zaire]: 0.93S, 29.33E).
May-Ya-Moto (3,117 ft./950 m.) is a fumarole field with no record of historic eruptions.

Mazama, Mt. *see* **Crater Lake.**

Meager (British Columbia, Canada: 50.63N, 123.50W).
Meager (8,793 ft./2,680 m.) is a Holocene complex volcano with no record of eruptions in historic time.

Medicine Lake (California, USA: 41.58N, 121.57W).
Medicine Lake (7,914 ft./2,412 m.) is a Holocene shield volcano with no record of eruptions in historic time.

Medvezhya (Russian, "bear") (Kuril Is.: 45.38N, 148.83E).
Medvezhya (3,687 ft./1,124 m) is a somma volcano located on Iturup Island in the southern Kuril Islands. There have been four recorded small and explosive eruptions between 1778 and 1958, all from the Kudriavy vent.

Mega Basalt Field (Ethiopia/Kenya: 4.08N, 37.42E).
The Mega Basalt Field (3,500 ft./1,067 m.) is composed of pyroclastic cones and Maars volcanoes. There is no record of historic eruptions, but there has likely been volcanic activity in the past 10,000 years.

Megata (Honshu, Japan: 39.95N, 139.73E).
Megata (955 ft./291 m.) is a Maars volcano with no recorded eruptions in historic time.

Mehetia (Society Is., Central Pacific: 17.87S, 148.07W).
Mehetia (1,425 ft./435 m.) is the youngest island of the Society Islands chain, located nearly 100 miles east of Tahiti. There is no record of a historic eruption, though earthquakes in 1981 indicate a possible submarine eruption on the southeast flank.

Meidob Volcanic Field (Sudan: 15.13N, 26.17E).
The Meidob Volcanic Field (3,281 ft./1,000 m.) is composed of Holocene scoria cones with no record of eruptions in historic time.

Melbourne (Antarctica: 74.35S, 164.70E).
Melbourne (8,964 ft./2,732 m.) is an undissected stratovolcano on the western coast of the Ross Sea. There is no record of historic eruptions, though fumarolic activity has been recorded.

Melimoyu (Chile: 44.08S, 72.88W).
Melimoyu (7,875 ft./2,400 m.) is a Holocene shield volcano with no record of eruptions in historic time.

Melos *see* **Milos.**

Mencheca (Chile: 40.53S, 72.04W).
Mencheca (6,037 ft./1,840 m.) is a Holocene stratovolcano with no record of eruptions in historic time.

Mendeleev (named 1946 for D.I. Mendeleev [1834–1907], Russian chemist) (Kuril Is.: 43.98N, 145.70E).
Mendeleev (2,910 ft./887 m.) is a stratovolcano on Kunashir Island in the southern Kuril Islands. The sole recorded eruption to date was a phreatic eruption in 1880.

Menengai (Kenya: 0.20S, 36.07E).
Menengai (7,472 ft./2,278 m.) is a Holocene shield volcano located in the Kenya Rift Valley. There is a five-mile-wide caldera. There is evidence of numerous eruptions though the only one dated occurred approximately 7,350 years ago.

Mentolat (Chile: 44.67S, 73.08W).
Mentolat (5,446 ft./1,660 m.) is a Holocene stratovolcano with no evidence of eruptions in historic time.

Merapi, Mt. (Java: 7.54S, 110.44E).
Mount Merapi (9,548 ft./2,911 m.) is a stratovolcano with an active lava dome at its summit. It is less than 50 miles north of the city of Yogyakarta. The earliest recorded eruption occurred in 1548. Since then Merapi has erupted over 60 times. Many eruptions caused fatalities; that of 1672 killed somewhere between 300 to 3,000 people. The next worst eruption occurred in 1930, in which 1,369 died, with 13 villages totally, and 29 partly, destroyed. An eruption in 1872 cost the lives of around 200. There was a major eruption in November of 1994, when the lava dome collapsed, sending pyroclastic flows as far as five miles from the summit. The eruption caused the death of 43 people and forced the evacuation of 6,000. Merapi remains active, with the most recent eruption reported in June of 1998.

Merbabu (Java: 7.45S, 110.43E).
Merbabu (10,315 ft./3,145 m.) is a stratovolcano in central Java. There have been two recorded historical eruptions. There was an explosive eruption in 1560 and a moderate-sized eruption in 1797.

Mere Lava (Vanuatu: 14.45S, 168.05E).
Mere Lava (3,372 ft./1,028 m.) is a Holocene stratovolcano. There was an unconfirmed eruption in 1606, but otherwise no record of eruptions in historic time.

Meru (Tanzania: 3.25S, 36.75E).

Meru (15,000 ft./4,565 m.) is a stratovolcano whose earliest recorded eruption occurred in 1878. The most recent eruption occurred in 1910.

Methana (Greece: 37.61N, 23.34E).

Methana (2,493 ft./760 m.) forms a peninsula composed of lava domes. The earliest recorded eruption occurred in approximately 258 B.C. There was an unconfirmed eruption reported in August of 1922.

Metis Shoal (Tonga Is.: 19.18S, 174.87W).

Metis Shoal (-13 ft./-4 m.) is a submarine volcano whose earliest recorded eruption occurred in 1851. The most recent eruption took place in 1979.

Mezhdusopochny (Russian, "between volcanoes") (Kamchatka, Russia: 57.43N, 60.20E).

Mezhdusopochny (5,384 ft./1,641 m.) is a Holocene shield volcano with no record of eruptions in historic time.

Michael, Mt. (South Sandwich Is.: 57.78S, 26.45W).

Mount Michael (3,250 ft./990 m.) is an ice-covered stratovolcano with a crater and somma ridge at its summit. The sole recorded eruption was explosive and occurred in 1819.

Michoacán-Guanajuato (Mexico: 19.48N, 102.25W).

Michoacán-Guanajuato (10,400 ft./3,170) is a stratovolcano. The earliest recorded eruption occurred in 1759. The most recent eruption was in 1943, when cone Paricutín arose in a cornfield, destroying and burying two villages and hundreds of homes. (A partially buried church is a local tourist attraction.) The cone reached a height of 325 meters in 1944. When it finally became inactive in 1952 it was 410 meters high. Paricutín is thus one of youngest volcanoes in the world.

Micotrin (Dominica, West Indies: 15.33N, 61.33W).

Micotrin (4,550 ft./1,387 m.) consists of two lava domes, Micotrin and Morne Trois Pitons, in central Dominica. The sole recorded eruption to date occurred in 1880.

Middle Gobi (Mongolia: 45.28N, 106.70E).

Middle Gobi (3,675 ft./1,120 m.) is composed of cinder cones with likely volcanic activity in the past 10,000 years.

Middle Sister (central of Three Sisters peaks) (Oregon, USA: 44.1N, 121.77W).

Middle Sister (10,050 ft./3,063 m.) was formed after North Sister and is composed of basalt, andesite lava, dacite and rhyodacite.

Mihara-yama *see* **Oshima.**

Milbanke Sound Group (British Columbia, Canada: 52.50N, 128.73W).
The Milbanke Sound Group (1,099 ft./335 m.) are Holocene cinder cones with no record of eruptions in historic time.

Milne (Shimushir I., Kuril Is.: 46.82N, 151.78E).
Milne (5,051 ft./1,540 m.) is a Holocene somma volcano on Shimushir Island in the central Kuril Islands. There has been no record of historic eruptions.

Milos [Melos] (Greece: 36.70N, 24.44E).
Milos (2,464 ft./751 m.) is a Pleistocene or Holocene stratovolcano with no known eruptions in historic time.

Minami-dake *see* **Sakura-jima.**

Minami-Hiyoshi (Volcano Is., Japan: 23.51N, 141.90E).
Minami-Hiyoshi (-98 ft./-30m.) is a seamount whose sole recorded submarine eruption to date occurred in 1975. Volcanic activity was reported in early 1996.

Minchinmavida (Chile: 42.78S, 72.43W).
Minchinmavida (7,887 ft./2,404 m.) is a stratovolcano whose earliest recorded eruption occurred in 1742. The most recent eruption took place in 1835.

Miravalles (Costa Rica: 10.75N, 85.15W).
Miravalles (6,654 ft./2,028 m.) is a stratovolcano in Costa Rica's northern volcanic arc. The sole recorded eruption to date occurred in 1946.

Misery, Mt. *see* **Liamuiga.**

Misti, El (Peru: 16.29S, 71.41W).
El Misti (19,102 ft./5,822 m.) is a stratovolcano whose earliest recorded eruption occurred in approximately 1454. The most recent certain eruption took place in 1787, but possible later eruptions were reported in 1826, 1830, 1831, 1869 and 1870. The volcano held religious significance in Inca culture.

Miyake-jima (Izu Is., Japan: 34.08N, 139.53E).
Miyake-jima (2,674 ft./815 m.) is an island stratovolcano whose earliest recorded eruption occurred in 1085. An eruption in 1940 caused 11 deaths, and injured 20. The most recent eruption occurred in 1983.

Mocho, El *see* **Mocho-Choshuenco.**

Mocho-Choshuenco (Chile: 39.93S, 72.03W).
Mocho-Choshuenco (7,946 ft./2,422 m.) is a stratovolcano whose earliest recorded eruption took place in 1864. The most recent eruption occurred in 1937.

Moffett (Adak I., Aleutian Is., Alaska, USA: 51.93N, 176.75W).
Moffett (3,923 ft./1,196 m.) is a Holocene stratovolcano which helps to form the northern peninsula of Adak Island. There have been no eruptions in historic time.

Moiro, Cerro (Bolivia: 21.68S, 67.47W).
Cerro Moiro (17,225 ft./5,250 m.) is a Holocene scoria cone with no record of eruptions in historic time.

Mojanda (Ecuador: 0.13N, 78.27W).
Mojanda (14,089 ft./4,294 m.) is a stratovolcano in the Andes' Eastern Cordillera. The only known eruption occurred approximately 1,450 years ago. There have been no eruptions in historic time.

Mokuaweoweo *see* **Mauna Loa.**

Mombacho (Nicaragua: 11.83N, 85.97W).
Mombacho (4,413 ft./1,345 m.) is a stratovolcano with fumarolic activity. An avalanche on the southern flank of the volcano in 1570, possibly caused by an eruption, destroyed an Indian village with the loss of around 400 lives.

Momotombo (Nicaragua: 12.42N, 86.54W).
Momotombo (4,126 ft./1,258 m.) is a young stratovolcano in western Nicaragua's volcanic arc. The earliest recorded eruption occurred in 1524. There have been 15 subsequent eruptions. The eruption of 1605-06 destroyed the city of Leon, Nicaragua's former capital. The most recent eruption occurred in 1905.

Monaco Bank (Azores: 37.60N, 25.88W).
A submarine volcano at Monaco Bank (-646 ft./-197 m.) erupted in 1907. The most recent eruption occurred in 1911.

Mondaca (Chile: 35.46S, 70.80W).
Mondaca (6,719 ft./2,048 m.) is a Holocene lava dome with no record of eruptions in historic time.

Mongibello *see* **Etna.**

Mono Craters (Native American *monache*, tribal name meaning "fly people") (California, USA: 37.88N, 119.00W).
The Mono Craters (9,174 ft./2,796 m.) are lava domes. Radiocarbon and

other (sometimes less reliable) datings indicate around 10 eruptions between approximately 6750 B.C. and 1345.

Mono Lake Volcanic Field (California, USA: 38.00N, 119.03W).

The Mono Lake Volcanic Field (6,959 ft./2,121 m.) is composed of cinder cones. There is evidence of volcanic activity in the past 300 years.

Monowai Seamount (north of Kermadec Is.: 25.89S, 177.19W).

The Monowai Seamount (-328 ft./-100 m.) is a submarine volcano between Kermadec and Tonga Islands. There was a possible eruption in 1944, and seven recorded eruptions between 1977 and 1991. There were several likely eruptions in 1997.

Motir (Halmahera, Indonesia: 0.45N, 127.40E).

Motir (2,264 ft./690 m.) is a stratovolcano with no record of eruptions in historic time.

Motlav (Vanuatu: 13.67S, 167.67E).

Motlav (1,348 ft./411 m.) is a Holocene stratovolcano with no record of eruptions in historic time.

Moua Pihaa (Society Is., Central Pacific: 18.32S, 148.67W).

Moua Pihaa (-590 ft./-180 m.) is a submarine volcano which possibly erupted in 1969 and 1970.

Mousa Alli (Ethiopia: 12.47N, 42.40E).

Mousa Alli (6,654 ft./2,028 m.) is a Holocene stratovolcano with no record of eruptions in historic time.

Moyuta (Guatemala: 14.03N, 90.10W).

Moyuta (5,453 ft./1,662 m.) is a stratovolcano with hot springs. There is no record of eruptions in historic time.

Muhavura (Uganda/Rwanda: 1.38S, 29.69E).

Muhavura (13,836 ft./4,127 m.) is a Holocene stratovolcano with no record of eruptions in historic time.

Mundua (New Britain, Papua New Guinea: 4.63S, 149.35E).

Mundua (587 ft./179 m.) is a Holocene complex volcano with no record of eruptions in historic time.

Musa River (New Guinea: 9.31S, 146.13E).

Musa River (2,651 ft./808 m.) is a hydrothermal field with hot springs. There have been no recorded eruptions in historic time.

Mutnovskaya Sopka (Kamchatka, Russia: 52.43N, 158.19E).
Mutnovskaya Sopka (7,616 ft./2,322 m.) is a composite stratovolcano with twin crater lakes at its summit. The earliest recorded eruption occurred in 1650, but ash layer datings show many previous eruptions going back to approximately 7550 B.C. An eruption in 1904 produced lava flows. The most recent eruption occurred in 1961. Although there was no eruption, 1991 saw the death of a geology student when he fell through a snowfield crust into a mudpot.

Mutsu-Hiuchi-Dake (Honshu, Japan: 41.43N, 141.07E).
Mutsu-Hiuchi-Dake (2,562 ft./781 m.) is a stratovolcano with fumarolic activity. There have been no eruptions recorded in historic time.

Myojin-sho *see* **Bayonnaise Rocks.**

Myoko (Honshu, Japan: 36.88N, 138.12E).
Myoko (8,025 ft./2,446 m.) is a stratovolcano with no record of eruptions in historic time.

N

Nabro (Ethiopia: 13.37N, 41.70E).
Nabro (7,277 ft./2,218 m.) is a Holocene stratovolcano with no record of eruptions in historic time.

Naka-dake *see* **Aso.**

Nakano-shima (Ryukyu Is., Japan: 29.85N, 129.87E).
Nakano-shima (3,212 ft./979 m.) is a stratovolcano whose sole recorded eruption to date occurred in 1914.

Namarunu (Kenya: 1.90N, 36.27E).
Namarunu (2,680 ft./817 m.) is a shield volcano with no record of eruptions in historic time.

Nantai (Honshu, Japan: 36.77N, 139.50E).
Nantai (8,148 ft./2,484 m.) is a Holocene stratovolcano. An ancient eruption of Mt. Nantai formed Lake Chuzhen. There is no record of an eruption in historic time. Saint Shodo was the first person to climb Mt. Nantain in 782, where he built the Chuzehen Temple two years later.

Narage (New Britain, Papua New Guinea: 4.55S, 149.12E).
Narage (1,007 ft./307 m.) is a Pleistocene stratovolcano with geysers. There is no record of eruptions in historic time.

Narcondum (Andaman Is.: 13.43N, 94.25E).
Narcondum (2,329 ft./710 m.) is a Holocene stratovolcano with no record of eruptions in historic time.

Narugo (Honshu, Japan: 38.73N, 140.73E).
Narugo (1,515 ft./462 m.) is composed of lava domes. The sole recorded eruption to date occurred in A.D. 837.

Nasu (Honshu, Japan: 37.12N, 139.97E).
Nasu (6,289 ft./1,917 m.) is composed of overlapping stratovolcanoes and lava domes. The earliest recorded eruption occurred from the Chausu-dake dome in 1397. There have been at least nine subsequent eruptions. An eruption in 1419 killed 180 people and many cattle. The most recent eruption occurred in 1963.

Natib (Luzon, Philippines: 14.70N, 120.40E).
Natib (4,222 ft./1,287 m.) is a Holocene stratovolcano with no record of eruptions in historic time.

Nazko (British Columbia, Canada: 52.90N, 123.73W).
Nazko (4,035 ft./1,230 m.) is composed of Holocene cinder cones with no record of eruptions in historic time.

Ndete Napu (Flores I., Indonesia: 8.72S, 121.78E).
Ndete Napu (2,460 ft./750 m.) is a fumarolic field with no record of eruptions in historic time.

Negra, Sierra (Spanish, "black range") (Isabela I., Galápagos Is.: 0.83S, 91.17W).
Sierra Negra (4,888 ft./1,490 m.) is a shield volcano whose earliest recorded eruption occurred in 1813. The most recent eruption from Volcán Chico ("little volcano") took place in 1979.

Negrillar, El (Chile: 24.18S, 68.25W).
El Negrillar (11,483 ft./3,500 m.) is composed of pyroclastic cones. There is no evidence of an eruption in historic time.

Negrillar, La (Chile: 24.28S, 68.60W).
La Negrillar (13,481 ft./4,109 m.) is composed of pyroclastic cones. There is no evidence of an eruption in historic time.

Negro, Cerro (Spanish, "black peak") (Nicaragua: 12.51N, 86.70W).
Cerro Negro (2,214 ft./675 m.) is a basaltic cinder cone, the most recent to form in the western hemisphere. There have been at least 20 recorded eruptions since 1850. There was a major eruption in 1960 that lasted three months. The most recent eruption occurred in May of 1995.

Negro de Mayasquer, Cerro (Colombia: 0.83N, 77.96W).

Cerro Negro de Mayasquer (14,584 ft./4,445 m.) is a Holocene stratovolcano whose sole recorded eruption to date occurred in 1936.

Nejapa-Ticomo (Nicaragua: 12.12N, 86.32W).

Nejapa-Ticomo (722 ft./220 m.) is a Holocene fissure vent with no record of eruptions in historic time.

Nemo Peak (Onekotan I., Kuril Is.: 49.57N, 154.81E).

Nemo Peak (3339 ft./1018 m.) is a caldera on Onekotan in the Northern Kuril Islands. There have been three moderate explosive eruptions recorded from 1710 until 1938.

Nemrut Dagi (Turkey: 38.65N, 42.02E).

Nemrut Dagi (10,007 ft./3,050 m.) is a stratovolcano. The sole recorded eruption to date occurred in 1441, but varve count shows 16 earlier eruptions dating from approximately 7769 B.C. Lava flow from one of these may have dammed river(s) to form Lake Van, Turkey's largest lake. (Varves, annually deposited layers of clay and silt in lakes, can be counted to establish dates for layers of volcanic ash in their midst.).

Nevada, Sierra (Chile/Argentina: 26.48S, 68.58W).

Sierra Nevada (20,102 ft./6,127 m.) is a Holocene volcanic field with no record of eruptions in historic time.

Nevis Peak (Nevis, West Indies: 17.15N, 62.58W).

Nevis Peak (3,231 ft./985 m.) is a Holocene stratovolcano with no record of eruptions in historic time.

Newberry Volcano (Oregon, USA: 43.72N, 121.23W).

Newberry Volcano (7,986 ft./2,434 m.) is the largest volcano in the Cascades. There is a large caldera at the summit containing Paulina and East lakes. There have been numerous eruptions in the past 10,000 years, with the most recent occurring approximately 1,440 years ago.

Newer Volcanics Province see Gambier, Mt.

Ngaoundere Plateau (Cameroon: 7.25N, 13.67E).

Ngaoundere Plateau is a Holocene volcanic field with no record of eruptions in historic time.

Ngauruhoe see Tongariro.

Ngozi (Tanzania: 8.97S, 33.57E).

Ngozi (8,703 ft./2,622 m.) is a Holocene caldera with no record of eruptions in historic time.

Nieuwerkerk (Banda Sea, Indonesia: 6.60S, 124.67E).
Nieuwerkerk (-7,497 ft./-2,285 m.) is a likely submarine volcano with no known eruptions.

Nigorigawa (Hokkaido, Japan: 42.12N, 140.45E).
Nigorigawa (1,168 ft./356 m.) is a Pleistocene hydrothermal field with fumarolic activity.

Niigata-yake-yama (Honshu, Japan: 36.92N, 138.03E).
Niigata-yake-yama (7,874 ft./2,400 m.) is a lava dome whose earliest recorded eruption occurred in A.D. 887. The most recent eruption took place in 1989.

Nii-jima (Izu Is., Japan: 34.37N, 139.27E).
Nii-jima (1,417 ft./432 m.) is an island composed of eight low rhyloite lava domes. There have been only two recorded eruptions in A.D. 840 and 886.

Nikko (Volcano Is., Japan: 23.07N, 142.31E).
Nikko (-1,283 ft./-391 m.) is a submarine volcano with no recorded eruptions.

Nikko-shirane (Honshu, Japan: 36.80N, 139.38E).
Nikko-shirane (8,458 ft./2,578 m.) is a shield volcano with a lava dome. The earliest recorded eruption occurred in 1625. There have been four subsequent eruptions, most recently in 1889.

Nila (Banda Sea, Indonesia: 6.73S, 129.50E).
Nila (2,562 ft./781 m.) is a stratovolcano whose earliest recorded eruption occurred in 1903. The most recent eruption occurred in 1968.

Nindiri *see* **Masaya.**

Nipesotsu-Upepesanke (Hokkaido, Japan: 43.45N, 143.03E).
Nipesotsu-Upepesanke (6,605 ft./2,013 m.) is composed of a cluster of lava domes. There have been two historic eruptions at the Maru-yama vent, in 1000 and 1898.

Nishino-shima (Volcano Is., Japan: 27.24N, 140.88E).
Nishimo-shima (171 ft./52 m.) is a caldera whose sole recorded eruption to date occurred in 1973.

Nishi-yama *see* **Oshima-Oshima.**

Nisyros (Greece: 36.58N, 27.18E).
Nisyros (2,290 ft./698 m.) is a stratovolcano at the eastern end of the Hellenic island arc. The earliest recorded eruption occurred in 1871, though there was a suspected eruption in 1422. The most recent eruption occurred in 1888.

Niuafo'ou (Tonga Is.: 15.60S, 175.63W).
Niuafo'ou (853 ft./260 m.) is a shield volcano. The earliest recorded eruption occurred in 1814. Approximately 25 people were killed during the 1853 eruption when a lava flow cut through a village. Eleven were dead or missing following a 1886 eruption, when several older men, including chiefs of rank, died of shock. Following the 1946 eruption, the island's inhabitants were evacuated to 'Eua. They only began to return in 1958. The most recent eruption occurred in 1985.

Nonda (Vella Lavella I., Solomon Is.: 7.67S, 156.60E).
Nonda (249 ft./76 m.) is a Pleistocene stratovolcano with fumarolic activity.

Norikura (Honshu, Japan: 36.12N, 137.55E).
Norikura (9,928 ft./3,026 m.) is a Holocene stratovolcano with no record of eruptions in historic time.

North Island (L. Turkana, Kenya: 4.07N, 36.05E).
North Island (1,706 ft./520 m.) is composed of tuff cones in the northern portion of Lake Turkana (formerly Lake Victoria) and has no record of eruptions in historic time. There was likely volcanic activity in the past 10,000 years.

North Sister Field (northernmost of Three Sisters peaks) (Oregon, USA: 44.17N, 121.77W).
North Sister (10,090 ft./3,075 m.) is a complex shield volcano made of basaltic andesite. It is the oldest of the Three Sisters.

North Vate (Vanuatu: 17.45S, 168.33E).
North Vate (1,948 ft./594 m.) is a group of Holocene stratovolcanoes.

Northeastern Udokan Plateau (Russia: 56.33N, 188.07E).
The Northeastern Udokan Plateau (7,152 ft./2,180 m.) is a Holocene volcanic field with no record of eruptions in historic time.

Nosy-Be (Madagascar: 13.32S, 48.48E).
Nosy-Be (702 ft./214 m.) is a Holocene cinder cone with no record of eruptions in historic time.

Novarupta (pseudo-Latin, "newly erupted") (Alaska, USA: 58.27N, 155.16W).
Novarupta (2,758 ft./841 m.) is now a pumice-filled depression following its sole recorded eruption to date in 1912. It was the world's largest eruption (simultaneously with neighboring **Katmai**) in the twentieth century and Novarupta was the vent. It caused only two deaths: one an elderly woman caught in ash fall, the other a man buried up to his arms in wet ash.

Nuevo Mundo (Bolivia: 19.78S, 66.48W).
Nuevo Mundo (18,170 ft./5,538 m.) is composed of Holocene lava domes. There is no record of eruptions in historic time.

Numazawa (Honshu, Japan: 37.43N, 139.58E).
Numazawa (3,609 ft./1,100 m.) is a shield volcano with no recorded historical eruptions.

Nunivak I. (Inuit [Eskimo], perhaps "big land") (Alaska, USA: 60.02N, 166.33W).
Nunivak Island (1,676 ft./511 m.) is a Holocene shield volcano with no record of eruptions in historic time.

Nyambeni Hills (Kenya: 0.23N, 37.87E).
The Nyambeni Hills (2,461 ft./750 m.) are Holocene shield volcanoes with no record of eruptions in historic time.

Nyamuragira (Dem. Rep. of Congo [Zaire]: 1.41S, 29.20E).
Nyamuragira (10,013 ft./3,053 m.) is a shield volcano about 10 miles northwest of Nyiragongo. The earliest recorded eruption occurred in 1865. Since then there have been 35 eruptions, with the latest in 1993. The eruption of 1912 killed 20 villagers when lava flow changed direction. The largest lava flow from the 1982 eruption destroyed a 13-kilometer-long stretch of forest.

Nyiragongo ((Dem. Rep. of Congo [Zaire]: 1.52S, 29.25E).
Nyiragongo (11,365 ft./3,465 m) is a stratovolcano and part of the Virunga Volcanic Chain. The earliest recorded eruption occurred in 1884. There were almost continuous eruptions from 1928 through 1977, when lava abruptly drained from the lava lake, killing around 100 and "molding" slow-moving elephants. The most recent eruption occurred in 1994.

O

Ofu-Olosega (American Samoa: 14.17S, 169.62W).
Ofu-Olosega (2,096 ft./639 m.) are shield volcanoes whose sole recorded eruption to date occurred in 1866.

Ohachi *see* **Kirishima.**

Ojos del Salado, Nevado
(Spanish, "eyes of the Salado [River]") (Chile/Argentina: 27.12S, 68.53W).
Nevado Ojos de Salado (22,596 ft./6,887 m.) is considered to be the world's highest active volcano. It is technically inactive, but has fumaroles, or vapor vents, on its summit, which in the opinion of some qualifies it for record.

Oka Volcanic Field (Russia: 52.70N, 98.98E).
The Oka Volcanic Field (6,815 ft./2,077 m.) is composed of Holocene cinder cones with no recorded eruptions in historic time.

Okama *see* **Zao.**

Okataina (Maori *oka*, "to prick," *taina*, "younger sibling") (New Zealand: 38.12S, 176.50E).
Okataina (3,644 ft./1,111 m.) includes the Haroharo caldera and the Haroharo and Tarawera rhyolite dome complexes. The earliest recorded eruption occurred in 1886 from fissure vent Tarawera (Maori *tara*, "peak," *wera*, "hot"), when 153 people died, buried by ash. All but six were Maoris. Four lost their lives in a 1903 eruption, and two in that of 1917. Most twentieth-century eruptions come from Echo Crater of Waimangu (Maori *wai*, "water," *mangu*, "black"). The most recent eruption occurred in 1973.

Oki-Dogo (west of Honshu, Japan: 36.17N, 133.33E).
Oki-Dogo (4.95 ft./151 m.) is a Holocene shield volcano with no record of eruptions in historic time.

Okinawa-tori-shima (Ryukyu Is., Japan: 27.85N, 128.25E).
Okinawa-tori-shima is a complex volcano whose earliest recorded eruption occurred in 1664. The most recent eruption took place in 1968.

Okmok (Umnak I., Aleutian Is., Alaska, USA: 53.42N, 168.13W).
Okmok (3,520 ft./1,073 m.) is a large caldera on the eastern end of Umnak Island. The earliest recorded eruption occurred in 1805. There were lava producing eruptions recorded in 1945 and 1958. A recent eruption occurred from November of 1986 through February of 1988. There was a small volcanic eruption reported in February of 1997.

Oku Volcanic Field (Cameroon: 6.35N, 10.50E).
The Oku Volcanic Field (9,879 ft./3,011 m.) is a Maars field. Although there was no eruption, around 1,700 died in 1986 when large volumes of carbon dioxide gas were released from Lake Nyos.

Ol Kokwe (Kenya: 0.63N, 36.08E).
Ol Kokwe (4,364 ft./1,130 m.) is a Holocene shield volcano with no record of eruptions in historic time.

Olca-Paruma (Chile/Bolivia: 20.93S, 68.48W).
Olca-Paruma (17,740 ft./5,407 m.) is a stratovolcano whose sole recorded eruption to date occurred in 1865.

Olkaria (Kenya: 0.90S, 36.29E).
Olkaria (7,986 ft./2,434 m.) is a pumice cone with a likely eruption in the 1700s.

Olkhovy (Russian, "alder tree") (Kamchatka, Russia: 52.08N, 157.48E).
Olkhovy (2,087 ft./636 m.) is a Holocene shield volcano with no record of eruptions in historic time.

Ollague (Chile/Bolivia: 21.30S, 68.18W).
Ollague (19,253 ft./5,868 m.) is a Holocene stratovolcano with no record of eruptions in historic time.

Olot Volcanic Field (Spain: 42.17N, 2.53E).
The Olot Volcanic Field (2,930 ft./893 m.) is composed of pyroclastic cones. There is no recorded historical eruption, but likely volcanic activity in the past 10,000 years.

Omachi Seamount (Izu Is., Japan: 29.22N, 140.80E).
The Omachi Seamount (-5,578 ft./-1,700 m.) is a submarine volcano with no recorded eruptions in historic time.

Omanago Group (Honshu, Japan: 36.78N, 139.50E).
The Omanago Group (7,792 ft./2,375 m.) is composed of Holocene lava domes. There is no record of eruptions in historic time.

On-Take (Honshu, Japan: 35.90N, 137.48E).
On-Take (10,049 ft./3,063 m.) is a massive stratovolcano in central Japan. The sole recorded eruption to date occurred in 1979. This ended in 1980, but an earthquake in 1984 caused the southern flank of the volcano to collapse, creating an avalanche that killed ten people in a hot spa. Another 19 died in landslides elsewhere. The mountain itself is the second most sacred (after **Fuji**) in Japan, and is climbed by thousands of pilgrims annually each summer.

On-take *see* **Suwanose-jima**.

Oo, Puu *see* **Kilauea**.

Opala (Kamchatka, Russia: 52.54N, 157.33E).
Opala (8,118 ft./2,475 m.) is an extinct stratovolcano, also known as Apalskaia Sopka. The Opala caldera was formed over 30,000 years ago. An explosive eruption occurred in 1776.

Öræfajökull (Iceland: 64.00N, 16.65W).
Öræfajökull (6,950 ft./2,119 m.) is a post-glacial stratovolcano and the highest peak in Iceland. The earliest recorded eruption occurred in 1362 and completely destroyed Herad district. There has been only one subsequent eruption in 1728.

Orizaba, Pico de (Citlaltépetl [Nahuatl, *citlal*, "star," *tepetl*, "mountain"]) (Mexico: 19.03N, 97.27W).
Pico de Orizaba (18,406 ft./5,610 m.) is a stratovolcano whose earliest recorded eruption occurred in 1537, although radiocarbon datings indicate at

least 15 previous eruptions, the first in approximately 7450 B.C. The most recent eruption took place in 1687.

Orosi (Costa Rica: 10.98N, 85.47W).

Orosi (5,443 ft./1,659 m.) is a stratovolcano with no record of eruptions in historic time.

Oshima (Izu Is., Japan: 34.73N, 139.38E).

Oshima (2,486 ft./758 m.) is an island stratovolcano with a large caldera on its summit in Sagami Bay. The earliest recorded eruption occurred in A.D. 605, with radiocarbon datings showing five eruptions before this, going back to approximately 50 B.C. Since then Oshima has erupted over 70 times, most recently in 1990. Most eruptions are from its cone, Mihara-yama, renowned for its high "fire fountains" of vertically jetting lava. That of 1986 reached a height of 1,600 meters.

Oshima-Oshima (Hokkaido, Japan: 41.50N, 139.37E).

Oshima-Oshima (2,385 ft./737 m.) is a small island composed of two coalescing volcanoes. The earliest recorded eruption occurred in 1741, when 729 houses were washed away by giant waves following an earthquake and avalanche from the northern flank of Nishi-yama cone, killing 1,475. Subsequent eruptions were reported in 1759, 1786 and, most recently, in 1790.

Osore-yama (Honshu, Japan: 41.32N, 141.08E).

Osore-yama (2,884 ft./879 m.) is a stratovolcano whose sole recorded eruption to date occurred in approximately 1787.

Osorno (Chile: 41.10S, 72.49W).

Osorno (8,701 ft./2,652 m.) is a stratovolcano whose earliest recorded eruption occurred in 1719. The most recent eruption took place in 1869.

Ostanets (Kamchatka, Russia: 52.15N, 157.32E).

Ostanets (2,359 ft./719 m.) is a Holocene shield volcano with no record of eruptions in historic time.

Ostry (Russian, "sharp") (Kamchatka, Russia: 58.18N, 160.82E).

Ostry (12,077 ft./3,682 m.) is a Holocene stratovolcano forming part of the Tolbachik massif.

Otdel'naya (Russian, "separate"; lies east of others) (Kamchatka, Russia: 52.22N, 157.43E).

Otdel'naya (2,559 ft./791 m.) is a Holocene shield volcano with no record of eruptions in historic time.

Overo, Cerro (Chile: 23.35S, 67.67W).

Cerro Overo (14,945 ft./4,555 m.) is a Holocene Maar volcano with no record of eruptions in historic time.

Oyoye (Tibesti, Chad: 17.32E, 20.49 N).

Oyoye (7,314 ft./2,230 m.) is a caldera volcano located between Lake Chad and the Gulf of Syrte in northern Chad's Tibesti volcanic region. There is no record of historical eruptions.

Ozernoy (Russian, "lake") (Kamchatka, Russia: 51.88N, 157.38E).

Ozernoy (1,844 ft./562 m.) is a Holocene shield volcano with no record of eruptions in historic time.

P

Pacaya (Guatemala: 14.38N, 90.60W).

Pacaya (8,371 ft./2,552 m.) is a compound volcano composed of a modern basaltic stratovolcano, an older stratovolcano, domes, flows and tephra. The earliest recorded eruption occurred in 1565 and there have been over 20 eruptions since. The volcano cone rose over 274 meters in height during the 1980s. It is known for its frequent activity since 1965, greater even than **Etna**. Pacaya's red glare can often be seen at night in Guatemala City, 32 kilometers away. Recent eruptions occurred in 1993 and 1996–98.

Paco (Mindanao, Philippines: 9.59N, 125.52E).

Paco (1,719 ft./524 m.) is a compound volcano with fumarolic activity.

Pagan (Mariana Is.: 18.13N, 145.80E).

Pagan (1,870 ft./570 m.) is a stratovolcano in the western Pacific Ocean. The earliest recorded eruption occurred in 1669. There have been nearly 20 eruptions in historic time. The largest eruption occurred in 1981. There were subsequent eruptions in 1987, 1988, 1992 and, most recently, 1993.

Pago (New Britain, Papua New Guinea: 5.58S, 150.52E).

Pago (2,434 ft./742 m.) is a caldera on New Britain Island in the south Bismarck Sea. There was a large eruption in 1350 B.C. The earliest recorded eruption occurred from 1911–1918. It was explosive and produced lava flows. Smaller eruptions occurred in 1920 and 1933.

Paka (Kenya: 0.92N, 36.18E).

Paka (2,287 ft./697 m.) is a shield volcano with no likelihood of an eruption in the past 2,000 years.

Palei-Aike Volcanic Field (Chile/Argentina: 52.00S, 70.00W).

The Palei-Aike Volcanic Field (820 ft./250 m.) is composed of Holocene cinder cones. There is no record of an eruption in historic time.

Palena Volcanic Group (Chile: 43.68S, 72.50W).

The Palena Volcanic Group is composed of Holocene cinder cones. There is no record of eruptions in historic time.

Pallas Peak *see* Ketoy.

Palomo (Chile: 34.61S, 70.29W).

Palomo (15,946 ft./4,860 m.) is a Holocene stratovolcano with no record of eruptions in historic time.

Paluweh (Indonesia: 8.32S, 121.71E).

Paluweh (2,871 ft./875 m.) is a stratovolcano whose earliest recorded eruption occurred in 1650. An eruption in 1928 caused the deaths of 226 people, 128 of these in giant waves generated by a landslide. The most recent eruption took place in 1985.

Pampa Luxsar (Bolivia: 20.85S, 68.20W).

Pampa Luxsar (18,186 ft./5,543 m.) is a Holocene volcanic field with no recorded eruptions in historic time.

Pan de Azúcar (Ecuador: 0.43S, 77.72W).

Pan de Azúcar (11,242 ft./3,482 m.) is a Holocene stratovolcano with no record of eruptions in historic time.

Panay (Luzon, Philippines: 13.72N, 120.89E).

Panay (1,644 ft./501 m.) is a Pleistocene stratovolcano with fumarolic activity.

Pantelleria (Italy: 36.77N, 12.02E).

Pantelleria (2,743 ft./836 m.) is a shield volcano. The sole recorded eruption to date was in 1891, but radiocarbon datings indicate earlier eruptions from approximately 6130 B.C., and potassium-argon dating shows an even earlier event around 7050 B.C.

Pantoja, Cerro (Chile: 40.77S, 71.95W).

Cerro Pantoja (6,929 ft./2,112 m.) is a Holocene stratovolcano with no record of eruptions in historic time.

Papandayan (Java: 7.32S. 107.73E).

Papandayan (8,700 ft./2,665 m.) is a stratovolcano whose earliest recorded eruption occurred in 1772. The northeastern part of the mountain collapsed and the resultant avalanche totally destroyed 40 villages with loss of almost 3,000 lives. There have been two eruptions since, most recently in 1942. There was a minor phreatic explosion reported in June of 1998.

Papayo (Mexico: 19.31N, 98.70W).
Papayo (11,811 ft./3,600 m.) is a Holocene stratovolcano with no record of eruptions in historic time.

Paricutín *see* **Michoacán-Guanajuato.**

Parinacota (Chile/Bolivia: 18.17S, 69.15W).
Parinacota (20,821 ft./6,348 m.) is a composite volcano on the border of Chile and Bolivia and, with the older volcano Pomerape, makes up the Nevados Payachata range. An avalanche in prehistoric times blocked the outlet to the Pacific, so forming Lake Chungara, one of the highest lakes in the world (4,550 m.).

Patah (Sumatra: 4.27S, 103.30E).
Patah (9,242 ft./2,817 m.) is a volcano with no record of eruptions in historic time.

Patates, Morne (Dominica, West Indies: 15.22N, 61.37W).
Morne Patates (3,149 ft./960 m.) is a stratovolcano located at Dominica's southern tip. There have been no recorded historic eruptions, though it is believed that Morne Patates' most recent eruption occurred approximately 500 years ago.

Patilla Pata (Bolivia: 18.05S, 69.03W).
Patilla Pata (17,389 ft./5,300 m.) is a Holocene stratovolcano with no record of eruptions in historic time.

Patoc (Luzon, Philippines: 17.15N, 120.98E).
Patoc (6,119 ft./1,865 m.) is a stratovolcano with fumarolic activity. There have been no recorded eruptions in historic time.

Patuha (Java: 7.15S, 107.37E).
Patuha (7,986 ft./2,434 m.) is a Holocene stratovolcano with no record of eruptions in historic time.

Paulet (Antarctica: 63.58S, 55.77W).
Paulet (1,158 ft./353 m.) is a Holocene cinder cone with no record of eruptions in historic time.

Pauzhetka (Kamchatka, Russia: 51.43N, 156.93E).
Pauzhetka (4,366 ft./1,331 m.) is a caldera and one of the largest volcanic structures in Kamchatka. A depression formed by the caldera contains Kurile Lake. There have been no eruptions in historic time.

Pavlof (Alaska, USA: 55.42N, 161.90W).
Pavlof (8,264 ft./2,519 m.) is a snow-covered cone-shaped stratovolcano on the Alaska Peninsula. The earliest recorded eruption occurred in 1790. Since then there have been nearly 40 eruptions recorded. The largest eruption at Pavlof

occurred in December of 1911, with lava flowing from a fissure vent. An eruption of 1981 sent vapor and ash some 5 kilometers into the atmosphere. The most recent eruption occurred in 1996.

Pavlof Sister (Alaska, USA: 55.45N, 161.87W).
Pavlof Sister (7,028 ft./2,142 m.) is a stratovolcano which neighbors Pavlof on the Alaska Peninsula. The only recorded eruption began in 1762 and lasted until 1786.

Payun Matru, Cerro (Argentina: 36.42S, 69.20W).
Cerro Payun Matru (12,110 ft./3,691 m.) is a Holocene shield volcano with no record of eruptions in historic time.

Peinado (Argentina: 26.62S, 68.15W).
Peinado (18,833 ft./5,740 m.) is a Holocene stratovolcano with no record of eruptions in historic time.

Pelée, Mt. (French, *montagne pelée*, "bald mountain") (Martinique, West Indies: 14.82N, 61.17W).
Mount Pelée (4,583 ft./1,397 m.) is a stratovolcano composed of pyroclastic rocks in the Lesser Antilles volcanic arc. Its earliest recorded eruption occurred in 1635. There was a devastating eruption in May of 1902, when approximately 28,000 people perished, including all inhabitants of the town of St. Pierre and many others who had sought refuge there. Mt. Pelée gave its name to the *Pelean* type of volcanic activity. The most recent eruption began in March of 1929, with volcanic activity finally subsiding in 1932.

Penanggungan (Java: 7.62S, 112.63E).
Penanggungan (5,423 ft./1,653 m.) is a Holocene stratovolcano with no record of eruptions in historic time.

Pendan (Sumatra: 2.82S, 102.02E).
Pendan is a likely Holocene volcano with no record of eruptions in historic time.

Peng-Chia-Hsu (north of Taiwan: 25.63N, 122.07E).
Peng-Chia-Hsu (423 ft./129 m.) is a Pleistocene stratovolcano with fumarolic activity. There is no record of eruptions in historic time.

Penguin I. (Antarctica: 62.10S, 57.93W).
Penguin Island (590 ft./180 m.) is a stratovolcano with evidence of volcanic activity in the past 100 years.

Perbakti (Java: 6.75S, 106.68E).
Perbakti (5,574 ft./1,699 m.) is a stratovolcano with fumarolic activity. There is no record of eruptions in historic time.

Petacas (Colombia: 1.57N, 76.78W).
Petacas (13,301 ft./4,054 m.) is a Holocene lava dome with no recorded eruptions in historic time.

Peter I I. (Antarctica: 68.85S, 90.58W).
Peter I Island (5,380 ft./1,640 m.) is a Holocene shield volcano with no recorded eruptions in historic time.

Peteroa *see* **Planchon-Peteroa.**

Peuet Sague ("square") (Sumatra: 4.92N, 96.33E).
Peuet Sague (9,121 ft./2,780 m.) is a stratovolcano with four summit peaks in northern Sumatra. The sole recorded eruption to date occurred in 1918, lasting three years. There were possible eruptions reported in 1949, 1979, 1986 and 1991.

Peulik *see* **Ugashik-Peulik.**

Phlegraean Fields *see* (1) **Campi Flegri;** (2) **Campi Flegri del Mar Sicilia.**

Pico (Portuguese, "peak") (Azores: 38.47N, 28.40W).
Pico (5,600 ft./2,351 m.) is a volcanic structure composed of a tall basaltic stratovolcano and an older volcanic ridge. It is the youngest island in the Azores. The earliest recorded eruption occurred in 1562. The most recent eruption occurred in 1720.

Piip (Kamchatka, Russia: 55.42N, 167.33E).
Piip (-984 ft./-300 m.) is a submarine volcano with no recorded eruptions.

Pilas, Las (Spanish, "the heaps") (Nicaragua: 12.49N, 86.69W).
Las Pilas (3,440 ft./1,050 m.) is a complex volcano whose first recorded historical eruption was in 1528. There were small phreatic eruptions in 1952 and 1954.

Pina, Cerro (Chile: 19.49S, 68.65W).
Cerro Pina (13,245 ft./4,037 m.) is a Holocene volcano with no record of eruptions in historic time.

Pinacate Peaks (Mexico: 31.77N, 113.50W).
Pinacate Peaks (3,937 ft./1,200 m.) are a 30-mile-wide volcanic field with numerous small volcanoes, cinder cones and Maars craters. There are estimated to be over 300 volcanic vents in the field. There are only two recorded eruptions at Pinacate, in 1928 and, most recently, in 1935.

Pinatubo, Mt. (Luzon, Philippines: 15.12N, 120.35E).
Mount Pinatubo (5,248 ft./1,600 m.) is a dome complex and stratovolcano. The sole recorded eruption to date occurred in 1991, but radiocarbon datings show three previous eruptions, the first in approximately 6100 B.C. The eruption of 1991, the world's third largest of the twentieth century, resulted in a total of around 800 deaths, either directly or as result of disease in evacuation camps. The situation was exacerbated because the eruption climax coincided with the passage of typhoon Yunya. Many mud flows were generated and thousands of houses were washed away or buried. Gases and particles expelled in this eruption led to a cooling of 0.5°C in the ozone layer. Three Japanese engineers and eight Filipino surveyors were rescued from mudflows in 1997.

Pinta (Galápagos Is.: 0.58N, 90.75W).
Pinta (2,559 ft./780 m.) is a shield volcano whose sole recorded eruption to date occurred in 1928.

Piratkovsky (Kamchatka, Russia: 52.11N, 157.85E).
Piratkovsky (4,337 ft./1,322 m.) is a Holocene stratovolcano with no record of eruptions in historic time.

Pitos, Sierra de las (Mexico: 19.92N, 98.75W).
Sierra de las Pitos (9,840 ft./3,000 m.) is a Holocene volcano with no record of eruptions in historic time.

Planchón-Peteroa (Chile: 35.24S, 70.57W).
Planchón-Peteroa (13,474 ft./4,107 m.) is a stratovolcano whose earliest recorded eruption occurred in 1660. The most recent eruption took place in 1991.

Platanar, Cerro (Costa Rica: 10.30N, 84.37W).
Cerro Platanar (7,162 ft./2,183 m.) is a stratovolcano at the northern end of the Cordillera Central. There is no historic record of volcanic activity, but there are indications of an eruption in the past few thousand years.

Pleiades, The (Antarctica: 72.67S, 165.50E).
The Pleiades (9,974 ft./3,040 m.) is a stratovolcano with no record of eruptions in historic time.

Plosky 1 (Russian, "flat") (Kamchatka, Russia: 55.20N, 158.47E).
Plosky 1 (4,055 ft./1,236 m.) is a shield volcano with no record of eruptions in historic time.

Plosky 2 (Russian, "flat") (Kamchatka, Russia: 57.83N, 160.25E).
Plosky 2 (4,117 ft./1,255 m.) is a shield volcano with no record of eruptions in historic time.

Plosky Volcanic Group (Russian, "flat") (Kamchatka, Russia: 52.02N, 157.53E).

The Plosky Volcanic Group (2,234 ft./681 m.) is a Holocene volcanic field with no record of eruptions in historic time.

Poás (Costa Rica: 10.20N, 84.23W).

Poás (8,870 ft./2,704 m.) is a stratovolcano with two crater lakes near the summit. The earliest recorded eruption occurred in 1828. There have been over 40 eruptions since then, most recently in 1992. A former tropical rain forest downwind of the volcano has been destroyed since the 1970s by sulfurous fumes and showers of acid rain jetted up from the crater lake.

Pocdol Mountains (Luzon, Philippines: 13.05N, 123.96E).

The Pocdol Mountains (3,616 ft./1,102 m.) are a Holocene volcanic complex with no record of eruptions in historic time.

Poco Leok (Flores I., Indonesia: 8.68S, 120.48E).

Poco Leok (5,496 ft./1,675 m.) is a fumarolic volcano with no recorded eruptions in historic time.

Poco Sol, Laguna (Costa Rica: 10.32N, 84.66W).

Laguna Poco Sol (2,589 ft./789 m.) is an explosion crater with no known eruptions in historic time.

Pogranichny (Russian, "border") (Kamchatka, Russia: 56.85N, 159.80E).

Pogranichny (5,010 ft./1,527 m.) is a Holocene shield volcano with no record of eruptions in historic time.

Popa (Myanmar: 20.87N, 95.23E).

Popa (4,980 ft./1,518 m.) is a Holocene stratovolcano with no record of eruptions in historic time.

Popocatépetl (Nahuatl *popokani*, "to smoke," *tepetl*, "mountain") (Mexico: 19.02N, 8.62W).

Popocatépetl (17,883 ft./5,452 m.) is a stratovolcano capped with snow in central Mexico. The earliest recorded eruption occurred in 1345, although radiocarbon datings indicate previous eruptions going back to approximately 7690 B.C. There have been at least 36 historic eruptions. An eruption of 1923 lasted four months. A relatively calm period ended in 1997 with 31 eruptions, when ash and acrid gases showered down on Mexico City and were carried 225 kilometers east to the Gulf of Mexico. A new eruption in early 1998 spewed out a massive gas cloud and set off tremors reaching 3.5 on the Richter scale. It was heard in Puebla, 20 miles away, where ash rained in the street. Popocatépetl remained active through late 1998.

Possession, Ile de la (Indian Ocean: 46.42S, 51.63E).
Ile de la Possession (934 m.) is a Holocene stratovolcano with no record of eruptions in historic time.

Potato Butte (California, USA: 40.63N, 121.43W).
Potato Butte (5,026 ft./1,532 m.) is composed of Holocene shield volcanoes. There is no record of eruptions in historic time.

Prestahnúkur (Iceland: 64.60N, 20.58W).
Prestahnúkur (4,560 ft./1,390 m.) is a subglacial volcano with no record of eruptions in historic time.

Prevo Peak (Shimushir I., Kuril Is.: 47.02N, 152.12E).
Prevo Peak (4,460 ft./1,360 m.) is a stratovolcano on Shimushir Island in the Central Kuril Islands. The earliest recorded eruption was an explosive one causing damage in 1764. The most recent eruption occurred in 1825.

Prieto, Cerro (Mexico: 32.42N, 115.30W).
Cerro Prieto (1,345 ft./410 m.) is a Holocene cinder cone with no record of eruptions in historic time.

Prince Edward I. (Indian Ocean: 46.63S, 37.95E).
Prince Edward Island (2,205 ft./672 m.) is a Holocene stratovolcano with no record of eruptions in historic time.

Protector Shoal (South Sandwich Is.: 55.92S, 28.08W).
Protector Shoal (-89 ft./-27 m) is a submarine volcano whose sole recorded eruption to date occurred in 1962.

Puchuldiza (Chile: 19.42S, 68.97W).
Puchuldiza (14,765 ft./4,500 m.) is a Pleistocene hydrothermal field with geysers. There have been no recorded eruptions in historic time.

Puesto Cortaderas (Argentina: 37.55S, 69.62W).
Puesto Cortaderas (3,182 ft./970 m.) is a Holocene pyroclastic cone with no record of eruptions in historic time.

Pular (Chile: 24.18S, 68.05W).
Pular (20,450 ft./6,233 m.) is composed of Holocene stratovolcanoes with no record of eruptions in historic time.

Pulau Weh (Sumatra: 5.88N, 95.33E).
Pulau Weh (1,916 ft./584 m.) is a stratovolcano that forms an island north of Flores. The earliest recorded eruption occurred in 1928. The eruption generated a tsunami which killed 1,928 people and tephra killed 98 more. There

have been seven subsequent eruptions. An eruption in 1964 killed one person and injured three others.

Pululagua (Ecuador: 0.04N, 78.46W).
Pululagua (11,011 ft./3,356 m.) is a Holocene caldera with no record of eruptions in historic time.

Puntiguido-Cordón Cenizos (Chile: 40.97S, 72.26W).
Puntiguido-Cordón Cenizos (8,179 ft./2,493 m.) is a stratovolcano whose sole recorded eruption to date occurred in 1850.

Puracé (Colombia: 2.32N, 76.40W).
Puracé (15,000 ft./4,600 m.) is an active volcano composed of a dacitic shield capped by an andesitic cone. The earliest recorded eruption occurred in 1816. Many were killed in an 1885 eruption, and 17 in that of 1949, all university students trying to reach the summit. The most recent eruption occurred in 1977.

Purico Complex (Chile: 23.00S, 67.75W).
The Purico Complex (18,711 ft./5,703 m.) is composed of Holocene stratovolcanoes. There is no record of eruptions in historic time.

Putana (Chile: 22.57S, 67.87W).
Putana (19,325 ft./5,890 m.) is a stratovolcano whose earliest recorded eruption occurred in approximately 1810. The most recent eruption took place in 1972.

Puyehue (Chile: 40.59S, 72.12W).
Puyehue (7,336 ft./2,236 m.) is a stratovolcano with no record of eruptions in historic time.

Puyuhuapi (Chile: 44.30S, 72.53W).
Puyuhuapi (837 ft./255 m.) is composed of Holocene cinder cones with no record of eruptions in historic time.

Q

Qal'eh Hasan Ali (Iran: 29.40N, 57.57E).
Qal'eh Hasan Ali is a Holocene Maars field with no record of eruptions in historic time.

Qualibou (St. Lucia, West Indies: 13.83N, 61.05W).
Qualibou (2,549 ft./777 m.) is a caldera on the southwest side of St. Lucia. The sole recorded eruption to date occurred in 1766.

Quetena (Bolivia: 22.25S, 67.42W).
Quetena (18,800 ft./5,730 m.) is a Holocene fissure vent with no record of eruptions in historic time.

Quetrupillan (Chile: 39.50S, 71.70W).
Quetrupillan (7,743 ft./2,360 m.) is a caldera whose sole recorded eruption to date occurred in 1872.

Quezaltepeque (Guatemala: 14.65N, 89.35W).
Quezaltepeque (3,937 ft./1,200 m.) is a Holocene volcano with no record of eruptions in historic time.

Quill, The (St. Eustatius, West Indies: 17.48N, 62.95W).
The Quill (1,972 ft./601 m.) is a stratovolcano with evidence of volcanic activity in the past 2,000 years.

Quilotoa (Ecuador: 0.85S, 78.90W).
Quilotoa (12,842 ft./3,914 m.) is a caldera with evidence of volcanic activity in the past 2,000 years.

Quimsachata (Peru: 14.37S, 71.17W).
Quimsachata (12,871 ft./3,923 m.) is a Holocene lava dome with no record of eruptions in historic time.

Quizapu *see* **Cerro Azul.**

R

Rabaul (New Britain, Papua New Guinea: 4.27S, 152.20E).
Rabaul (2,257 ft./688 m.) is a caldera whose earliest recorded eruption was 1767. Rabaul's natural harbor was formed by an eruption and collapse in the sixth century A.D. Earliest radiocarbon dating shows eruption in approximately 1550 B.C. An eruption of Vulcan and Matupi craters in 1937 killed about 500 people and partially destroyed Rabaul, then New Guinea's capital. The capital moved to Lae in 1941. An eruption occurred at Tavurvur vent in 1943. In 1990, although there was no eruption, an adult and two children died of suffocation while hunting for wildfowl eggs. Three friends and relatives died the next day trying to recover their bodies. An eruption occurred at both the Tavurvur and Vulcan vents in 1994, forcing the evacuation of the island.

Ragang (Mindanao, Philippines: 7.67N, 124.50E).
Ragang (9,233 ft./2,815 m.) is a stratovolcano at the end of a row of volcanic cones. There have been nine eruptions since the earliest recorded in 1765. The most recent eruption occurred in 1915.

Rahah, Harrat Ar- (Saudi Arabia: 27.80N, 36.17E).
Harrat Ar-Rahah (5,446 ft./1,660 m.) is a volcanic field with no record of eruptions in historic time.

Rahat, Harrat (Saudi Arabia: 23.08N, 39.78E).
Harrat Rahat (5,722 ft./1,744 m.) is a volcanic field. The earliest recorded eruption occurred in A.D. 641. The most recent eruption occurred in 1256.

Raikoke (Kuril Is.: 48.29N, 153.25E).
Raikoke (1,807 ft./551 m.) is a stratovolcano in the central Kuril Islands. The earliest recorded eruption occurred in 1765. A major eruption in 1778 caused 15 deaths. A third, and most recent, eruption occurred in 1924.

Rainier, Mt. (for Peter Rainier [1742–1808], British admiral) [**Tacoma** (from Native American word meaning "mountain")] (Washington, USA: 46.87N, 121.76W).
Mount Rainier (14,409 ft./4,392 m.) is a stratovolcano and the highest in the Cascade Ranger. Radiocarbon datings indicate at least 11 eruptions from approximately 6800 B.C. Several eruptions were reported in the nineteenth century, but none substantiated as genuine. Tree ring count shows that the most recent eruption was in 1825. Mt. Rainier is one of largest the volcanoes in North America.

Rajabasa (Sumatra: 5.78S, 105.62E).
Rajabasa (4,203 ft./1,281 m.) is a stratovolcano with fumarolic activity. There is no record of eruptions in historic time.

Ranakah, Gunung (Flores I., Indonesia: 8.62S, 120.52E).
Gunung Ranakah (6,890 ft./2,100 m.) is composed of lava domes. The earliest recorded eruption occurred in 1987. The most recent eruption took place in 1991.

Ranau (Sumatra: 4.83S, 103.92E).
Ranau (6,172 ft./1,881 m.) is a Holocene caldera with no record of eruptions in historic time.

Raoul I. (Kermadec Is.: 29.27S, 177.92W).
Raoul Island (1,692 ft./516 m.) is a stratovolcano in the Kermadec Islands. The earliest recorded eruption occurred in 1814. There have been 13 subsequent eruptions, most recently in 1965.

Rasshua (Kuril Is.: 47.77N, 153.02E).
Rasshua (3,135 ft./956 m.) is a stratovolcano in the central Kuril Islands. The only two recorded eruptions occurred in 1846 and 1957.

Raton-Clayton (*Raton* from Spanish, "mouse"; *Clayton* for Clayton C. Dorsey, landowner's son) (New Mexico, USA: 36.42N, 104.08W).
Raton-Clayton (10,990 ft./3,350 m.) is a Holocene volcanic field with no record of eruptions in historic time.

Raung (Java: 8.12S, 114.04E).
Raung (10,928 ft./3,332 m.) is a stratovolcano with a circular summit caldera. The earliest recorded eruption occurred in 1593, with 10,000 fatalities reported. There have been over 50 eruptions since then, most recently in June of 1997. Thousands died in a 1638 eruption when they were caught in a flood and mud flow between the Stail and Klatak Rivers.

Rausu (Hokkaido, Japan: 44.07N, 145.12E).
Rausu (5,445 ft./1,660 m.) is a Holocene stratovolcano. There is no record of eruptions in historic time.

Recheschnoi (Umnak I., Aleutian Is., Alaska, USA: 53.15N, 168.55W).
Recheschnoi (6,509 ft./1,984 m.) is a Holocene stratovolcano near the Vseidof volcano on Umnak Island. There is no evidence of historical eruptions.

Reclus (Chile: 50.98S, 73.70W).
Reclus is a Holocene stratovolcano with no record of eruptions in historic time.

Red Cones (California, USA: 37.58N, 119.05W).
Red Cones (9,016 ft./2,748 m.) are Holocene cinder cones with no record of eruptions in historic time.

Redondo, Cerro (Spanish, "round peak") (Chile: 39.27S, 71.70W).
Cerro Redondo is composed of Holocene cinder cones with no recorded eruptions in historic time.

Redoubt (for mountain's resemblance to fortification) (Alaska, USA: 60.48N, 152.75W).
Redoubt (10,194 ft./3,108 m.) is a stratovolcano in Cok Inlet in the eastern Aleutian arc. The earliest recorded eruption occurred in 1902, but radiocarbon and ash layer datings show several eruptions before this; the first in approximately 5740 B.C. There have been at least 30 eruptions in the past 10,000 years. During the most recent eruption in 1990, KLM 747 aircraft flew into the ash cloud, lost engine power, and made an emergency landing at Anchorage. This eruption was one of the most damaging eruptions in United States history.

Reporoa (Maori *repo*, "swamp," *roa*, "long") (New Zealand: 38.42S, 176.33E).
Reporoa (1,942 ft./592 m.) is a caldera with likely volcanic activity in the past 2,000 years.

Resago, Volcán (Chile: 36.45S, 70.92W).
Volcán Resago (5,085 ft./1,550 m.) is a Holocene cinder cone with no record of eruptions in historic time.

Reventador (Spanish, "troublemaker") (Ecuador: 0.08S, 77.66W).
Reventador (11,687 ft./3,562 m.) is a stratovolcano in the Eastern Cordillera of the Andes. The earliest recorded eruption occurred in 1541. There have been at least 24 subsequent eruptions, most recently in January of 1976.

Revillagigedo I. (for Juan Vicente de Güemes Pacheco de Padilla, conde de Revillagigedo [1740–1799], Spanish viceroy of Mexico) (Alaska, USA: 55.32N, 131.05W).
Rivillagigedo Island (1,640 ft./500 m.) is likely composed of Holocene cinder cones with no record of eruptions in historic time.

Reykjanes (Icelandic, "smoky head") (Iceland: 63.88N, 22.50W).
Reykjanes (755 ft./230 m.) is composed of crater rows. The earliest recorded eruption occurred in 1211, with radiocarbon dating indicating prior events in approximately 400 and 200 B.C. and ash layer dating giving the earliest eruption around 1800 B.C. The last certain recorded eruption was in 1226.

Reykjaneshryggur (Icelandic, "smoky head mountain") (southwest of Iceland: 63.67N, 23.33W).
Reykjaneshryggur (262 ft./80 m.) is a submarine volcano whose earliest recorded eruption occurred in approximately 1179. The most recent eruption took place in 1970.

Riang Kotang (Flores I., Indonesia: 8.30S, 122.89E).
Riang Kotang (656 ft./200 m.) is a fumarolic field with no record of eruptions in historic time.

Rincón de la Vieja (Costa Rica: 10.83N, 85.32W).
Rincón de la Vieja (6,285 ft./1,916 m.) is a stratovolcano with six active vents in the northwestern corner of Costa Rica. The volcano's name came from a legend of a native princess, Curabanda, who fell in love with Mixcoac, the chief of an enemy tribe. Curabanda's father captured Mixcoac and threw him into the volcano. After Mixcoac's death Curabanda went to live on the side of the volcano, where she gave birth to a child. She threw her child into the volcano, where he could be with his father. Curabanda spent the rest of her life living near the volcano's crater. The local people named her home Rincón de le Vieja, meaning "the nook where the old one lives." The earliest recorded eruption occurred in 1765. There were recent eruptions in 1992 and February of 1998.

Rinjani (Lombok I., Indonesia: 8.42S, 116.47E).
Gunung Rinjani (12,225 ft./3,726 m.) is a stratovolcano which is part of the Segara Anak Caldera on Lombok Island. The earliest recorded eruption occurred in 1847. The most recent eruption occurred in July of 1994.

Rishiri (Hokkaido, Japan: 45.18N, 141.25E).
Rishiri (5,640 ft./1,719 m.) is a Holocene stratovolcano with no record of eruptions in historic time.

Ritter I. (northeast of New Guinea: 5.52S, 148.12E).
Ritter Island (459 ft./140 m.) is a stratovolcano in Papua New Guinea. The earliest recorded eruption occurred in 1700. An avalanche of debris during an 1888 phreatic eruption caused a giant wave that killed hundreds along the coasts of neighboring islands. The two most recent eruptions in 1972 and 1974 were submarine, causing tsunamis but no fatalities.

Robinson Crusoe I. [Más a Tierra] (Juan Fernández Is., Chile: 33.66S, 78.85W).
Robinson Crusoe Island (3,025 ft./922 m.) is composed of shield volcanoes. The sole eruption to date was recorded by Charles Darwin in 1835. Alexander Selkirk (Robinson Crusoe) did not report any eruptions when living there from 1704 to 1709.

Robledo (Argentina: 26.77S, 67.72W).
Robledo (14,436 ft./4,400 m.) is a Holocene caldera with no record of eruptions in historic time.

Rocard (Society Is., Central Pacific: 17.64S, 148.60W).
Rocard (-6,890 ft./-2,100 m.) is a submarine volcano. There were possible eruptions in 1966, 1971 and 1972.

Rokatenda *see* **Paluweh.**

Romanovka (Kamchatka, Russia: 55.65N, 158.80E).
Romanovka (4,731 ft./1,442 m.) is a Holocene stratovolcano with no record of eruptions in historic time.

Rota (Nicaragua: 12.55N, 86.75W).
Rota (2,743 ft./836 m.) is a Holocene shield volcano with no record of eruptions in historic time.

Rotorua (Maori *roto,* "lake," *rua,* "second") (New Zealand: 38.08S, 176.27E).
Rotorua (2,484 ft./757 m.) is a Pleistocene caldera with geysers.

Roundtop (Unimak I., Aleutian Is., Alaska, USA: 54.80N, 163.60W).
Roundtop (6,139 ft./1,871 m.) is a glaciated stratovolcano in the Aleutian

Island chain. There are no recorded eruptions in historic time, though hot-springs activity was reported on the slopes in the 1930s.

Royal Society Range (Antarctica: 78.25S, 163.60E).

The Royal Society Range (9,843 ft./3,000 m.) is composed of Holocene cinder cones. There have been no recorded eruptions in historic time.

Ruang (Sangihe Is., Indonesia: 2.28N, 125.42E).

Ruang (2,379 ft./725 m.) is an island stratovolcano near the southern end of Sangihi Island. The earliest recorded eruption occurred in 1808. An eruption of 1871 may have caused the deaths of as many as 400 people in giant waves generated by the partial collapse of the lava dome. A subsequent eruption occurred in 1949 and there were reports of an eruption in June of 1996.

Ruapehu (Maori *rua*, "hole," "chasm," *pahu*, "drum") (New Zealand: 39.28S, 175.57E).

Ruapehu (9,174 ft./2,797 m.) is an andesite stratovolcano, and the tallest mountain on North Island. The earliest recorded eruption occurred in 1861, but radiocarbon and ash layer datings indicate four eruptions before this; the first in approximately 7840 B.C. Since then there have been over 50 eruptions recorded, most recently in September of 1995. Although there was no eruption, 151 died in 1953 when the summit crater lake drained following the collapse of an ash barrier retaining it. A mud flow swept away part of Tangiwi bridge just before the arrival of the Wellington-Auckland express. The locomotive, tender, and five cars plunged into the river.

Ruby (Mariana Is.: 15.62N, 145.57E).

Ruby (-755 ft./-230 m.) is a submarine volcano whose sole recorded eruption to date occurred in 1966.

Ruby Mountain (British Columbia, Canada: 59.68N, 133.32W).

Ruby Mountain (4,997 ft./1,523 m.) is composed of cinder cones whose sole recorded eruption to date occurred in 1898.

Rudakov (Kuril Is.: 45.88N, 149.83E).

Rudakov (1,777 ft./542 m.) is a Holocene stratovolcano located on Urup Island in the southern Kuril Islands. There are no recorded historic eruptions.

Ruiz, Nevado del (Colombia: 4.89N, 75.53W).

Nevado del Ruiz (17,453 ft./5,321 m.) is an active stratovolcano capped with snow and ice. The earliest recorded eruption occurred in 1570. Mud flows during the 1595 eruption killed around 630 people, and perhaps as many as 1,000 lost their lives from the same cause during the 1845 eruption. An eruption of 1985, the most devastating to date, had a death toll put at around 23,000, most

of them inhabitants of town of Armero. This was the second most deadly eruption in the twentieth entury. The most recent eruption occurred in 1991.

Rumble I (New Zealand: 35.50S, 178.87E).
Rumble I (-3,610 ft./-1,100 m.) is one of five volcanic centers on White
Island. There is evidence of activity in the past 10,000 years, but no record of
historic eruptions.

Rumble II (New Zealand: 35.43S, 178.65E).
Rumble II (-2,890 ft./-880 m.) is one of five volcanic centers on White
Island. There is evidence of activity in the past 10,000 years, but no record of
historic eruptions.

Rumble III (New Zealand: 35.74S, 178.48E).
Rumble III (-460 ft./-140 m.) is one of five volcanic centers on White
Island. It is the most active volcano on the island with recorded eruptions in
1958, 1963, 1970, 1973 and, most recently, in 1986.

Rumble IV (New Zealand: 36.22S, 178.05E).
Rumble IV (-1,480 ft./-450 m.) is one of five volcanic centers on White
Island. There is evidence of activity in the past 10,000 years, but no record of
historic eruptions. Fumaroles have been detected at Rumble IV.

Rumble V (New Zealand: 36.14S, 178.18E).
Rumble V (-3,610 ft./-1,100 m.) is one of five volcanic centers on White
Island. There is evidence of activity in the past 10,000 years, but no record of
historic eruptions. Fumaroles have been detected at Rumble V.

Rungwe (Tanzania: 9.13S, 33.67E).
Rungwe (9,715 ft./2,961 m.) is a Holocene stratovolcano with no record
of eruptions in historic time.

Rusekere (Uganda: 0.73N, 30.38E).
Rusekere (5,299 ft./1,615 m.) are Holocene tuff cones with no record of
eruptions in historic time.

S

Saba (West Indies: 17.63N, 63.23W).
Saba (2,910 ft./887 m.) is the northernmost active stratovolcano in the
West Indies. The sole recorded eruption to date occurred in approximately 1636.

Sabancaya (Peru: 15.78S, 71.85W).
Sabancaya (19,578 ft./5,967 m.) is a glacier-topped stratovolcano in
the Andes Mountains. There were no known historical eruptions prior to

December of 1986, when volcanic ash and gases killed cattle, but there were no reported fatalities of people. A lava dome was built at the summit crater over the next 18 months.

Sacabaya, Volcán de (Bolivia: 18.62S, 68.75W).
Volcán de Sacabaya (13,829 ft./4,215 m.) is composed of Holocene cinder cones. There have been no recorded eruptions in historic time.

Saddle Butte (Oregon, USA: 43.00N, 117.80W).
Saddle Butte (5,578 ft./1,700 m.) is a Holocene volcanic field with no record of eruptions in historic time.

St. Andrew Strait (Admiralty Is.: 2.38S, 147.35E).
St. Andrew Strait (885 ft./270 m.) is a complex volcano. The earliest recorded eruption occurred in 1883. The most recent eruption, from Tuluman cone, began in 1953 and ended in 1957.

St. Catherine (West Indies: 12.15N, 6167W).
St. Catherine (2,756 ft./840 m.) is a Holocene stratovolcano with no record of eruptions in historic time.

St. Helens, Mt. (for Alleyne Fitzherbert, Baron St. Helens [1753–1839], British ambassador to Spain) (Washington, USA: 46.20N, 122.18W).
Mount St. Helens (8,363 ft./2,549) is a stratovolcano in Washington State. The earliest recorded eruption occurred in 1831, but radiocarbon and tree ring datings indicate at least a dozen events before this, beginning in approximately 2335 B.C. A major eruption in 1980 caused 57 deaths, all attributable to lateral air blast, ash falls, and mud flows. (Half of the casualties were asphyxiated by ash.) Some isolated deaths were caused indirectly. A crop duster pilot hit powerlines during ash fall; elderly folk collapsed while shoveling ash from property. Millions of trees were flattened by the air blast over an area of almost 600 square kilometers . The most recent eruption occurred in 1990.

St. Michael (Alaska, USA: 63.45N, 162.12W).
St. Michael (2,346 ft./715 m.) is composed of cinder cones with no record of historic eruptions, but likely volcanic activity in historic times.

St. Paul I. (Alaska, USA: 57.18N, 17030W).
St. Paul Island (666 ft./203 m.) is composed of Holocene cinder cones with no record of eruptions in historic time.

St. Paul I. (Indian Ocean: 38.72S, 77.53E).
St. Paul Island (879 ft./268 m.) is a stratovolcano whose sole recorded eruption to date occurred in 1793.

Sairecabur (Chile/Bolivia: 22.73S, 67.88W).
Sairecabur (19,591 ft./5,971 m.) is a Holocene stratovolcano with no record of eruptions in historic time.

Sajama (Bolivia: 18.1S, 68.9W).
Sajama (21,391 ft./6,522 m.) is a stratovolcano in the Bolivian Andes. There have been no eruptions in the past 10,000 years.

Sakar (Papua New Guinea: 5.41S, 148.09E).
Sakar (3,255 ft./992 m.) is a Holocene stratovolcano which has had no recorded historical eruptions.

Sakura-jima (Kyushu, Japan: 31.58N, 130.67E).
Sakura-jima (3,663 ft./1,117 m.) is an active stratovolcano within the Aira Caldera in Kagoshima Bay. The earliest recorded eruption was in 708 A.D., with nine radiocarbon datings before this going back to approximately 7750 B.C. These came from Kita-dake, while later eruptions were from Minami-dake. There have been between 100 to 200 eruptions on Sakura-jima. The eruption of 1779 caused 153 deaths, mainly in giant waves, lava flows, and village burials. An eruption in 1914 caused an earthquake and landslide that killed around 60 people. The most recent eruption began in 1955 and is still ongoing, dumping 1–6 kilograms per square meter of ash on the nearby seaport city of Kagoshima annually.

Salak (Java: 6.72S, 106.73E).
Salak (7,254 ft./2,211 m.) is a stratovolcano whose earliest recorded eruption occurred in 1780. There have been at least four subsequent eruptions, all at the flank vents, most recently in 1938.

San Agustín, Cerro (Bolivia: 21.25S, 67.75W).
Cerro San Agustín (16,339 ft./4,980 m.) is a Holocene stratovolcano with no record of eruptions in historic time.

San Borja Volcanic Field (Mexico: 28.50N, 113.75W).
The San Borja Volcanic Field is composed of Holocene cinder cones. There have been no recorded eruptions in historic time.

San Carlos (Bioko, Equatorial Guinea: 3.35N, 8.52E).
San Carlos (7,415 ft./2,260 m.) is a Holocene shield volcano with no record of eruptions in historic time.

San Cristóbal 1 (Galápagos Is.: 0.88S, 89.50W).
San Cristóbal (2,490 ft./759 m.) is a Holocene shield volcano with no recorded eruptions in historic time.

San Cristóbal 2 (Nicaragua: 12.70N, 87.00W).
San Cristóbal (5,724 ft./1,745 m.) is a stratovolcano with a basaltic cone with a flattened top. It is the youngest volcano in the San Cristobal complex. The earliest recorded eruption occurred in 1528. There have been at least seven subsequent eruptions, most recently in 1997.

San Diego (El Salvador: 14.27N, 89.47W).
San Diego (2,821 ft./860 m.) is a Holocene volcanic field with no record of eruptions in historic time.

San Félix (Pacific Ocean, west of Chile: 26.27S, 80.12W).
San Félix (5,916 ft./1,803 m.) is a Holocene shield volcano with no recorded eruptions in historic time.

San Joaquín (Bioko, Equatorial Guinea: 3.35N, 8.63E).
San Joaquín (6,592 ft./2,009 m.) is a Holocene shield volcano with no record of eruptions in historic time.

San José (Chile: 33.78S, 69.90W).
San José (19,213 ft./5,856 m.) is a stratovolcano whose earliest recorded eruption took place in 1822. The most recent eruption occurred in 1960.

San Luis Gonzaga, Isla (Mexico: 29.81N, 114.38W).
Isla San Luis Gonzaga (525 ft./160 m.) is composed of Holocene explosion craters. There have been no recorded eruptions in historic time.

San Martín, Volcán de (Mexico: 18.57N, 95.17W).
Volcán de San Martín (5,414 ft./1,650 m.) is a shield volcano whose earliest recorded eruption occurred in 1664. The most recent eruption took place in 1796.

San Miguel (El Salvador: 13.43N, 88.27W).
San Miguel (6,988 ft./2,130 m.) is a stratovolcano whose earliest recorded eruption occurred in approximately 1510. The most recent eruption took place in 1986.

Sano, Wai (Flores I., Indonesia: 8.68S, 120.02E).
Wai Sano (2,963 ft./903 m.) is a caldera with fumarolic activity. There have been no eruptions reported in historic time.

San Pedro (Chile: 21.88S, 68.40W).
San Pedro (20,162 ft./6,145 m.) is a stratovolcano whose earliest recorded eruption occurred in approximately 1877. The most recent eruption took place in 1938.

San Pedro-Pellado (Chile: 35.99S, 70.85W).

San Pedro-Pellado (11,880 ft./3,621 m.) is composed of Holocene strato-volcanoes. There have been no recorded eruptions in historic time.

San Quintín Volcanic Field (Mexico: 30.47N, 116.00W).

The San Quintín Volcanic Field (876 ft./267 m.) is composed of Holocene cinder cones. There have been no recorded eruptions in historic time.

San Salvador (El Salvador: 13.74N, 89.29W).

San Salvador (6,211 ft./1,893 m.) is a stratovolcano whose earliest recorded eruption occurred in approximately 1572.

San Vicente (El Salvador: 13.62N, 88.85W).

San Vicente (6,560 ft./2,000 m.) is a stratovolcano with fumarolic activity. There is no record of eruptions in historic time.

San Vicente (Cape Verde Islands: 16.9N, 25.0W).

San Vicente (2,286 ft./697 m.) is a Holocene stratovolcano. There is no record of an eruption in historic time.

Sanbe (Honshu, Japan: 35.13N, 132.62E).

Sanbe (3,694 ft./1,126 m.) is a Holocene caldera with no record of eruptions in historic time.

Sand Mountain Field (Oregon, USA: 44.38N, 121.93W).

The Sand Mountain Field (5,459 ft./1,664 m.) are Holocene cinder cones with likely volcanic activity in the past 2,000 years.

Sanford (for Sanford family) (Alaska, USA: 62.22N, 144.13W).

Sanford (16,233 ft./4,949 m.) is a shield volcano, and the largest in the Wrangell volcanic field. There is no indication of an eruption in historic time.

Sanganguey (Mexico: 21.45N, 104.73W).

Sanganguey (7,720 ft./2,353 m.) is a Holocene stratovolcano with no record of eruptions in historic time.

Sangay (Ecuador: 2.03S, 78.33W).

Sangay (17,154 ft./5,230 m.) is a stratovolcano in the Andes, and the southernmost of the northern volcanic zone. The earliest recorded eruption occurred in 1628. It has been erupting nearly continuously since 1934. Two people died from their injuries in August of 1976 when caught during an explosion near the summit. The most recent eruption occurred in 1993.

Sangeang Api (Indonesia: 8.18S, 119.01E).

Sangeang Api (6,395 ft./1,949 m.) is a complex volcano whose earliest recorded eruption took place in 1512. The most recent eruption occurred in 1988.

Santa Ana (El Salvador: 13.85N, 89.63W).
Santa Ana (7,757 ft./2,365 m.) is a stratovolcano whose earliest recorded eruption occurred in 1521. There were 11 subsequent eruptions, most recently in 1920.

Santa Catarina Range (Mexico: 19.32N, 99.00W).
The Santa Catarina Range (8.970 ft./2,734 m.) is a volcanic field with no record of eruptions in historic time.

Santa Clara (for St. Clare) (Utah, USA: 37.26N, 113.62W).
Santa Clara (4,807 ft./1,465 m.) is a Holocene volcanic field with no recorded eruptions in historic time.

Santa Cruz (Galápagos Is.: 0.62S, 90.33W).
Santa Cruz (2,835 ft./864 m.) is a Holocene shield volcano with no record of eruptions in historic time.

Santa Isabel (Bioko, Equatorial Guinea: 3.58N, 8.75E).
Santa Isabel (6,585 ft./2,007 m.) is a shield volcano whose earliest recorded eruption was in approximately 1898. The most recent eruption occurred in 1923.

Santa Isabel (Colombia: 4.82N, 75.37W).
Santa Isabel (16,241 ft./4,950 m.) is a Holocene shield volcano with no recorded eruptions in historic time.

Santa Isabel, Cerro (Bolivia: 21.67S, 66.50W).
Cerro Santa Isabel (16,732 ft./5,100 m.) is a Holocene stratovolcano with no record of eruptions in historic time.

Santa María (Guatemala: 14.76N, 91.55W).
Santa María (12,372 ft./3,772 m.) is a stratovolcano composed of basaltic andesite. The earliest recorded eruption in 1902 was one of the world's greatest in the twentieth century. Hundreds were killed in collapsing houses. A subsequent malaria outbreak caused the deaths of at least 2,000 and much of Guatemala's coffee industry was destroyed. (Ash fall killed birds but not mosquitoes.). An eruption in 1929 killed at least 200 in lava and pumic flows. Four hikers on a government-sponsored filming mission died during a 1990 eruption. The most recent eruptions occurred in 1993 and 1996.

Santiago (Galápagos Is.: 0.22S, 90.77W).
Santiago (3,018 ft./920 m.) is a shield volcano whose earliest recorded eruption took place in 1897. The most recent eruption occurred in 1906.

Santiago *see* **Masaya.**

Santiago, Cerro (Guatemala: 14.33N, 89.87W).
Cerro Santiago (3,911 ft./1,192 m.) is a Holocene volcanic field with no record of eruptions in historic time.

Santo Antão (Cape Verde Is.: 17.07N, 25.17W).
Santo Antão (6,491 ft./1,979 m.) is a Holocene stratovolcano with no record of an eruption in historic time.

Santoríni (for St. Irina) [**Thera** (for Theras, Spartan leader who colonized island)] (Greece: 36.40N, 25.37E).
Santoríni (1,850 ft./564 m.) is an overlapping complex of shield volcanoes. The earliest recorded eruption occurred in 197 B.C., when the world's first documented "new island" was created. Radiocarbon dating indicates a devastating eruption in approximately 1650 B.C., however, and it was then that the ancient town of Akrotiri was buried in volcanic ash. (Some claim this eruption created the legend of the "lost" continent of Atlantis, because much of island of Thera was submerged then.) An eruption of 1650 killed around 120; some suffocated by sulfurous vapor, others by black dust. The most recent eruption occurred on Nea Kameni, the northern island, in 1950. It was phreatic and lasted less than a month.

Santo Tomas (Luzon, Philippines: 16.33N, 120.55E).
Santo Tomas (7,415 ft./2,260 m.) is likely a stratovolcano with no record of eruptions in historic time.

São Jorge (Azores: 38.65N, 28.08W).
São Jorge (3,455 ft./1,053 m.) is composed of fissure vents. The earliest recorded eruption occurred in 1580. Hundreds of people died during a 1757 submarine eruption, which coincided with Azores' most violent earthquake to date. The most recent eruption took place in 1907.

São Tomé (São Tomé and Príncipe: 0.32N, 6.72E).
São Tomé (6,640 ft./2,024 m.) is a Holocene shield volcano with no record of eruptions in historic time.

Sarigan (Mariana Is.: 16.71N, 145.78E).
Sarigan (1,765 ft./538 m.) is a Holocene stratovolcano with no record of eruptions in historic time.

Sarychev Peak (Matua I., Kuril Is.: 48.09N, 153.20E).
Sarychev Peak (4,906 ft./1,496 m.) is the most active stratovolcano in the Kuril Islands. There have been over 14 eruptions recorded since the earliest in 1765. The most recent eruption occurred in 1989.

Satah Mountain (British Columbia, Canada: 52.47N, 124.70W).
Satah Mountain is a Holocene volcanic field with no record of eruptions in historic time.

Savai'i (Western Samoa: 13.61S, 172.52W).
Savai'i (6,096 ft./1,858 m.) is a shield volcano whose earliest recorded eruption occurred in 1725. The most recent eruption occurred in 1911.

Savo (Solomon Is.: 9.13S, 159.82E).
Savo (2,792 ft./851 m.) is a stratovolcano near Guadalcanal. The earliest recorded eruption occurred in 1568. In a 1840 eruption, most of the population of the island was killed when caught by ash and stones. The most recent eruption occurred in 1847–50.

Sawad, Harrat es- (Yemen: 13.58N, 46.12E).
Harrat es-Sawad (5,699 ft./1,737 m.) is a volcanic field whose sole recorded eruption to date occurred in 1253.

Seal Nunataks Group (Antarctica: 65.03S, 60.05W).
The Seal Nunataks Group (1,207 ft./368 m.) are a group of 16 nunataks (pyroclastic cones) in the Larsen Ice Shelf east of Graham Land Peninsula. The sole recorded eruption to date occurred in 1893. Fumarolic activity was observed in 1982.

Sedankinsky (Kamchatka, Russia: 57.23N, 160.08E).
Sedankinsky (4,072 ft./1,241 m.) is a Holocene shield volcano with no record of eruptions in historic time.

Segererua Plateau (Kenya: 1.57N, 37.90E).
The Segererua Plateau (2,293 ft./699 m.) is composed of pyroclastic cones. There is no record of eruptions in historic time, but it is likely there was volcanic activity in the past 10,000 years.

Seguam (Aleutian Is., Alaska, USA: 52.32N, 172.52W).
Seguam (3,458 ft./1,054 m.) is a stratovolcano whose earliest recorded eruption occurred in 1786. The most recent eruption took place in 1993.

Segula (Aleutian Is., Alaska, USA: 52.02N, 178.13E).
Segula (3,782 ft./1,153 m.) is a Holocene stratovolcano with no record of an eruption in historic time.

Sekincau Belirang (Sumatra: 5.12S, 104.32E).
Sekincau Belirang (5,640 ft./1,719 m.) is a caldera with evidence of fumarolic activity. There have been no recorded eruptions in historic time.

Semeru (Java: 8.11S, 112.92E).
Semeru (12,057 ft./3,676 m.) is a stratovolcano whose earliest recorded eruption occurred in 1818. There have been over 50 eruptions since then. An avalanche of debris during a 1885 eruption killed 74 people, while mud flow in a 1909 eruption caused the deaths of 221. A secondary mud flow in 1981 cost the lives of around 370. The most recent eruption began in 1995. Two German mountain climbers were killed in September of 1997 from a ballistic eruption.

Semisopochnoi (Russian, "seven hills") (Aleutian Is., Alaska, USA: 51.95N, 179.62E).
Semisopochnoi (4,005 ft./1,221 m.) is a volcanic island composed of a shield volcano, a caldera and several stratovolcanoes. The earliest recorded eruption occurred in 1873. The sole recorded eruption since then was recorded in 1987, though there were four unconfirmed eruptions between 1772 and 1830.

Sempu (Sulawesi, Indonesia: 1.14N, 124.73E).
Sempu (5,082 ft./1,549 m.) is a caldera with evidence of fumarolic activity. There is no recorded eruption in historic time.

Sergief (Atka I., Aleutian Is., Alaska, USA: 52.03N, 174.93W).
Sergief (1,837 ft./560 m.) is a stratovolcano with no record of eruptions in historic time.

Serua (Banda Sea, Indonesia: 6.30S, 130.00E).
Serua (2,103 ft./641 m.) is a stratovolcano whose earliest recorded eruption occurred in 1683, when an unspecified number of people were killed in a stream of "burning brimstone." The most recent eruption took place in 1921.

Sessagara (New Guinea: 9.48S, 149.13E).
Sessagara (1,214 ft./370 m.) is a Holocene volcano with no record of eruptions in historic time.

Sete Cidades (San Miguel, Azores: 37.87N, 25.78W).
Sete Cidades (2,807 ft./856 m.) is a stratovolcano with a summit caldera. The earliest recorded eruption occurred in 1638, which formed the islet of Sabrina. The most recent eruption came from a submarine vent in 1880.

Seulawah Agam (Sumatra: 5.42N, 95.60E).
Seulaway Agam (5,663 ft./1,726 m.) is a Holocene stratovolcano with no evidence of eruptions in historic time.

Severgin *see* **Harimkotan**.

Severny (Russian, "northern") (Kamchatka, Russia: 58.28N, 160.87E).
Severny (6,352 ft./1,936 m.) is a Holocene shield volcano with no record of eruptions in historic time.

Shala (Ethiopia: 7.47N, 38.55E).

Shala (6,806 ft./2,075 m.) is a caldera that likely collapsed during the late Pleistocene Era, forming the deepest lake in Ethiopia.

Sharat Kovakab (Syria: 36.53N, 40.85E).

Sharat Kovakab (1,752 ft./534 m.) is a Holocene volcanic field with no eruption recorded in historic time.

Shasta, Mt. (for Native American tribal name) (California, USA: 41.42N, 122.20W).

Mount Shasta (14,161 ft./4,317 m.) is the second highest mountain in the Cascade Range near the California-Oregon border. The sole recorded eruption to date from this stratovolcano occurred in 1786. There are over 20 radiocarbon and ash layer datings before this, going back to approximately 8050 B.C.

Sherman Crater *see* **Mt. Baker.**

Shiga (Honshu, Japan: 36.70N, 138.52E).

Shiga (6,680 ft./2,036 m.) is a Holocene shield volcano with no record of eruptions in historic time.

Shikaribetsu Group (Hokkaido, Japan: 43.28N, 143.08E).

The Shikaribetsu Group (4,692 ft./1,430 m.) is composed of Holocene lava domes. There is no evidence of eruptions in historic time.

Shikotsu (Hokkaido, Japan: 42.70N, 141.33E).

Shikotsu (4,331 ft./1,320 m.) is a caldera near the southwestern end of the Kuril arc. The earliest recorded eruption occurred in 1667. There have been over 30 eruptions since then, all from the Tarumai vent. The most recent eruption was phreatic and occurred in 1982.

Shin-dake *see* **Kuchinoerabu-jima.**

Shin-Iwo-jima (Volcano Is., Japan: 24.28N, 141.52E).

Shin-Iwo-jima (-46 ft./-14 m.), also known as Fukutoku-okanaba, is an andesitic submarine volcano. The earliest recorded submarine eruption was in 1904. There were subsequent eruptions in 1914, 1974, 1986 and, most recently, in November of 1992.

Shinmoe-dake *see* **Kirishima.**

Shira *see* **Kilimanjaro.**

Shiretoko-Iwa-Zan (Hokkaido, Japan: 44.13N, 145.17E).

Shiretoko-Iwa-Zan (5,126 ft./1,563 m.) is a stratovolcano with two craters at its summit at Hokkaido's northeast tip. The earliest recorded eruption occurred in 1876. There have been at least three eruptions since, most recently in 1936.

Shiribetsu (Hokkaido, Japan: 42.77N, 140.92E).

Shiribetsu (3,632 ft./1,107 m). is a Holocene stratovolcano with no evidence of eruptions in historic time.

Shirinki (Kuril Is.: 50.20N, 154.98E).

Shirinki (2,496 ft./761 m.) is a Holocene stratovolcano on Onekotan in the northern Kuril Islands. There have been no recorded historic eruptions.

Shishaldin (Unimak I., Aleutian Is., Alaska, USA: 54.75N, 163.97W).

Shishaldin (9,374 ft./2,857 m.) is a stratovolcano with a small summit crater. The earliest recorded eruption occurred in 1775. There have been nearly 30 eruptions since, including several months of activity in 1986-87. There have been nearly continuous eruptions since 1993.

Shishel (Kamchatka, Russia: 57.45N, 160.37E).

Shishel (8,284 ft./2,525 m.) is a Holocene shield volcano with no record of eruptions in historic time.

Shiveluch (Kamchatka, Russia: 56.65N, 161.36E).

Shiveluch (10,768 ft./3,283 m.) is a stratovolcano with faults that split it into two parts. The earliest recorded eruption occurred in 1854, but radiocarbon and ash layer datings before this indicate eruptions going back to approximately 7150 B.C. There were violent eruptions in 1854 and 1964. There have been over 28 eruptions, most recently in 1993.

Shoshone Lava Field (Idaho, USA: 43.07N, 114.43W).

The Shoshone Lava Field (5,003 ft./1,525 m.) is composed of Holocene cinder cones. There have been no recorded eruptions in historic time.

Sibayak (Sumatra: 3.21N, 98.47E).

Sibayak (7,257 ft./2,212 m.) is a stratovolcano whose sole recorded eruption to date occurred in 1881.

Silali (Kenya: 1.15N,36.23E).

Silali (5,013 ft./1,528 m.) is a shield volcano with no likely eruptions in the past 2,000 years.

Silay (Negros, Philippines: 10.77N, 123.33E).

Silay (5,036 ft./1,535 m.) is a Holocene stratovolcano with no record of eruptions in historic time.

Silverthrone (Canada: 51.43N, 126.30W).

Silverthrone (10,368 ft./3,160 m.) is a Holocene caldera with no record of eruptions in historic time.

Simbo (Solomon Is.: 8.29S, 156.52E).

Simbo (1,099 ft./335 m.) is likely a stratovolcano with no record of eruptions in historic time.

Sinabung (Sumatra: 3.17N, 98.39E).

Sinabung (8.071 ft./2,460 m.) is a stratovolcano with fumarolic activity. There have been no recorded eruptions in historic time.

Sinarka (Kuril Is.: 48.87N, 154.17E).

Sinarka (3064 ft./934 m.) is a stratovolcano on Shiashkotan in the northern Kuril Islands. The first recorded eruption occurred in 1725. A major eruption occurred in 1872, lasting through 1878. The Ainu village was destroyed during this period and a lava dome was constructed.

Singu Plateau (Myanmar: 22.70N, 95.98E).

The Singu Plateau (1,663 ft./507 m.) is composed of Holocene fissure vents with no recorded eruptions in historic time.

Singuil, Cerro (El Salvador: 14.05N, 89.63W).

Cerro Singuil (3,143 ft./958 m.) is a Holocene cinder cone with no record of eruptions in historic time.

Siple (named for Paul A. Siple [1908–1968], American polar explorer) (Antarctica: 73.43S, 126.67W).

Siple (10,204 ft./3,110 m.) is a shield volcano with a summit caldera forming an island on the Pacific coast of Marie Byrd Land. There have been no eruptions recorded in historic time.

Sirung (Pantar I., Indonesia: 8.51S, 124.15E).

Sirung (2,828 ft./862 m.) is a complex volcano whose earliest recorded eruption occurred in 1934. The most recent eruption took place in 1970.

Slamet (Java: 7.24S, 109.21E).

Slamet (11,260 ft./3,432 m.) is a stratovolcano with a cluster of 17 cinder cones. The earliest recorded eruption occurred in 1772. There have been over 30 eruptions since then, most recently in 1989.

Smirnov (Kuril Is.: 44.43N, 146.13E).

Smirnov (3,900 ft./1189 m.) is a Holocene stratovolcano on Kunashir Island in the southern Kuril Islands. There have been no recorded eruptions in historical time.

Smith Rock (Izu Is., Japan: 31.32N, 140.05E).

Smith Rock (446 ft./136 m.) is a submarine volcano whose earliest recorded eruption occurred in approximately 1672. The most recent eruption took place in 1916.

Snæfellsjökull (Icelandic, "snowy peak glacier") (Iceland: 64.80N, 23.78W). Snæfellsjökull (4,751 ft./1,448 m.) is a stratovolcano with radiocarbon and ash layer datings showing nine eruptions between approximately 6050 B.C. and 200 A.D.

Snegovoy (Russian, "snow-covered") (Kamchatka, Russia: 58.20N, 160.97E). Snegovoy (7,116 ft./2,169 m.) is a Holocene shield volcano with no record of eruptions in historic time.

Snezhny (Russian, "snowy") (Kamchatka, Russia: 58.02N, 160.75). Snezhny (2,169 m.) is a Holocene shield volcano with no record of eruptions in historic time.

Snowy (Alaska, USA: 58.33N, 154.68W). Snowy (7,090 ft./2,161 m.) is a stratovolcano with fumarolic activity. There have been no recorded eruptions in historic time.

Soche (Ecuador: 0.55N, 77.58W). Soche (12,976 ft./3,955 m.) is a Holocene stratovolcano with no record of eruptions in historic time.

Socompa (Chile/Argentina: 24.40S, 68.25W). Socompa (19,853 ft./6,051 m.) is a stratovolcano with carbon dating suggesting the earliest eruption occurring in approximately 5250 B.C., when the western flank collapsed, causing a massive avalanche. Deposit from it is preserved over an area of nearly 500 square kilometers in the Atacama Desert.

Socorro (Mexico: 18.78N, 110.95W). Socorro (3,445 ft./1,050 m.) is an island formed by a large shield volcano containing a summit caldera. The earliest recorded eruption occurred in 1905. There was a submarine eruption recorded in 1993.

Sodore (Ethiopia: 8.43N, 39.35E). Sodore (5,791 ft./1,765 m.) consists of pyroclastic cones likely formed during the Holocene Era.

Sollipulli (Chile: 38.97S, 71.52W). Sollipulli (7,487 ft./2,282 m.) is a dormant stratovolcano topped with an ice-filled caldera. The last major eruption occurred over 3,000 years ago. The most recent eruption occurred in 1240. There is still evidence of fumaroles at the volcano site.

Soputan (Sulawesi, Indonesia: 1.11N, 124.72E). Soputan (5,853 ft./1,784 m.) is a small conical stratovolcano on the rime of Tondaro Caldera on Sulawesi. The earliest recorded eruption occurred in 1785. The most recent eruption lasted from October of 1991 through mid–1993. Volcanic activity continued to be reported in late 1996.

Soretimeat (Vanua Lava I., Vanuatu: 13.80S, 167.47E).
Soretimeat (3,021 ft./921 m.) is a complex volcano at the center of Vanua Lava Island. There were two recorded explosive eruptions in the nineteenth century from the central vent in 1860 and 1865. The most recent eruption in 1966 was phreatic and from the northwest flank.

Sorikmarapi (Sumatra: 0.69N, 99.58E).
Sorikmarapi (7,038 ft./2,145 m.) is a stratovolcano with a summit crater containing a lake. The earliest recorded eruption occurred in approximately 1829. An eruption in 1892 cost the lives of 180 people in Sibangor village, seven kilometers from the summit. The most recent eruption occurred in 1986.

Sorkale (Ethiopia: 13.18N, 41.72E).
Sorkale (5,286 ft./1,611 m.) is a Holocene stratovolcano with no record of eruptions in historic time.

Sotara (Colombia: 2.12N, 76.58W).
Sotara (14,436 ft./4,400 m.) is a Holocene stratovolcano with no record of eruptions in historic time.

Soufrière Guadeloupe (French *soufrière*, "sulfur mine," from *soufre*, "sulfur") (Guadeloupe, West Indies: 16.05N, 1.67W).
Soufrière Guadeloupe (4,812 ft./1,467 m.) is a stratovolcano in the western half of the island of Guadeloupe. It produced the first observed volcanic eruption in the West Indies in 1660. Radiocarbon datings indicate at least 10 before this, from approximately 6550 B.C. The most recent eruption occurred in 1976. French *soufrière* is an alternate term for a *solfatara*. *See* **Campi Flegrei**.

Soufrière Hills (French *soufrière*, "sulfur mine," from *soufre*, "sulfur") (Montserrat, West Indies: 16.72N, 2.18W).
Soufrière Hills (3,002 ft./915 m.) is a stratovolcano located on the southern end of the island of Montserrat. An eruption from Castle Peak is indicated by radiocarbon dating in approximately 1630. Two thirds of Montserrat's population evacuated to the sparsely populated northern region when Chances Peak erupted in 1995. The capital, Plymouth, was evacuated in 1996. High-speed lava flows killed 26 people, and whole valleys and forests vanished under thick mud, during an eruption in 1997.

Soufrière St. Vincent (French *soufrière*, "sulfur mine," from *soufre*, "sulfur") (St. Vincent, West Indies: 13.33N, 1.18W).
Soufrière St. Vincent (4,000 ft./1,220 m.) is a stratovolcano with a crater lake. It is the youngest volcano on St. Vincent Island. The earliest recorded eruption occurred in 1718, but radiocarbon datings reveal 14 before this, going back to approximately 2380 B.C. There were violent eruptions in 1718, 1812 and 1902, the latter killing over 1,600 people. Recent eruptions occurred in 1972 and 1979.

South Island (L. Turkana, Kenya: 2.63N, 36.60E).

South Island (2,300 ft./700 m.), also known as Hohnel Island, is located in Lake Turkana (formerly Lake Rudolf) in northern Kenya. It is a volcano complex composed of a central ridge of ash cones. The sole recorded eruption to date occurred in 1888, but this was possibly only sulfur steam.

South Sister (for southernmost of Three Sisters peaks) (Oregon, USA: 44.10N, 121.77W).

South Sister (10,360 ft./3,158 m.) is the youngest of the Three Sisters. The complex volcano is composed of andesite, dacite and rhyodacite. The most recent eruption occurred approximately 1,900 years ago.

Southern Sikhote-Alin (Russia: 44.50N, 135.50E).

The Southern Sikhote-Alin is a Holocene volcanic field with no record of eruptions in historic time.

Southwest Usangu Basin (Tanzania: 8.75S, 33.80E).

The Southwest Usangu Basin (7,149 ft./2,179 m.) is a Holocene volcanic field with no record of eruptions in historic time.

Spectrum Range (British Columbia, Canada: 57.43N, 130.68W).

Spectrum Range (7,973 ft./2,430 m.) is a Holocene shield volcano with no record of eruptions in historic time.

Spurr, Mt. (for J.E. Spurr [1870–1950], geologist and explorer of Alaska) (Alaska, USA: 61.30N, 152.25W).

Mount Spurr (11,066 ft./3,374 m.) is a stratovolcano composed of andesite at the center of an older caldera. It is the highest volcano of the Aleutian arc. The earliest recorded eruption occurred in 1953, sending ash more than 19 km. into the atmosphere. The most recent eruption occurred in 1992 and also deposited ash on the city of Anchorage.

Squaw Ridge Field (Oregon, USA: 43.47N, 120.75W).

The Squaw Ridge Field (5,614 ft./1,711 m.) is a Holocene volcanic field with no record of eruptions in historic time.

Srednii (Russian, "middle") (northwest of Ushishur I., Kuril Is.: 47.60N, 152.92E).

Srednii (108 ft./36 m.) is a submarine volcano northwest of Ushishur Island in the central Kuril Islands. There was an unconfirmed eruption in 1880.

Steamboat Springs (springs sound like chugging steamboat) (Nevada, USA: 39.37N, 119.72W).

Steamboat Springs (4,643 ft./1,415 m.) is composed of Pleistocene lava domes with fumarolic activity.

Steller (for G.W. Steller, naturalist) (Alaska, USA: 58.43N, 154.40W).
Steller (7,454 ft./2,272 m.) is a volcano with no known eruptions in historic time.

Stromboli (Greek *strongule*, "round one") (Lipari Is., Italy: 38.79N, 15.21E).
Stromboli (2,900 ft./926 m.) is a stratovolcano on one of Italy's Aeolian Islands. It is one of the most active volcanoes on the planet. The earliest recorded eruption occurred in approximately 450 B.C. There have been over 60 eruptions since then, and some are still ongoing. (Regular nighttime explosions of glowing lava have given the volcano the nickname "Lighthouse of the Mediterranean." *Cf.* **Izalco**.). A biologist close to the crater rim during a 1986 eruption died when he was hit on his head by a falling rock. The eruptions of 1919 and 1930 killed four each. Stromboli gave its name to the *Strombolian* type of volcanic activity.

Stubel *see* **Ksudach.**

Sturge I. (Balleny Is., Antarctica: 67.40S, 164.83E).
Sturge Island (3,829 ft./1,167 m.) is a stratovolcano with no record of eruptions in historic time.

Suchitán Volcanic Field (Guatemala: 14.40N, 89.78W).
The Suchitán Volcanic Field (6,700 ft./2,042 m.) is composed of Holocene stratovolcanoes with no record of eruptions in historic time.

Sukaria Caldera (Flores I., Indonesia: 8.79S, 121.77E).
The Sukaria Caldera (4,920 ft./1,500 m.) is a caldera with fumarolic activity. There have been no recorded eruptions in historic time.

Sumaco (Ecuador: 0.54S, 77.63W).
Sumaco (13,090 ft./3,990 m.) is a stratovolcano with recorded eruptions in 1650, 1895 and, most recently, in 1933.

Sumbing 1 (Java: 7.38S, 110.06E).
Sumbing (11,056 ft./3,371 m.) is a stratovolcano in central Java. The sole recorded eruption to date occurred from the central vent in 1730.

Sumbing 2 (Sumatra: 2.42S, 101.73E).
Sumbing (8,229 ft./2,508 m.) is a stratovolcano with two recorded eruptions to date, 1909 and 1921.

Sumiyoche-ike (Kyushu, Japan: 31.77N, 130.59E).
Sumiyochi-ike (328 ft./100 m.) is a Maars volcano with no record of eruptions in historic time.

Sundoro (Java: 7.30S, 109.99E).

Sundoro (10,335 ft./3,151 m.) is a stratovolcano in central Java. There have been eight historic eruptions since the earliest recorded in 1818. The most recent occurred in 1971.

Sunset Crater (Arizona, USA: 35.37N, 111.50W).

Sunset Crater (8,026 ft./2,447 m.) is a scoria cone in the eastern part of the San Francisco volcanic field. Native American legends describe eruptions here, now dated by tree ring count in approximately 1065. Magnetic dating indicates subsequent eruptions in the approximate years 1100, 1180, and 1220. The crater was named in 1892 for cinder colors, which grade down from the summit through yellow, orange, and red to black ash at the base of the cone. A National Monument was established here in 1930.

Suoh (Sumatra: 5.25S, 104.27E).

Suoh (3,280 ft./1,000 m.) is a Maars volcano whose sole recorded eruption to date occurred in 1933.

Suphan Dagi (Turkey: 38.92N, 42.82E).

Suphan Dagi (14,548 ft./4,434 m.) is a Holocene stratovolcano with no record of eruptions in historic time.

Supply Reef (Mariana Is.: 20.13N, 145.10E).

Supply Reef (-26 ft./-8 m.) is a submarine volcano with two eruptions recorded to date, 1969 and 1989.

Surtsey *see* **Eldfell**.

Suswa (Kenya: 0.92S, 36.45E).

Suswa (7,728 ft./2,356 m.) is a Holocene shield volcano in the center of the Kenya Rift Valley. It is also known as Ol Doinyo Nyukie ("The Red Mountain"). There is no evidence of eruptions in historical time.

Suwanose-jima (Ryukyu Is., Japan: 29.53N, 129.72E).

Suwanose-jima (2,621 ft./799 m.) is a volcanic island whose earliest recorded eruption occurred in 1813. There was a major eruption in 1884-85, forcing the evacuation of the island, which remained uninhabited for nearly 70 years. Recent eruptions occurred in 1993 and 1996-97.

T

Taal (Luzon, Philippines: 14.00N, 120.99E).

Taal (1,312 ft./400 m.) is a stratovolcano whose earliest recorded eruption was in 1572. There have been over 30 eruptions logged since then, most recently in 1977. The most disastrous eruption was that of 1911, with at least 1,330 deaths in flows of lava and pumice. The eruption of 1965 caused around 200 deaths, most of them in giant waves which capsized boats full of fleeing inhabitants. The volcano has been restless since 1991, with earthquakes and ground fracturing. It is considered by volcanologists to be one of the most potentially damaging volcanoes in the next decade.

Table Top-Wide Bay (Unalaska I., Aleutian Is., Alaska, USA: 53.98N, 166.67W).
Table Top-Wide Bay (2,625 ft./800 m.) is composed of cinder cones with likely volcanic activity in the past 10,000 years. There is no record of eruptions in historic time.

Taburete (El Salvador: 13.45N, 88.53W).
Taburete (3,845 ft./1,172 m.) is a Holocene stratovolcano with no record of eruptions in historic time.

Tacana (Mexico: 15.13N, 92.11W).
Tacana (13,485 ft./4,110 m.) is a stratovolcano whose earliest recorded eruption occurred in 1878. The most recent eruption took place in 1986.

Tacoma, Mt. *see* **Mt. Rainier.**

Tacora (Chile: 17.72S, 69.77W).
Tacora (19,620 ft./5,980 m.) is a stratovolcano with fumarolic activity. There have been no recorded eruptions in historic time.

Taftan (Iran: 28.60N, 61.60E).
Taftan (13,288 ft./4,050 m.) is a Holocene stratovolcano with no record of eruptions in historic time.

Tajumulco (Guatemala: 15.03N, 91.90W).
Tajumulco (13,846 ft./4,220 m.) is a Holocene stratovolcano with no record of eruptions in historic time.

Takahara (Honshu, Japan: 36.90N, 139.78E).
Takahara (5,889 ft./1,795 m.) is a Holocene stratovolcano with no record of eruptions in historic time.

Takahe (Antarctica: 76.28S, 112.08W).
Takahe (11,352 ft./3,460 m.) is a shield volcano with an ice core. There have been no recorded eruptions in historic time.

Takawangha (Tanaga I., Aleutian Is., Alaska, USA: 51.87N, 178.02W).
Takawangha (4,795 ft./1,462 m.) is a Holocene stratovolcano in the Aleutian arc that has not erupted in historical time.

Takuan Group (Bougainville: 6.44S, 155.61E).

The Takuan Group (7,251 ft./2,210 m.) is a Holocene volcanic complex on Bougainville Island in the Solomon Islands chain. There is no evidence of historic eruptions.

Talagabodas (Java: 7.21S, 108.07E).

Talagabodas (3,347 ft./1,020 m.) is a stratovolcano with fumarolic activity. There have been no recorded eruptions in historic time.

Talakmau (Sumatra: 0.08N, 99.98E).

Talakmau (9,554 ft./2,912 m.) is a Holocene complex volcano with no record of eruptions in historic time.

Talang (Sumatra: 0.98S, 100.68E).

Talang (9,502 ft./2,896 m.) is a stratovolcano whose earliest recorded eruption occurred in 1883. There have been at least eight subsequent eruptions, most recently in 1968.

Tambora (Sumbawa I., Indonesia: 8.25S, 118.00E).

Tambora (9,348 ft./2,850 m.) is a stratovolcano that forms the Sanggar peninsula of Sumbawa Island. The earliest recorded eruption was in 1812, with radiocarbon datings showing three before this, the first in approximately 3910 B.C. A huge eruption in 1815 caused the deaths of around 10,000 people from ejected lava impacts, ash falls, and giant waves, while further estimates indicate 82,000 perished as the result of starvation and disease. The eruption was the largest in history, discharging nearly 150 km 3 of fragmented rock, with ash fallout reaching to 1,300 kilometers and plunging the region up to 60 kilometers west of the volcano into darkness for almost three days. Tambora may have been 4,000 meters high before the eruption, but the summit is now 2,850 meters high and occupied by a crater 6 kilometers wide, 1,100 meters deep. The most recent eruption occurred in 1967.

Tampomas (Java: 6.77S, 107.95E).

Tampomas (5,525 ft./1,684 m.) is a Holocene stratovolcano with no record of eruptions in historic time.

Tanaga (Aleut, "big land") (Aleutian Is., Alaska, USA: 51.88N, 178.13W).

Tanaga (5,924 ft./1,806 m.) is a stratovolcano in the Aleutian arc. Its earliest recorded eruption occurred in 1763. There have been two eruptions since, most recently in 1914.

Tandikat (Sumatra: 0.43S, 100.32E).

Tandikat (7,999 ft./2,438 m.) is a stratovolcano whose earliest recorded eruption occurred in 1889. The most recent eruption took place in 1924.

Tangkubanparahu (Java: 6.77S, 107.60E).
Tangkubanparahu (6,836 ft./2,084 m.) is an active stratovolcano inside the Sunda Caldera in Java, about 18 miles north of the city of Bandung. The earliest recorded eruption occurred in 1826. Since then Tangkubanparahu has erupted 15 times, most recently a small phreatic eruption in 1983. Three high school boys were killed by asphyxiating gas in 1923, although no eruption occurred then.

Tao-Rusyr Caldera (Kuril Is.: 49.35N, 154.70E).
Tao-Rusyr (4346 ft./1325 m.) is a stratovolcano on Onekotan in the northern Kuril Islands. It was formed during a major explosive eruption in approximately 5550 B.C. The Eastern Krenitzyn Peak erupted explosively in 1952 and a lava dome was constructed.

Tara, Batu (Komba I., Indonesia: 7.79S, 123.58E).
Batu Tara (2,431 ft./741 m.) is a stratovolcano whose sole recorded eruption to date occurred in 1847. The eruption continued five years until 1852.

Taranaki *see* **Egmont, Mt.**

Tarawera *see* **Okataina.**

Tarumai *see* **Shikotsu.**

Taryatu-Chulutu (Mongolia: 48.17N, 99.70E).
Taryatu-Chulutu (7,874 ft./2,400 m.) is a Holocene volcanic field with no record of eruptions in historic time.

Tat Ali (Ethiopia: 13.28N, 41.07E).
Tat Ali (2,297 ft./700 m.) is a Holocene shield volcano with no record of eruptions in historic time.

Tata Sabaya (Bolivia: 19.13S, 68.53W).
Tata Sabaya (17,816 ft./5,430 m.) is a Holocene stratovolcano with no recorded eruptions in historic time.

Tate-yama (Honshu, Japan: 36.57N, 137.60E).
Tate-yama (6,631 ft./2,021 m.) is a stratovolcano whose sole recorded eruption to date occurred in 1839, but ash layer datings indicate two earlier events, in approximately 2550 and 1000 B.C.

Tateshina (Honshu, Japan: 36.10N, 138.30E).
Tateshina (8,301 ft./2,530 m.) is a Holocene stratovolcano with no record of eruptions in historic time.

Tatio (Chile: 22.35S, 68.03W).
Tatio (14,043 ft./4,280 m.) is a Pleistocene hydrothermal field with geysers.

Ta'u (American Samoa: 14.23S, 169.45W).
Ta'u (3,055 ft./931 m.) is a Holocene shield volcano with no record of eruptions in historic time.

Taunshits (Kamchatka, Russia: 54.53N, 159.80E).
Taunshits (7,720 ft./2,353 m.) is a Holocene stratovolcano with no record of eruptions in historic time.

Taupo (Maori, "cloak") (New Zealand: 38.82S, 176.00E).
Taupo (2,494 ft./760 m.) is a caldera. Radiocarbon datings reveal around 25 eruptions from approximately 9850 B.C. through 180 A.D., with ash layer dating showing a later eruption in A.D. 210. New Zealand was still uninhabited then, so there were no casualties. Although there was no eruption, 63 perished in 1846 when a mud flow destroyed the village of Te Heu Heu, a famous Maori chieftain.

Tavai Ruro (Vanuatu: 16.80S, 168.43E).
Tavai Ruro (1,818 ft./554 m.) is a Holocene stratovolcano with no record of eruptions in historic time.

Taveuni (Fiji Is.: 16.82S, 179.97W).
Taveuni (4,072 ft./1,241 m.) is a Holocene shield volcano with no record of eruptions in historic time.

Tavurvur *see* **Rabaul.**

Teahitia (Society Is., Central Pacific: 17.57S, 148.85W).
Teahitia (-5,250 ft./-1,600 m.) is a seamount which had several possible eruptions in the early 1980s.

Tecapa (El Salvador: 13.50N, 88.50W).
Tecapa (5,223 ft./1,592 m.) is a stratovolcano with fumarolic activity. There have been no recorded eruptions in historic time.

Tecuamburro (Guatemala: 14.16N, 90.41W).
Tecuamburro (6,053 ft./1,845 m.) is a Holocene stratovolcano with no record of eruptions in historic time.

Teide, Pico del *see* **Tenerife.**

Teleki's Volcano *see* **The Barrier.**

Telica (Nicaragua: 12.60N, 86.84W).
Telica (3,481 ft./1,061 m.) is a volcano group consisting of several overlapping cones and vents. It is one of Nicaragua's most active volcanoes. The earliest

recorded eruption occurred in 1529. At least 27 eruptions have occurred since. An eruption of 1982 reached almost five kilometers into the atmosphere and deposited ash nearly 48 kilometers away. The most recent eruption occurred in 1987, and fumarolic activity was reported in 1998.

Telomoyo (Java: 7.37S, 110.40E).

Telomoyo (6,214 ft./1,894 m.) is a Holocene stratovolcano in central Java. There is no evidence of historical eruptions.

Telong, Bur Ni (Sumatra: 4.77N, 96.81E).

Bur Ni Telong (8,609 ft./2,624 m.) is a stratovolcano whose earliest recorded eruption occurred in 1837. The most recent eruption took place in 1937.

Tenayo Group (Mexico: 19.17N, 98.82W).

The Tenayo Group (10,105 ft./3,080 m.) is composed of Holocene cinder cones. There have been no recorded eruptions in historic time.

Tenduruk Dagi (Turkey: 39.33N, 43.83E).

Tenduruk Dagi (11,759 ft./3,584 m.) is a Holocene shield volcano with no record of eruptions in historic time.

Tenerife (Canary Is.: 28.27N, 16.64W).

Tenerife is a stratovolcano topped by the Las Canadas caldera. The major vent, Pico del Teide (12,175 ft./3,715 m.), is Earth's third largest volcano. The earliest recorded eruption was in 1396. Pico del Teide was erupting in 1492 as Columbus passed by on his epic voyage. An eruption in 1705 buried the town of Garachico and filled in its harbor. The most recent eruption occurred in 1909 on the volcano's northwest flank, producing lava flows and causing some damage.

Tengchong (China: 25.32N, 98.47E).

Tengchong (9,400 ft./2,865 m.) is composed of pyroclastic cones whose sole recorded eruption to date occurred in 1609.

Tengger Caldera (Java: 7.94S, 112.95E).

The Tengger Caldera (7,639 ft./2,329 m.) is three miles in diameter atop a stratovolcano. The earliest recorded eruption was in 1804. Since then there have been over 50 eruptions, all from Bromo, most recently in 1984.

Tenorio Group (Costa Rica: 10.67N, 85.01W).

The Tenorio Group (6,286 ft./1,916 m.) is a cluster of volcanic cones near the crest of Costa Rica's Guanacaste Range in the northern volcanic arc. There is a legend of an eruption in 1816, but the physical nature of the area indicated no eruptions in historic time.

Teon (Banda Sea, Indonesia: 6.92S, 129.12E).

Teon (2,149 ft./655 m.) is a stratovolcano whose earliest recorded eruption occurred in 1659. The most recent eruption took place in 1904.

Tepetiltic, Volcán (Mexico: 21.27N, 104.70W).

Volcán Tepetiltic (6,627 ft./2,020 m.) is a Holocene stratovolcano with no record of eruptions in historic time.

Tepi (Ethiopia: 7.42N, 35.43E).

Tepi (8,950 ft./2,728 m.) is a Holocene shield volcano with no record of eruptions in historic time.

Terceira (Azores: 38.73N, 27.32W).

Terceira (3,356 ft./1,023 m.) is composed of stratovolcanoes whose earliest recorded eruption took place in 1761. The most recent eruption occurred in 1867.

Terror, Mt. (James Ross I., Antarctica: 77.52S, 168.55E).

Mount Terror (10,770 ft./3,2,62 m.) is an extinct shield volcano forming the eastern part of Ross Island. Named for HMS *Terror*, the second ship of British naval commander James Ross, whose first ship, HMS *Erebus*, gave its name to the nearby active Mt. **Erebus**. Most of Mount Terror is covered in ice and snow.

Teyr, Jebel (Red Sea: 15.70N, 41.74E).

Jebel Teyr (800 ft./244 m.) is a Holocene stratovolcano. The earliest recorded eruption occurred in 1750. The most recent eruption occurred in 1883.

Theistareykjarbunga (Icelandic, "dark smoky hill") (Iceland: 65.88N, 16.83W).

Theistareykjarbunga (1,850 ft./564 m.) is a Holocene shield volcano with no recorded eruptions in historic time.

Thera *see* **Santoríni**.

Thielsen, Mt. (Oregon, USA: 43.2N, 122.1W).

Mount Thielsen (9185 ft./2,800 m.) is an extinct shield volcano that is nearly 300,000 years old. Much of the volcano has been removed by glaciers, leaving a jagged central plug surrounded by pyroclastic rocks.

Thompson I. (Southern Atlantic: 53.93S, 5.50E).

Thompson Island is presumed to be a submarine volcano with no record of eruptions in historic time.

Three-Fingered Jack (Oregon, USA: 44.5N, 121.8W).

Three-Fingered Jack (7,840 ft./2,390 m.) is an extinct basaltic shield volcano that has been deeply eroded by glaciers. The volcano is between 500,000 and 250,000 years old.

Three Sisters *see* **North Sister; Middle Sister; *and* South Sister.**

Thule Is. (South Sandwich Is.: 59.45S, 27.37W).

Thule Island (3,525 ft./1,075 m.), near Cook Island, is composed of the southernmost volcanoes in the South Sandwich Islands volcanic arc. There was volcanic activity on Thule in 1962, when steam was observed rising from the water in the volcano's summit crater.

Tianshan Volcanic Group (China: 42.50N, 86.50E).

The Tianshan Volcanic Group is a volcanic field. Two eruptions have been recorded, in A.D. 50 and in A.D. 650.

Tiatia *see* **Tyatya.**

Ticsani (Peru: 16.75S, 70.59W).

Ticsani (17,744 ft./5,408 m.) is a Holocene stratovolcano with no record of eruptions in historic time.

Tidichi *see* **Tousside.**

Tigre, Isla el (Honduras: 13.27N, 87.63W).

Isla el Tigre (2,494 ft./760 m.) is a Holocene stratovolcano with no record of eruptions in historic time.

Tiho (Djibouti: 11.53N, 42.05E).

Tiho (1,640 ft./500 m.) is a Quaternary fumarole field likely formed in the Pleistocene Era.

Tinakula (Santa Cruz Is.: 10.38S, 165.80E).

Tinakula (2,792 ft./851 m.) is a stratovolcano whose earliest recorded eruption occurred in 1595. The most recent eruption to date occurred in 1985.

Tindfjallajökull (Icelandic, "peaked mountain glacier") (Iceland:63.78N, 19.57W).

Tindfjallajökull (4,800 ft./1,463 m.) is a Holocene stratovolcano with no record of eruptions in historic time.

Tinguiririca [Tinquirica] (Chile: 34.81S, 70.35W).

Tinguiririca (14,043 ft./4,280 m.) is a stratovolcano whose sole recorded eruption to date took place in 1917.

Tipas (Argentina: 27.20S, 68.55W).

Tipas (21,851 ft./6,660 m.) is a Holocene complex volcano with no record of eruptions in historic time.

Titila (Kamchatka, Russia: 57.40N, 160.10E).

Titila (5,115 ft./1,559 m.) is a Holocene shield volcano with no record of eruptions in historic time.

Tjornes Fracture Zone (Iceland: 66.30N, 17.10W).

The Tjornes Fracture Zone is a submarine volcano whose sole recorded submarine eruption to date occurred in 1867.

Tlevak Strait-Suemez Is. (Alaska, USA: 55.25N, 133.30W).

Tlevak Strait-Suemez Island is a Holocene volcanic field with no record of eruptions in historic time.

To-shima (Izu Is., Japan: 34.52N, 139.28E).

To-shima (1,667 ft./508 m.) is a Holocene stratovolcano with no record of eruptions in historic time.

Toba (Sumatra: 2.58N, 98.83E).

Toba Caldera (7,077 ft./2,157 m.) has the world's largest crater, covering an area of 1,775 square kilometers. This was formed by an eruption in the Holocene epoch, nearly 75,000 years ago, when ash fell as far away as India.

Toconce, Cerro (Chile: 22.20S, 68.10W).

Cerro Toconce (17,829 ft./5,434 m.) is a Holocene stratovolcano with no record of eruptions in historic time.

Tocorpuri, Cerros de (Chile/Bolivia: 22.43S, 67.90W).

Cerros de Tocorpuri (19,300 ft./5,800 m.) is a compound stratovolcano consisting of several eruptive centers on the border between Chile and Bolivia. The volcano's age is estimated to be between the Pleistocene and Holocene periods.

Todoko-Ranu (Halmahera, Indonesia: 1.30N, 127.43E).

Todoko-Ranu (3,212 ft./979 m.) is a caldera with active fumaroles. There have been no reported eruptions in historic time.

Tofua (Tonga Is.: 19.75S,175.07W).

Tofua (1,680 ft./512 m.) is a caldera whose earliest recorded eruption occurred in 1774. The most recent eruption occurred in 1958.

Toh, Tarso (Chad: 21.33N, 16.33E).

Tarso Toh (6,560 ft./2,000 m.) is a Holocene volcanic field with no record of eruptions in historic time.

Tokachi (Hokkaido, Japan: 43.42N, 142.68E).

Tokachi (6,815 ft./2,077 m.) is composed of overlapping stratovolcanoes. The earliest recorded eruption occurred in 1857. There have been over 15 eruptions since. An eruption in 1926 killed 146 people in lava flows, floods, and explosions. There were also reported fatalities in an eruption in 1962, when five people were killed by falling blocks. The most recent eruption occurred in 1989.

Tolbachiksky (Kamchatka, Russia: 55.83N, 160.33E).

Tolbachiksky (10,119 ft./3,085 m.) is a stratovolcano which, with Ostry, forms the Tolbachik massif. The earliest recorded eruption was in 1739. Ash layer datings reveal around 25 eruptions before this, with radiocarbon dating indicating the first in approximately 6050 B.C. There have been recent eruptions in 1967, 1970 and 1975-76.

Tolguaca (Chile: 38.31S, 71.64W).

Tolguaca (9,206 ft./2,806 m.) is a Holocene stratovolcano with no record of eruptions in historic time.

Tolima (Colombia: 4.67N, 85.33W).

Tolima (17,061 ft./5,200 m.) is a stratovolcano whose earliest recorded eruption occurred in 1822. The most recent eruption took place in 1953.

Toliman (Guatemala: 14.61N, 91.19W).

Toliman (10,358 ft./3,158 m.) is a Holocene stratovolcano with two cones. There have been no eruptions in historic time.

Tolmachev Dol (Kamchatka, Russia: 52.63N, 157.58E).

Tolmachev Dol (3,350 ft./1,021 m.) is composed of Holocene cinder cones with no record of eruptions in historic time.

Tompaluan *see* **Lokon-Empung**.

Tondano Caldera (Sulawesi, Indonesia: 1.23N, 124.83E).

The Tondano Caldera (3,944 ft./1,202 m.) is a caldera with fumarolic activity. There have been no recorded eruptions in historic time.

Toney Mountain (Antarctica: 75.80S, 115.83W).

Toney Mountain (11,795 ft./3,595 m.) is a Holocene shield volcano with no record of eruptions in historic time.

Tongariro (Maori *tonga*, "south wind," *riro*, "to come away") (New Zealand: 39.13S, 175.64E).

Tongariro (6,487 ft./1,978 m.) is a compound stratovolcano composed of several volcanic cones. The volcanic center is largely composed of four andesite massifs: Kakaramea, Pihanga, Tongariro and Ruapehu. The Ngauruhoe (Maori *nga*, "the," *uru*, "descendants," *hoe*, "paddle") is the youngest vent, and the most active volcano in New Zealand. The earliest recorded eruption occurred in 1839. There have been nearly 70 eruptions since then, most recently in 1977.

Tongkoko (Sulawesi, Indonesia: 1.52N, 125.20E).
Tongkoko (3,770 ft./1,149 m.) is a stratovolcano whose earliest recorded eruption occurred in 1680. The most recent eruption took place in 1880.

Toon (Chad: 21.33N, 16.33E).
Toon (8,200 ft./2,500 m.) is a caldera volcano located in the Tibesti volcanic region between Lake Chad and the Gulf of Syrte. There is no record of historic eruptions.

Tore (Bougainville: 5.83S, 154.93E).
Tore (7,218 ft./2,200 m.) is a Holocene lava cone with no record of eruptions in historic time.

Torfajökull (Iceland: 63.92N, 19.17W).
Torfajökull (4,131 ft./1,259 m.) is a stratovolcano whose earliest recorded eruption occurred in 1477. Nine prior eruptions are indicated by ash layer dating, the first in approximately 6050 B.C.

Tori-shima (Izu Is., Japan: 30.48N, 140.32E).
Tori-shima (1,322 ft./403 m.) is a stratovolcano whose earliest recorded eruption occurred in 1871. An eruption of 1902 killed all 125 islanders. The most recent eruption took place in 1975.

Toroeng Prong (Vietnam: 14.93N, 108.00E).
Toroeng Prong (2,625 ft./800 m.) is likely a Holocene volcano with no record of eruptions in historic time.

Tortuga, Isla (Mexico: 27.39N, 111.86W).
Isla Tortuga (1,017 ft./310 m.) is a Holocene shield volcano with no record of eruptions in historic time.

Tosa Sucha (Ethiopia: 5.92N, 37.57E).
Tosa Sucha (5,414 ft./1,650 m.) is composed of cinder cones. There is no record of eruptions in historic time, but likely volcanic activity in the past 10,000 years.

Tousside, Tarso (Chad: 21.03N, 16.45E).
Tarso Tousside (10,712 ft./3,265 m.), also known as Tidichi, is a Holocene stratovolcano in the Northwest Tibesti region. There have been no eruptions in historic time.

Towada (Honshu, Japan: 40.47N, 140.92E).
Towada (3,803 ft./1,159 m.) is a Holocene stratovolcano with a summit caldera. The sole recorded eruption to date was a large explosive one that occurred in 915 A.D., although radiocarbon and ash ring dating indicate six before this, with the earliest in approximately 7550 B.C.

Traitor's Head (Erromango I., Vanuatu: 18.75S, 169.23E).
Traitor's Head (2,745 ft./837 m.) is a stratovolcano with submarine vents. There have been only two recorded eruptions, in 1881 and 1959.

Tres Virgines, Volcán de las (Spanish, "three virgins") (Mexico: 27.47N, 112.59W).
Volcán de las Tres Virgines (6,365 ft./1.940 m.) is a volcano located near the eastern coast of Baja California. The sole recorded eruption to date occurred in 1746.

Tri Sestry (Russian, "three sisters") (Kuril Is.: 45.93N, 149.92E).
Tri Sestry (3,273 ft./998 m.) is a Holocene stratovolcano located on Urup Island in the southern Kuril Islands. There is no record of historical eruptions.

Trident (Alaska, USA: 58.23N, 155.08W).
Trident (6,116 ft./1,864 m.) is a stratovolcano whose earliest recorded eruption occurred in 1913. The most recent eruption took place in 1975.

Trindade (Southern Atlantic: 20.51S, 29.33W).
Trindade (1,970 ft./600 m.) is a Holocene stratovolcano with no record of eruptions in historic time.

Tristan da Cunha (Southern Atlantic: 37.09S, 12.28W).
Tristan da Cunha (6,759 ft./2,060 m.) is a stratovolcano with an eruption in approximately 1700, indicated by ash ring dating. The sole documented eruption to date occurred in 1961, when the island's entire population of 198 were evacuated to England. Most returned in 1963.

Tromen (Argentina: 37.14S, 70.03W).
Tromen (13,052 ft./3,978 m.) is a Holocene stratovolcano with no record of eruptions in historic time.

Tseax River Cone (British Columbia, Canada: 55.12N, 128.90W).
The Tseax River Cone (1,998 ft./609 m.) is a pyroclastic cone with likely volcanic activity in the past 300 years.

Tshibinda (Dem. Rep. of Congo [Zaire]: 2.32S, 28.75E).
Tshibinda (4,790 ft./1,460 m.) is composed of Holocene cinder cones with no record of eruptions in historic time.

Tsurumi (Kyushu, Japan: 33.28N, 131.43E).
Tsurumi (4,508 ft./1,374 m.) is composed of lava domes. The earliest recorded eruption occurred in A.D. 771. The most recent eruption in A.D. 867 lasted for over two months and caused some damage.

Tujle, Cerro (Chile: 23.83S, 67.95W).
Cerro Tujle (11,648 ft./3,550 m.) is a Holocene Maar volcano with no record of eruptions in historic time.

Tulabug (Ecuador: 1.78S, 78.61W).
Tulabug (10,942 ft./3,335 m.) is composed of Holocene scoria cones. There have been no recorded eruptions in historic time.

Tullu Moje (Ethiopia: 8.16N, 39.13E).
Tullu Moje (7,707 ft./2,349 m.) is a pumice cone. The sole recorded eruption to date occurred in 1900.

Tuluman *see* **St. Andrew Strait**.

Tumble Buttes (California, USA: 40.68N, 121.55W).
Tumble Buttes (7,189 ft./2,191 m.) is composed of Holocene cinder cones. There have been no recorded eruptions in historic time.

Tundrovy (Russian, "tundra") (Kamchatka, Russia: 52.25N, 157.60E).
Tundrovy (2,425 ft./739 m.) is a Holocene shield volcano with no record of eruptions in historic time.

Tungnafellsjökull (Iceland: 64.73N, 17.92W).
Tungnafellsjökull (5,036 ft./1,535 m.) is a Holocene stratovolcano with no record of eruptions in historic time.

Tungurahua (Ecuador: 1.47S, 78.44W).
Tungurahua (16,475 ft./5,023 m.) is an active volcano near the city of Banos, Ecuador. Also known as "the Black Giant," its earliest recorded eruption was in 1641. There have been at least 16 eruptions since, most recently in 1944, when the central crater erupted explosively.

Tunkin Depression (Russia: 51.50N, 102.50E).
The Tunkin Depression (3,937 ft./1,200 m.) is a volcanic field with no record of eruptions in historic time.

Tupungatito (Chile/Argentina: 33.40S, 69.80W).
Tupungatito (19,690 ft./6,000 m.) is a stratovolcano whose earliest recorded eruption occurred in 1829.

Turfan (China: 42.90N, 89.25E).
Turfan is a cone whose sole recorded eruption to date occurred in 1120.

Turrialba (Costa Rica: 10.03N, 83.77W).
Turrialba (10,959 ft./3,340 m.) is a cratered stratovolcano. The earliest recorded eruption occurred in 1853. The most recent eruption occurred in 1866.

Tutuila (American Samoa: 14.29S, 170.70W).
Tutuila (2,142 ft./653 m.) is composed of Holocene tuff cones with no record of eruptions in historic time.

Tutupaca (Peru: 17.02S, 70.36W).
Tutupaca (19,079 ft./5,815 m.) is a stratovolcano whose earliest recorded eruption took place in 1780. The most recent eruption occurred in 1902.

Tuzgle, Cerro (Argentina: 24.05S, 66.48W).
Cerro Tuzgle (18,210 ft./5,550 m.) is a Holocene stratovolcano with no record of eruptions in historic time.

Tuzovsky (Kamchatka, Russia: 57.32N, 159.97E).
Tuzovsky (5,030 ft./1,533 m.) is a Holocene shield volcano with no record of eruptions in historic time.

Twin Buttes (California, USA: 40.78N, 121.60W).
Twin Buttes (6,336 ft./1,631 m.) are Holocene cinder cones with no recorded eruptions in historic time.

Tyatya (Kuril Is.: 44.36N, 146.27E).
Tyatya (or Tiatia) (3,900 ft./1,819 m.) is a stratovolcano on Kunashir Island in the southern Kuril Islands. There have been at least five eruptions since the earliest recorded one in 1812. A major explosive eruption occurred from a flank vent in 1973. The most recent eruption was in 1981-82.

Tzanjuyub, Volcán de (Guatemala: 14.75N, 91.43W).
Volcán de Tzanjuyub (21,464 ft./3,542 m.) is a Pleistocene stratovolcano with evidence of fumarolic activity. There have been no known eruptions in historic time.

U

Ubehebe Craters (Shoshonean, meaning unknown) (California, USA: 37.02N, 117.45W).
The Ubehebe Craters (2,467 ft./752 m.), in the north end of Death Valley National Monument, include over a dozen Maar volcanoes.

Ubinas (Peru: 16.35S, 70.90W).
Ubinas (18,612 ft./5,672 m.) is a stratovolcano in southern Peru and is the most active volcano in the country. The earliest recorded eruption occurred in approximately 1550. Ubinas' most recent eruption was in 1969. Fumarolic activity has been persistent in recent years, increasing in 1995.

Udina (Kamchatka, Russia: 55.75N, 160.53E).

Udina (9,587 ft./2,923 m.) is a Holocene stratovolcano composed of two cones within the Kliuchevskoi Group. There is no evidence of eruptions in historic time.

Udokan Volcanic Field (Russia: 56.18N, 117.47E).

The Udokan Volcanic Field (6,496 ft./1,980 m.) is a Holocene shield volcano with no record of eruptions in historic time.

Ugashik-Peulik (Inuit [Eskimo], meaning unknown) (Alaska, USA: 57.75N, 156.37W).

Ugashik-Peulik (4,835 ft./1,474 m.) is a stratovolcano with a three-mile-wide caldera, Ugashik. The sole recorded eruption to date occurred in 1814.

Uinkaret Field (from Native American tribal name) (Arizona, USA: 36.38N, 113.13W).

Uinkaret (5,100 ft./1,555 m.) is a volcanic field in the western Grand Canyon, covering nearly 600 square miles. Basaltic cinder cones and lava flows, formed in the last 2 million years, are found within the field.

Uka (Kamchatka, Russia: 57.70N, 160.40E).

Uka (5,390 ft./1,643 m.) is a Holocene shield volcano with no record of eruptions in historic time.

Ukinrek Maars (Alaska, USA: 57.83N, 156.52W).

Ukinrek Maars (299 ft./91 m.) is a volcanic field whose sole recorded eruption to date occurred in 1977.

Uksichan (Kamchatka, Russia: 56.08N, 158.38E).

Uksichan (5,551 ft./1,692 m.) is a Holocene shield volcano with no record of eruptions in historic time.

Ulawun (New Britain, Papua New Guinea: 5.05S,151.33E).

Ulawun (7,655 ft./2,334 m.) is a stratovolcano on New Britain Island in the South Bismarck Sea. It is the most active volcano on the island with over 20 recorded eruptions since 1700. Most of the eruptions have been moderate explosive, generating pyroclastic flows. An eruption in 1884-85 produced a lava dome and flows. The most recent eruption occurred in 1993.

Uliaga (Aleutian Is., Alaska, USA: 53.07N, 169.77W).

Uliaga (2,914 ft./888 m.) is a likely Holocene stratovolcano with no record of eruptions in historic time.

Ulreung (Korea: 37.50N, 130.87E).

Ulreung (3,229 ft./984 m.) is a Holocene stratovolcano with no record of eruptions in historic time.

Ulug-Arginsky (Russia: 52.33N, 98.00E).

Ulug-Arginsky (5,906 ft./1,800 m.) is a Holocene cinder cone with no record of eruptions in historic time.

Umboi (Papua New Guinea: 5.59S, 147.87E).

Umboi (5,079 ft./1,548 m.) is a Holocene complex volcano that forms an island in Papua New Guinea. There has been no evidence of historic eruptions.

Umm Marafieb, Jebel (Sudan: 18.20N, 33.80E).

Jebel Umm Marafieb are Holocene scoria cones with no record of eruptions in historic time.

Una Una *see* **Cola.**

Ungaran (Java: 7.18S, 110.33E).

Ungaran (6,726 ft./2,050 m.) is a Holocene stratovolcano in central Java. There is no evidence of historical eruptions.

Unzen, Mt. (Kyushu, Japan: 32.75N, 130.30E).

Mount Unzen (4,457 ft./1,359 m.) is a large complex volcano with overlapping lava domes on the Shimabara Peninsula. The earliest recorded eruption occurred in 1663. A devastating eruption occurred in 1792, with over 14,000 fatalities, mainly in resulting giant waves which hit Shimabara peninsula and the Higo and Amakusa provinces, across Ariake Sea. The volcano was then inactive until 1991, when a lava dome began to grow, causing avalanches. One hit the town of Kamikoba, killing 42, mainly journalists who had gone too close, but also three experienced volcanologists. The most recent eruption occurred in 1993.

Upolu (Western Samoa: 13.93S, 171.72W).

Upolu (3,609 ft./1,100 m.) is a Holocene shield volcano with no record of eruptions in historic time.

Urataman (Shimushir I., Kuril Is.: 47.12N, 152.23E).

Urataman (2,223 ft./678 m.) is a Holocene somma volcano on Shimushir Island in the central Kuril Islands. There have been no known historic eruptions.

Ushishur (Kuril Is.: 47.52N, 152.80E).

Ushishur (1,316 ft./401 m.) is a caldera in the central Kuril Islands. The earliest recorded eruption occurred in 1710. There was a submarine eruption in 1769 which formed a lava dome. The most recent eruption occurred in 1884.

Ushkovsky (Kamchatka, Russia: 56.10N, 160.47E).

Ushkovsky (12,937 ft./3,943 m.) is a compound volcano whose sole recorded eruption to date occurred in 1890.

Usu (Hokkaido, Japan: 42.53N, 140.83E).
Usu (2,398 ft./731 m.) is a stratovolcano whose earliest recorded eruption occurred in 1626. An eruption in 1822 caused the deaths of 50 people in the village of Abuta on the southern side of volcano. The village itself was destroyed and over 1,000 horses were also killed. There were also eruptions in 1910, 1944–45 and 1977–82, all of which caused fatalities due to ashfall and mud flows. During the 1945 eruption the Showa-Shinzan dome grew on the eastern flank of Usu.

Usulután (El Salvador: 13.42N, 88.47W).
Usulután (4,757 ft./1,450 m.) is a Holocene stratovolcano with no record of eruptions in historic time.

Utashut *see* **Zheltovskaya Sopka.**

Utila I. (Honduras: 16.10N, 86.90W).
Utila Island (295 ft./90 m.) is composed of Holocene pyroclastic cones. There have been no recorded eruptions in historic time.

Uturunco (Bolivia: 22.27S, 67.22W).
Uturunco (19,712 ft./6,008 m.) is a Holocene stratovolcano with no record of eruptions in historic time.

'Uwayrid, Harrat (Saudi Arabia: 27.08N, 37.25E).
Harrat 'Uwayrid (6,234 ft./1,900 m.) is a volcano with likely volcanic activity in the past 2,000 years.

Uzon (Kamchatka, Russia: 54.50N, 159.97E).
Uzon (5,305 ft./1,617 m.) is a Holocene caldera with no record of eruptions in historic time.

V

Vakak Group (Afghanistan: 34.25N, 67.97E).
The Vakak Group (10,466 ft./3,190 m.) is a Holocene volcanic field with no record of eruptions in historic time.

Valles Caldera (Spanish, "valleys") (New Mexico, USA: 35.87N, 106.57W).
Valles Caldera (11,254 ft./3,430 m.) is a Pleistocene caldera with fumarolic activity. There have been no recorded eruptions in historic time.

Vatnafjöll (Icelandic, "lake mountain") (Iceland: 63.92N, 19.67W).
Vatnafjöll (4,052 ft./1,235 m.) is composed of fissure vents. Ash layer datings indicate there have been at least 26 eruptions from approximately 5050 B.C. through 750 A.D.

Veer (Russian, "fan") (Kamchatka, Russia: 53.63N, 158.42E).
Veer (1,148 ft./350 m.) is composed of cinder cones whose sole recorded eruption to date occurred in 1856.

Veniaminof (for I.P. Veniaminof [1797–1879], bishop of Russian America) (Alaska, USA: 46.17N, 159.38W).
Veniaminof (8,223 ft./2,507 m.) is a large active stratovolcano. A massive eruption approximately 3,700 years ago formed a six-mile caldera. The earliest recorded eruption occurred in 1838. Recent eruptions from 1983 to 1984 and from 1993 to the present have occurred from the caldera's central cinder cone.

Verde, Laguna (El Salvador: 13.89N, 89.79W).
Laguna Verde (6,001 ft./1,829 m.) is composed of Holocene stratovolcanoes with no record of eruptions in historic time.

Verkhovoy (Russian, "upper") (Kamchatka, Russia: 56.52N, 159.53E).
Verkhovoy (4,593 ft./1,400 m.) is a Holocene shield volcano with no record of eruptions in historic time.

Vernadsky Ridge (Kuril Is.: 50.55N, 155.97E).
Vernadsky Ridge (3880 ft./1183 m.) is located on Paramushir in the northern Kuril Islands. Made of Holocene cinder cones, there have been no historic eruptions.

Vestmannaeyjar *see* **Eldfell**.

Vesuvius (Pre-Celtic *ves*, "mountain," or Oscan *fesf*, "smoke") (Italy: 40.82, 14.43E).
Mount Vesuvius (4,200 ft./1,281 m.) is a complex volcano formed around 300,000 B.C. when molten rock at the edge of the Eurasian and African geological "plates" welled up. The earliest recorded eruption occurred in 79 A.D., notoriously killing at least 3,000 people in Pompeii and Herculaneum, but radiocarbon dating indicates eruptions dating from approximately 5960 B.C. The Pompeii population was trapped by a sudden deluge of suffocating ash and poison gas and mummified by a mix of boiling pumice and rainwater. The remains of 2,000 people were since discovered. The description of the eruption by Pliny the Younger gave the name of *Plinian* to this type of volcanic activity. There have been over 40 eruptions since then, most recently in 1944. Around 4,000 people died in the 1631 eruption, most being caught in lava and pumice flows. The eruption of 1794 killed around 400, with lava destroying Torre del Greco for the third time in 170 years. Around 350 died in the 1905 eruption, 105 of these when a church roof collapsed. A roof collapse under the weight of ash in the 1944 eruption killed 21. Since then Vesuvius has remained dormant in its longest quiet period since the 1631 explosion. Many experts think Vesuvius is

preparing for a colossal eruption that could kills tens of thousands in a matter of minutes.

Veteran (Vietnam: 9.83N, 109.05E).
Veteran is a submarine volcano with fumarolic activity.

Victory (New Guinea: 9.20S, 149.07E).
Victory (6,316 ft./1,925 m.) is a stratovolcano with volcanic activity in the twentieth century.

Viedma, Volcán (Argentina: 49.36S, 73.28W).
Volcán Viedma (4,265 ft./1,300 m.) is a subglacial volcano whose sole recorded eruption to date occurred in 1988.

Villarrica (Chile: 39.42S, 71.93W).
Villarrica (9,338 ft./2,847 m.) is an active stratovolcano in central Chile. The earliest recorded eruption occurred in 1558, with radiocarbon datings showing several before this, beginning in approximately 6690 B.C. Since then there have been at least 70 eruptions, most recently in August of 1997. Around 350 were killed in Villarrica village by the 1575 earthquake, but this was not an eruption. A mud flow caused by the 1964 eruption killed 22, and 15 lost their lives in that of 1971.

Vilyuchinskaya Sopka (Kamchatka, Russia: 52.68N, 158.30E).
Vilyuchinskaya Sopka (7,127 ft./2,173 m.) is a conical stratovolcano with a lava flow at the summit. There is no evidence of eruptions in historic time.

Visoke (Dem. Rep. of Congo [Zaire]/Rwanda: 1.47S, 29.49E).
Visoke (12,008 ft./3,660 m.) is a stratovolcano and part of the Virunga volcanic complex in the East African Rift Valley. There have been two eruptions recorded to date, in 1891 and 1957.

Volcancito, El *see* **Colima Volcanic Complex.**

Volcánico, Cerro (Spanish, "volcanic peak") (Argentina: 42.07S, 71.65W).
Cerro Volcánico is a Holocene cinder cone with no record of eruptions in historic time.

Volcán Nuevo *see* **Nevados de Chillán.**

Volcán Viejo *see* **Nevados de Chillán.**

Voon, Tarso (Chad: 20.92N, 17.28E).
Tarso Voon (10,168 ft./3,100 m.) is a fumarolic stratovolcano in the northeastern section of Chad's Tibesti volcanic field.

Voyampolsky (Kamchatka, Russia: 58.37N, 160.62E).
Voyampolsky (4,019 ft./1,225 m.) is a Holocene shield volcano with no record of eruptions in historic time.

Vsevidov (Umnak I., Aleutian Is., Alaska, USA: 53.13N, 168.68W).
Vsevidov (7,050 ft./2,149 m.) is a conical stratovolcano in the center of Umnak Island. The earliest recorded eruption was in 1784. There have been three recorded eruptions and four more suspected eruptions since, most recently in 1878.

Vulcano (Latin *Vulcanus*, earlier *Volcanus*, "Vulcan," Roman god of fire) (Lipari Is., Italy: 38.40N, 14.96E).
Vulcano (1,600 ft./500 m.) is a stratovolcano forming the southernmost of the Aeolian Islands. The earliest recorded eruption was in 475 B.C. There have been over 30 eruptions since then, most recently in 1890 from the Fossa cone within the Lentia caldera. Vulcano gave its name to the *Vulcanian* type of volcanic activity.

Vulsini (Italy: 42.60N, 11.93E).
Vulsini (2,645 ft./800 m.) is a caldera whose sole recorded eruption to date occurred in 104 B.C.

Vysoky (Russian, "high") (Kamchatka, Russia: 52.43N, 157.93E).
Vysoky (4,045 ft./1,234 m.) is a Holocene stratovolcano with no record of eruptions in historic time.

W

Waesche (Antarctica: 77.17S, 126.88W).
Waesche (10,801 ft./3,292 m.) are shield volcanoes in Marie Byrd Land. There is a possibility of Holocene activity.

Waimangu *see* **Okataina.**

Waiowa (New Guinea: 9.57S, 149.07E).
Waiowa (2,100 ft./640 m.) is a pyroclastic cone whose sole recorded eruption to date occurred in 1943.

Wallis Is. (Wallis and Futuna Is.: 13.30S, 176.17W).
Wallis Island (469 ft./143 m.) is composed of Holocene shield volcanoes with no record of eruptions in historic time.

Walo (New Britain, Papua New Guinea: 5.53S, 150.90E).
Walo (49 ft./15 m.) is a hydrothermal field with hot springs on New Britain Island in the south Bismarck Sea. There has been no record of an eruption in the past 10,000 years.

Wapi Lava Field (Idaho, USA: 42.88N, 113.22W).
The Wapi Lava Field (5,263 ft./1,604 m.) is a Holocene shield volcano with no record of eruptions in historic time.

Washington, Mt. (for George Washington [1732–1799], US president) (Oregon, USA: 44.33N, 121.84W).
Mount Washington (7,790 ft./2,376 m.) is a shield volcano with a summit cone composed of cinder lava flows. There have been no eruptions in modern time, with the most recent occurring over 1,330 years ago.

Waw an Namus (Namus is Arabic for "mosquito) (Libya: 27.25N, 17.50E).
Waw an Namus (3,936 ft./1,200 m.) is a caldera with a high cinder cone in the center located in the Libyan desert. There are no known historic eruptions.

Wayang-Windu (Java: 7.21S, 107.63E).
Wayang-Windu (7,159 ft./2,182 m.) is a stratovolcano with evidence of fumarolic activity. There is no record of an eruption in historic time.

Wells Gray-Clearwater (British Columbia, Canada: 52.33N, 120.57W).
Wells Gray-Clearwater (6,611 ft./2,015 m.) are cinder cones with likely volcanic activity in the past 500 years.

West Crater (Washington, USA: 45.88N, 122.08W).
West Crater (3,000 ft./914 m.) is a Holocene volcanic field with no record of eruptions in historic time.

West Eifel Volcanic Field (Germany: 50.17N, 6.85E).
The West Eifel Volcanic Field (1,969 ft./600 m.) is a Holocene Maars field.

Westdahl (Unimak I., Aleutian Is., Alaska, USA: 54.52N, 164.65W).
Westdahl (5,118 ft./1,560 m.) is a shield volcano covered with glaciers. The earliest recorded eruption occurred in 1795. There has been volcanic activity since February of 1978, with the most recent eruption occurring in 1992.

Whale I. (New Zealand: 37.86S, 176.98E).
Whale Island (1,142 ft./348 m.) is a Pleistocene fumarolic complex volcano with no record of eruptions in historic time.

Whangarei (Maori, *whanga*, "harbor," *rei*, "cherished") (New Zealand: 35.75S, 174.27E).
Whangarei (1,303 ft./397 m.) are Holocene cinder cones with no record of eruptions in historic time.

White I. (New Zealand: 37.52S, 177.18E).
White Island (1,053 ft./321 m.) is the summit of two overlapping stratovolcanoes. The subject of Maori legends, the earliest recorded eruption occurred

in 1826. There have been over 35 eruptions since then, making it one of New Zealand's most active volcanoes. In 1914 an avalanche of debris killed 11 sulfur workers, although no actual eruption occurred then. The most recent eruption took place in June of 1995.

Wilis (Java: 7.81S, 111.76E).
Wilis (8,410 ft./2,563 m.) is a Holocene stratovolcano with no record of eruptions in historic time.

Witori *see* **Pago**.

Wolf, Volcán (Isabela I., Galápagos Is.: 0.02N, 91.35W).
Volcán Wolf (5,611 ft./1,710 m.) is a shield volcano whose earliest recorded eruption occurred in 1797. The most recent eruption took place in 1982.

Wrangell, Mt. (for F.P. Wrangel [1797–1870], director of Russian-American Company) (Alaska, USA: 62.00N, 144.02W).
Mt. Wrangell (15,233 ft./4,949 m.) is a huge shield volcano in south central Alaska. It is covered with glaciers with a collapsed caldera on the summit. Mt. Wrangell has erupted five times between 1819 and 1902.

Wudalianchi (China: 48.72N, 126.12E).
Wudalianchi (1,791 ft./597 m.) is a volcanic field in eastern China's Heilongjiang province. The sole recorded eruption to date in 1719–21 formed two main vents, Laoheishan ("old black mountain") and Huoshhaoshan ("fire burn mountain").

Wurlali (Damar I., Banda Sea, Indonesia: 7.12S, 128.65E).
Wurlali (2,850 ft./868 m.) is a stratovolcano whose sole recorded eruption to date occurred in 1892.

X

Xianjindao (Korea: 41.33N, 128.00E).
Xianjindao is a volcano whose sole recorded eruption to date occurred in 1597.

Y

Yake-dake (Honshu, Japan: 36.22N, 137.58E).
Yake-dake (8,055 ft./2,455 m.) is a stratovolcano overlooking Honshu's Kamikochi valley. The earliest recorded eruption occurred in A.D. 686. There have been over 25 phreatic eruptions since then from Yake-dake's central, flank

and fissure vents. Eruptions in 1585, 1915, 1931 and, most recently, 1962-63, produced mudflows which caused damage.

Yali (Greece: 36.63N, 27.10E).
Yali (577 ft./176 m.) consists of lava domes formed during the Holocene period.

Yangudi (Ethiopia: 10.58N, 41.04E).
Yangudi (4,538 ft./1,383 m.) is a Holocene volcano complex. There is no record of eruptions in historic time.

Yantarni (Russian, "amber") (Alaska, USA: 57.02N, 157.18W).
Yantarni (4,382 ft./1,336 m.) is a stratovolcano with a caldera composed of andesite and dacite. The only known eruption occurred approximately 2,800 years ago.

Yanteles, Cerro (Chile: 43.42S, 72.83W).
Cerro Yanteles (6,727 ft./2,050 m.) is a stratovolcano whose sole recorded eruption to date occurred in 1835.

Yar, Jabal (Saudi Arabia: 17.05N, 42.83E).
Jabal Yar (1,001 ft./305 m.) is a volcanic field whose sole recorded eruption to date occurred in 1810.

Yasur (Tanna I., Vanuatu: 19.52S, 169.42E).
Yasur (1,184 ft./361 m.) is an active stratovolcano on Tanna Island in the Southwest Pacific. It began erupting sometime prior to 1774 and has continued to be active ever since. Yasur's Strombolian and Vulcanian explosions have caused damage and have been responsible for at least three deaths in recent years. Several eruptions were reported in 1996 and 1997.

Yate, Mt. (Chile: 41.75S, 72.40W).
Mount Yate (7,176 ft./2,187 m.) is a Holocene stratovolcano with no record of eruptions in historic time.

Yega (Chad: 20.36N, 17.24E).
Yega (8,200 ft./2,500 m.) is located in the Tibesti volcanic region between Lake Chad and the Gulf of Syrte. There is no record of historic eruptions.

Yegualda, La (Panama: 8.52N, 80.91W).
La Yegualda (4,255 ft./1,297 m.) is a Holocene stratovolcano with evidence of volcanic activity in the past 500 years.

Yelia (New Guinea: 7.05S, 145.86E).
Yelia (11,103 ft./3,384 m.) is a Holocene stratovolcano with no record of eruptions in historic time.

Yellowstone (for yellow rocks in the river) (Wyoming, USA: 44.43N, 110.67W).

Yellowstone (9,203 ft./2,805 m.) has had three massive eruptions in the past 2 million years. The last eruption occurred approximately 600,000 years ago, showering ash and rocks over much of North America, and as far as Louisiana. Old Faithful and other geysers in Yellowstone National Park are living witness to continuing volcanic activity (as a subterranean "hot spot").

Yersey (Wetar I., Indonesia: 7.53S, 123.95E).

Yersey (-12,468 ft./-3,800 m.) is likely a submarine volcano with no known eruptions.

Yojoa, Lake (Honduras: 14.98N, 87.98W).

Lake Yojoa (3,576 ft./1,090 m.) is a Holocene volcanic field with no record of eruptions in historic time.

Yomba (northeast of New Guinea: 4.92S, 146.75E).

Yomba is a submarine volcano with no record of eruptions in historic time.

Yotei (Hokkaido, Japan: 42.83N, 140.82E).

Yotei (6,211 ft./1,893 m.) is a Holocene stratovolcano with no record of eruptions in historic time.

Young I. (Balleny Is., Antarctica: 66.42S, 162.45E).

Young Island (4,397 ft./1,340 m.) is a stratovolcano with fumarolic activity. There have been no recorded eruptions in historic time.

Yucamane (Peru: 17.18S, 70.20W).

Yucamane (18,210 ft./5,550 m.) is a stratovolcano whose sole recorded eruption to date occurred in 1787.

Yumia, Cerro (Bolivia: 21.50S, 67.50W).

Cerro Yumia (13,290 ft./4,050 m.) is a Holocene cone with no record of eruptions in historic time.

Yunaska (Aleutian Is., Alaska, USA: 52.63N, 170.63W).

Yunaska (1,805 ft./550 m.) is a shield volcano whose earliest recorded eruption took place in 1824. The most recent eruption occurred in 1937.

Z

Zacate Grande, Isla (Honduras: 13.33N, 87.63W).

Isla Zacate Grande (1,970 ft./600 m.) is a Holocene stratovolcano with no record of eruptions in historic time.

Zao (Honshu, Japan: 38.15N, 140.45E).
Zao (6,040 ft./1,841 m.) is a complex volcano whose earliest recorded eruption occurred in A.D. 884. There have been approximately 30 eruptions since then, most recently in 1940. Overflow of water from the Okama crater lake during the 1867 eruption killed three hot spring bathers.

Zaozerny (Russian, "over the lake") (Kamchatka, Russia: 56.88N, 159.95E).
Zaozerny (4,426 ft./1,349 m.) is a Holocene shield volcano with no record of eruptions in historic time.

Zapatera I. (Nicaragua: 11.73N, 85.82W).
Zapatera Island (2,051 ft./625 m.) is a Holocene stratovolcano with no record of eruptions in historic time.

Zarechny (Russian, "over the river") (Kamchatka, Russia: 56.38N, 160.83E).
Zarechny (2,494 ft./760 m.) is a Holocene somma volcano with no record of eruptions in historic time.

Zavaritsky (Kamchatka, Russia: 53.90N, 158.38E).
Zavaritsky (5,141 ft./1,567 m.) is a Holocene stratovolcano with no record of eruptions in historic time.

Zavaritsky Caldera (Shimushir I., Kuril Is.: 46.92N, 151.95E).
Zavaritsky Caldera (2,046 ft./624 m.) is located on Shimushir Island in the central Kuril Islands. The earliest recorded eruption was in 1923. A second, and most recent, eruption in 1957 was explosive and generated lava flows and a dome.

Zavodovsky I. (South Sandwich Is.: 56.30S, 27.57W).
Zavodovsky Island (1,808 ft./551 m.) is a stratovolcano whose earliest recorded eruption occurred in 1819, when the Russian explorer Bellingshausen discovered the island and reported a black ash cloud issuing from the summit.

Zengyu (north of Taiwan: 26.18N, 122.46E).
Zengyu (-1,371 ft./-418 m.) is a submarine volcano whose sole recorded eruption to date occurred in 1916.

Zheltovskaya Sopka (Kamchatka, Russia: 51.57N, 157.32E).
Zheltovskaya Sopka (6,406 ft./1,953 m.), also known as Utashut, is a conical stratovolcano. An explosive eruption in April of 1923 blew off a portion of Zheltovskaya's summit. The most recent eruption occurred in 1972.

Zhupanovskaya Sopka (Kamchatka, Russia: 53.59N, 159.15E).
Zhupanovskaya Sopka (9,702 ft./2,958 m.) is a compound volcano with four summits. There have been at least a dozen vulcanian eruptions. The earliest

recorded eruption was in 1776, with ash layer datings indicating at least four before this; the first in approximately 5050 B.C. The most recent eruption occurred in 1959.

Zimina (Kamchatka, Russia: 55.86N, 160.60E).

Zimina (10,230 ft./3,119 m.) is a large stratovolcano with two ice-covered summits named Bolshaya Zimina and Malaya Zimina. There have been no eruptions in historic time.

Zubayr, Jebel (Red Sea: 15.08N, 42.17E).

Jebel Zubayr (627 ft./191 m.) is a shield volcano whose sole recorded eruption to date occurred in 1824.

Zuñi-Bandera (*Zuñi* for Native American tribe; *Bandera* from Spanish, "flag") (New Mexico, USA: 34.80N, 108.00W).

Zuñi-Bandera (2,367 ft./2,550 m.) is a Holocene volcanic field with no record of eruptions in historic time.

Appendix 1:
Unnamed Volcanoes

The following volcanoes were still unnamed in 1993.

1. (Georgia: 42.45N, 44.25E). Volcano (12,304 ft./3,750 m.) composed of cinder cones formed during the Holocene Era.

2. (Georgia: 41.55N, 43.60E). Volcano (11,155 ft./3,400 m.) composed of cones formed during the Holocene Era.

3. (Ethiopia: 8.70N, 39.63E). Pyroclastic Holocene volcano (4,265 ft./1,300 m.) with no record of eruptions in historic time.

4. (Ethiopia: 8.62N, 38.95E). Volcano (5,906 ft./1,800 m.) composed of fissure vents with no record of eruptions in historic time.

5. (Ethiopia: 8.07N, 39.07E). Volcano (5,906 ft./1,800 m.) composed of fissure vents with no record of eruptions in historic time.

6. (Ethiopia: 7.95N, 38.93E). Volcano (6,198 ft./1,889 m.) composed of fissure vents with no record of eruptions in historic time.

7. (Ethiopia: 5.65N, 37.67E). Volcano (3,937 ft./1,200 m.) composed of cinder cones formed during the Holocene Era.

8. (Tanzania: 8.63S, 33.57E). Volcano composed of Holocene pyroclastic cones with no record of eruptions in historic time.

9. (Syria: 36.67N, 37.00E). Holocene volcano with no record of eruptions in historic time.

10. (Syria: 33.31N, 36.92E). Holocene volcanic field (6,382 ft./1,945 m.) with no record of eruptions in historic time.

11. (Syria: 33.15N, 36.26E). Holocene volcanic field (3,927 ft./1,197 m.) with no record of eruptions in historic time.

12. (Syria: 32.67N, 36.42E). Holocene volcanic field (4,711 ft./1,436 m.) with no record of eruptions in historic time.

13. (Gulf of Aden: 12.25N, 45.00E). Submarine volcano with no recorded eruptions.

14. (Iran: 28.17N, 60.67E). A Holocene volcanic field with no record of eruptions in historic time.

15. (Indian Ocean: 11.75N, 80.75E). Submarine volcano with no recorded eruptions.

16. (Kermadec Is.: 29.18S, 177.87W). Submarine volcano (-1,837 ft. -560 m.) with an eruption recorded in 1886.

17. (Tonga: 21.38S, 175.65W). Submarine volcano (-1,641 ft./-500 m.) with eruptions recorded in 1907 and 1832.

18. (Tonga: 20.85S, 175.53W). Submarine volcano (-43 ft./-13 m.) with eruptions recorded in 1911 and 1923.

19. (Tonga: 20.57S, 175.38W). Submarine volcano with eruptions recorded in 1912, 1937 and 1988.

20. (American Samoa: 14.23S, 169.07W). Submarine volcano (-2,133 ft./-650 m.) with a possible eruption recorded in 1973.

21. (Admiralty Is.: 3.03S, 147.78E). Submarine volcano (-4,265 ft./-1,300 m.) with an eruption recorded in 1972.

22. (Northeast of New Guinea: 4.31S, 146.26E). Submarine volcano (-6,560 ft./-2,000 m.) with possible eruptions recorded in 1951 and 1970.

23. (New Britain, Southwestern Pacific: 5.20S, 148.57E). Submarine volcano with no record of historic eruptions.

24. (New Britain, Southwestern Pacific: 4.75S, 150.85E). Submarine volcano with no record of historic eruptions.

25. (Solomon Is.: 8.92S, 158.03E). Submarine volcano (-787 ft./-240 m.) with no record of historic eruptions.

26. (Vanuatu: 16.99S, 168.59E). Holocene stratovolcanoes (709 ft./216 m.) with no record of historic eruptions.

27. (Southwestern Pacific: 25.78S, 168.63E). Submarine volcano (-7,874 ft./-2,400 m.) with a hydrophonic eruption recorded in 1963.

28. (Sangihe Is.: 3.97N, 124.17E). Submarine volcano (-16,405 ft./-5,000 m.) with possible eruptions recorded in 1922 and 1955.

29. (Mindanao, Philippines: 7.44N, 126.07E). Hot springs (4,265 ft./1,300 m.) with no record of historic eruptions.

30. (North of Luzon, Philippines: 20.33N, 121.75E). Submarine volcano (-79 ft./-24 m.) with eruptions recorded in 1773, 1850, and 1854.

31. (East of Taiwan: 20.93N, 134.75E). Submarine volcano (-19,686 ft./-6,000 m.) with a possible eruption recorded in 1850.

32. (East of Taiwan: 19.17N, 132.25E). Submarine volcano (-33 ft./-10 m.) with a possible eruption recorded in 1955.

33. (East of Taiwan: 21.83N, 121.18E). Submarine volcano (-377 ft./-115 m.) with an eruption recorded in 1854.

34. (East of Taiwan: 24.00N, 121.83E). Submarine volcano with an eruption recorded in 1853.

35. (North of Taiwan: 25.42N, 122.33E). Submarine volcano (-328 ft./-100 m.) with an eruption recorded in 1867.

36. (Volcano Is., Japan: 26.13N, 144.48E). Submarine volcano (-105 ft./-32 m.) with a possible eruption recorded in 1974.

37. (Mariana Is.: 21.00N, 142.90E). Submarine volcano with a possible eruption recorded in 1975.

38. (Mariana Is.: 20.30N, 143.20E). Submarine volcano with a possible eruption recorded in 1975.

39. (Northwest of Iturup I., Kuril Is.: 45.03N, 147.21E). Submarine volcano (-3,051 ft./-930 m.) with a possible eruption recorded in 1967.

40. (East of Urup I., Kuril Is.: 46.10N, 150.50E). Submarine volcano (-328 ft./-100 m.) with a possible eruption recorded in 1978.

41. (Kuril Is.: 46.47N, 151.28E). Submarine volcano (-1,647 ft./-502 m.) with an eruption recorded in 1972.

42. (East of Matua I., Kuril Is.: 48.08N, 153.33E). Submarine volcano (-492 ft./-150 m.) with an eruption recorded in 1924.

43. (Kamchatka, Russia: 51.60N, 156.55E). Holocene cinder cones (978 ft./ 298 m.) with no record of eruptions in historic time.

44. (Kamchatka, Russia: 52.33N, 157.33E). Holocene pyroclastic cones (2,093 ft./638 m.) with no record of eruptions in historic time.

45. (Kamchatka, Russia: 52.57N, 157.02E). Holocene cinder cones (2,001 ft./ 610 m.) with no record of eruptions in historic time.

46. (Kamchatka, Russia: 52.92N, 158.52E). Holocene shield volcanoes (1,476 ft./450 m.) with no record of eruptions in historic time.

47. (Kamchatka, Russia: 52.88N, 158.30E). Holocene shield volcanoes (2,297 ft./700 m.) with no record of eruptions in historic time.

48. (Kamchatka, Russia: 53.63N, 158.10E). Holocene cinder cones (656 ft./ 200 m.) with no record of eruptions in historic time.

49. (Kamchatka, Russia: 55.92N, 161.75E). Holocene cinder cones with no record of eruptions in historic time.

50. (Kamchatka, Russia: 56.53N, 160.87E). Holocene cinder cones (646 ft./ 200 m.) with no record of eruptions in historic time.

51. (Kamchatka, Russia: 56.82N, 158.95E). Holocene shield volcano (3,888 ft./1,185 m.) with no record of eruptions in historic time.

52. (China: 35.85N, 91.70E). Holocene volcanic field (17,717 ft./5,400 m.) with no record of eruptions in historic time.

53. (Alaska, USA: 55.93N, 160.00W). Holocene cinder cones (5,102 ft./ 1,555 m.) with no record of eruptions in historic time.

54. (Alaska, USA: 57.87N, 155.42W). Holocene lava dome (984 ft./ 300 m.) with no record of eruptions in historic time.

55. (Northeastern Pacific: 46.52N, 129.58W). Submarine volcano (-7,874 ft./ -2,400 m.) with an eruption recorded in 1993.

56. (Northeastern Pacific: 45.03N, 130.20W). Submarine volcano (-7,546 ft./ -2,300 m.) with an eruption recorded in 1986.

57. (Northeastern Pacific: 31.75N, 124.25W). Submarine volcano (-8,311 ft./ -2,533 m.) with a possible eruption recorded in 1972.

58. (Northwest of Oahu, Hawaii, USA: 21.75N, 158.75W). Submarine volcano (-9,943 ft./-3,000 m.) with a possible eruption recorded in 1956.

59. (Northwest of Necker, Hawaii, USA: 23.58N, 163.83W). Submarine volcano (-13,124 ft./-4,000 m.) with a possible eruption recorded in 1955.

60. (Eastern Pacific: 9.82N, 104.30W). Submarine volcano (-8,203 ft./ -2,500 m.) with an eruption recorded in 1991.

61. (Southern Pacific: 53.90S, 140.30W). Submarine volcano (-3,281 ft./ -1,000 m.) with a possible eruption recorded in 1991.

62. (Southern Pacific: 55.97S, 143.17W). Submarine volcano with a possible eruption recorded in 1990.

63. (Mexico: 28.00N, 115.00W). Submarine volcano with a possible eruption recorded in 1953.

64. (Chile: 20.83S, 68.63W). Holocene pumice cone (13,780 ft./4,200 m.) with no recorded eruptions in historic time.

65. (Juan Fernández Is., Chile: 33.62S, 76.83W). Submarine volcano (-211 ft./-64 m.) with a possible eruption recorded in 1839.

66. (Arctic Ocean: 88.27N, 65.60W). Submarine volcano (-4,922 ft./-1,500 m.) with eruptions recorded in approximately 1475, 1725, and 1957.

67. (Northern Atlantic: 49.00N, 34.50W). Submarine volcano (-5,414 ft./ -1,650 m.) with an eruption recorded in 1884.

68. (Northern Atlantic: 39.95N, 25.83W). Submarine volcano (-9,302 ft./ -2,835 m.) with a possible eruption recorded in 1856.

69. (Northern Atlantic: 38.75N, 38.08W). Submarine volcano (-13,780 ft./ -4,200 m.) with an eruption recorded in 1865.

70. (San Miguel, Azores: 37.78N, 25.67W). Pyroclastic cones (1,148 ft./ 350 m.) with carbon dating indicating the earliest eruption in approximately 4040 B.C. The most recent recorded eruption occurred in 1652.

71. (Central Atlantic: 7.00N, 21.83W). Submarine volcano (-4,643 ft./ -1,415 m.) with a possible eruption recorded in 1824.

72. (Central Atlantic: 4.20N, 21.45W). Submarine volcano (-9,515 ft./ -2,900 m.) with a possible eruption recorded in 1878.

73. (Central Atlantic: 0.58S, 15.83W). Submarine volcano (-5,013 ft./ -1,528 m.) with possible eruptions recorded in 1761 and 1816. A certain eruption was recorded in 1836.

74. (Central Atlantic: 3.50S, 24.50W). Submarine volcano (-17,389 ft./ -5,300 m.) with a possible eruption recorded in 1852.

75. (Antarctica: 73.45S, 164.58E). Holocene scoria cones (-9,800 ft./ -2,987 m.) with no recorded eruptions in historic time.

76. (Antarctica: 76.83S, 163.00E). Holocene submarine volcano (-1,641 ft./ -500 m.) with no recorded eruptions in historic time.

77. (Antarctica: 56.25S, 72.17W). Likely submarine volcano with a possible eruption recorded in 1876.

Appendix 2:
Non-volcanoes

The following, formerly recorded as volcanoes, have now been shown not to be volcanoes.

Cook I. (Solomon Is.: 8.41S, 157.10E).
Hodder's Volcano (West Indies: 14.03N, 61.07W).
Llanganate (Ecuador: 1.22S, 78.25W).
Mesa Nevada de Herveo (Colombia: 5.30N, 75.47W).
Nar, Jabal an- (Yemen: 13.33N, 43.73E).
Ormus Is. (East of Oman: 26.00N, 56.50E).
Susaki (Greece: 37.93N, 23.07E).
Umsini (New Guinea: 1.18S, 134.00E).

Appendix 3:
Generic Terms in
Volcano Names

The following generic terms are found in volcano names, alphabetized in the main listing under the proper name, for example, **Cerro del Azufre** as **Azufre, Cerro del**.

Alto Spanish, "peak"

Ausoles Spanish, "fumarole field"

Banos Spanish, "spa"

Batu Indonesian, "mountain"

Boer Indonesian, "hill," "mountain"

Bukit Indonesian, "hill," "mountain"

Cerro Spanish, "peak"

Cipanas Indonesian, "hot springs"

Cuddia Italian, "hill"

Danau Indonesia, "lake"

Djebel (French form of) Arabic, "mountain"

Doinyo Masai, "mountain"

Dolok Indonesian, "mountain"

Duenjo Masai, "mountain"

Ehi Chad, "mountain"

Emi Chad, "mountain"

Gebel (Italian form of) Arabic, "mountain"

Gof Kenyan, "hill"

Gunung Indonesian, "mountain"

Hala Arabic, "volcanic cone"

Harra Arabic, "lava field"

Harras Arabic, "lava field"

Harrat Arabic, "lava field"

Hervideros Spanish, "hot springs"

Ile French, "island"

Isola Italian, "island"

Isla Spanish, "island"

Jabal Arabic, "mountain"

Jebel Arabic, "mountain"

Kaba Indonesian, "crater"

Kapundan Indonesian, "crater"

Kawah Indonesian, "crater"

Kepundan Indonesian, "crater"

Lago Spanish, "lake"

Lagoa Portuguese, "lake"

Loma Spanish, "hill"

Lua Hawaiian, "crater"

Massif French, "mountain range"

Maunga Polynesian, "mountain"

Mont French, "hill," "mountain"

Montagne French, "mountain"

Montaña Spanish, "mountain"

Monte Italian, Spanish, "hill," "mountain"

Morne French Creole, "hill"

Nevado Spanish, "mountain"

Oldoinyo Masai, "mountain"

Pic French, "peak"

Pico Spanish, Portuguese, "peak"

Piek Dutch, "peak"

Pitón Spanish, **Piton** French, "peak"

Puig Spanish, "hill"

Puu Hawaiian, "hill"

Puy French, "hill"

Sierra Spanish, "mountain range"

Sopka Russian, "volcano"

Tarso Chad, "mountain"

Tavani Melanesian, "mountain"

Termas Spanish, "spa"

Tjipanas (Dutch form of) Indonesian, "hot spring"

Volcán Spanish, "volcano"

Vusi Melanesian, "hill"

Vuti Melanesian, "hill"

Wai Indonesian, "stream"

Wolo Indonesian, "mountain"

Appendix 4:
Extraterrestrial Volcanoes

Volcanoes exist, or have existed, elsewhere than on Earth. Scientists have established that there was volcanic activity on the Moon, for example, because of the presence of basalt lava. But the activity dates back literally millions of years and there is no feature on the Moon today that is worthy of the name. (The famous craters on the Moon were caused by the impact of meteorites, not by the eruption of volcanoes, although the great basins made by the impacts were later largely filled by lava floods from the Moon's interior.)

Volcanoes also played an important role in the formation of the planets of Venus and Mars. Venus is noted for the huge lava fields that cover most of its plains. Hundreds of small volcanic domes have been detected in the plains, and two volcanoes, Theia and Rheia, exist in the region known as Beta Regio. (The names are those of Titanesses in Greek mythology.)

The American spacecraft Mariner 9 discovered four volcanoes on Mars when orbiting the planet in 1971. One of them, Olympus Mons, turned out to be the largest known volcano in the whole of the solar system. (It is 25 kilometers high, three times that of Everest, with a base diameter of over 600 kilometers.) The other three came to be called Ascraeus Mons, Pavonis Mons, and Arsia Mons, all classical placenames.

Olympus Mons is awesome enough, but is probably inactive today. The story of positively *active* extraterrestrial volcanoes begins in 1979, when the two American spacecraft Voyager 1 and Voyager 2 flew by Jupiter and discovered nine active volcanoes on its satellite, Io. They were given names derived from mythological characters linked in some way with fire (thunder, lightning, volcanoes, the Sun, light, metal forging), as follows:

Amirani: a hero of Georgian mythology, who taught humans how to obtain fire. He entered into conflict with the gods, for which he was punished by being chained to a rock. (*Cf.* **Prometheus**, below.) His name means "child of the Sun."

Loki: the Scandinavian god of fire. His name is also that of a volcano in Iceland (*see* **Loki-Fogrufjöll**).

Marduk: the supreme god in the Babylonian pantheon, a personification of the sun. He led the gods in combat against primordial monsters and, having conquered them, created the earth and humans.

Masubi: a god of fire, marriage, birth, and agriculture in Japanese mythology.

Maui: a demigod in Polynesian mythology. He helped the gods to raise the vault of heaven and order the course of the stars, then caught the sun in his net and stole fire to give it to humans (*see* **Haleakala**).

Pele: the goddess of fire and volcanoes in Hawaiian mythology. She now inhabits **Kilauea**.

Prometheus: a Titan of Greek mythology. He stole fire from the gods to give to humans, for which Zeus punished him by chaining him to a rock, where a vulture daily ate his liver. (*Cf.* **Amirani**, above.)

Surt: a giant in Scandinavian mythology who defended Muspelheim (the kingdom of fire) with a flaming sword. He also gave his name to a volcano (and island) in Iceland (*see* **Surtsey**).

Volund: a skilled smith in Scandinavian mythology, lord of the elves and gnomes (who live underground and are famed for their metal forging). He is known to the Germans as Wieland and to English speakers as Wayland the Smith (or Wayland Smith).

Select Bibliography

Bullard, Fred M. *Volcanoes of the Earth*. Austin: University of Texas Press, 2d rev.ed., 1984.

Decker, Robert W., and Barbara B. Decker. *Volcanoes*. San Francisco: W.H. Freeman, 1997.

____. *Mountains of Fire*. Cambridge: Cambridge University Press, 1991.

Fisher, R.V., G. Heiken, and J.B. Hulen. *Volcanoes: Crucibles of Change*. Princeton: Princeton University Press, 1997.

Francis, Peter. *Volcanoes: A Planetary Perspective*. Oxford: Clarendon Press, 1993.

Furneaux, Rupert. *Krakatoa*. Englewood Cliffs, NJ: Prentice-Hall, 1964.

Gorshkov, Gweorgii S. *Volcanism and the Upper Mantle*. New York: Plenum Press, 1970.

Green, J., and N.M. Short, eds. *Volcanic Landforms and Surface Features: A Photographic Atlas and Glossary*. New York: Springer-Verlag, 1971.

Greene, Mott T. *Natural Knowledge in Preclassical Antiquity*. Baltimore: Johns Hopkins University Press, 1992.

Johnson, C., and D. Weisel. *Fire on the Mountain*. San Francisco: Chronicle Press, 1994.

Macdonald, Gordon A. *Volcanoes*. Englewood Cliffs, NJ: Prentice Hall, 1972.

Mulford, John W. *Volcano Watcher's Guide to the Caribbean*. Bloomfield Hills, MI: Cranbrook Institute of Science, 1969.

Oakeshott, Gordon B. *Volcanoes & Earthquakes: Geologic Violence*. New York: McGraw-Hill, 1976.

Ollier, Cliff. *Volcanoes*. Cambridge: The MIT Press, 1969.

Ritchie, D. *The Encyclopedia of Earthquakes and Volcanoes*. New York: Facts on File, 1994.

Scarth, Alwyn. *Volcanoes: An Introduction*. London: UCL Press, 1994.

____. *Savage Earth*. London: HarperCollins, 1997.

Simkin, Tom, *et al. Volcanoes of the World: A Regional Directory, Gazetteer and Chronology of Volcanism During the Last 10,000 Years*. Dowden, Hutchinson & Ross, 1981.

Simkin, Tom, and Lee Siebert. *Volcanoes of the World*. Tucson, AZ: Geoscience Press, 2d ed., 1994.

Tazieff, Haroun. *Craters of Fire*. New York: Harper & Brothers, 1952.

Wilcoxson, Kent. *Volcanoes*. London: Cassell, 1967.

Hundreds of articles on volcanoes have been published, ranging from the popular to the high-grade scientific. Since the approach of the present book is populist rather than specialist, a reference to the more accessible items and articles is desirable. Those taking their first steps in volcanology could do no worse than see the following. They are easy to read and still recent enough (1995 or later) to be topical:

185

Ahuja, Anjana. "Sitting on a time bomb." *The Times* (London), April 7, 1997.

Chen, Y. "The edge of time: dating young volcanic ash layers with the 40 Ar — 39 Ar laser probe." *Science*, Nov. 15, 1996, p. 1,176.

De Roy, T. "The day the earth blew." *International Wildlife*, Sept. 1995, p. 4.

Dingwell, D.B. "Volcanic dilemma: flow or blow?" *Science*, Aug. 23, 1996, p. 1,054.

Duncan, D.E. "Volcanoes." *Life*, June 1996, p. 52.

Hildreth, Digby. "Fun with fire and brimstone." *The Times* (London), July 19, 1997.

Kernan, M. "Geology that's alive." *Smithsonian*, Dec. 1997, p. 29.

Kerr, R.A. "Geophysicists peer into fiery core and icy ocean depths." *Science*, Jan. 10, 1997, p. 160.

Kluger, J. "Volcanoes with an attitude." *Time*, Feb. 24, 1997, p. 56.

Matthews, Robert. "The Vesuvius dilemma." *Sunday Telegraph* (London), April 12, 1998.

McGuire, R. "The fire next time." *World Press Review*, Feb. 1997, p. 35.

Monastersky, R. "California volcano starts to stir." *Science News*, Dec. 20, 1997, p. 396.

_____. "Caribbean blasts sparked global warmth." *Science News*, Nov. 15, 1997, p. 319.

_____. "Volcanoes under ice: recipe for a flood." *Science News*, Nov. 2, 1996, p. 327.

_____. "When lava and ice clashed on Mount Rainier." *Science News*, April 18, 1998, p. 245.

Oeland, Glenn. "Iceland's trial by fire." *National Geographic*, May 1997.

Roggensack, K. "Volatiles from the 1994 eruptions of Rabaul; understanding large caldera systems." *Science*, July 26, 1996, p. 490.

Tyson, P. "Under the volcano." *Technology Review*, Jan. 1996, p. 38.

Williams, A.R. "Montserrat: under the volcano." *National Geographic*, July 1997.

Zielinsky, G.A. "The Gisp ice core record of volcanism since 7,000 B.C." *Science*, Jan. 13, 1995.

REFERENCES FOR APPENDIX 4

Background information on volcanic history and activity in the solar system is based on Chapter 18, "Extraterrestrial volcanism," in Francis (above) and on: Miller, Ron, and William K. Hartmann. *The Grand Tour: A Traveler's Guide to the Solar System*. New York: Workman, rev. ed., 1993.

The discovery of the nine active volcanoes on Io was reported in: Morabito, L.A., S.P. Synnott, P.N. Kupferman, and S.A. Collins. "Discovery of currently active extraterrestrial volcanism." *Science*, 1979. Vol. 204, no. 4396, p. 972.

Information on the names of Io's nine volcanoes is based on: G.A. Burba, *Nomenklatura detalej rel'jefa galilejevykh sputnikov Jupitera* [*Names of Surface Features on the Galilean Satellites of Jupiter*]. Moscow: Nauka, 1984.

Index